Institutional Economics

INSTITUTIONAL ECONOMICS

THE CHANGING SYSTEM
By Wendell Gordon

University of Texas Press

AUSTIN AND LONDON

Copyright © 1980 by the University of Texas Press
All rights reserved
Printed in the United States of America

Requests for permission to reproduce material from this work should be sent to
Permissions, University of Texas Press, Box 7819, Austin, Texas 78712.

Library of Congress Cataloging in Publication Data

Gordon, Wendell Chaffee, 1916–
    Institutional economics.
    Bibliography: p.
    Includes index.
    1. Institutional economics. 2. Economics. I. Title.
HB99.5.G67   330.15′5   79-25660
ISBN 0-292-77022-7
ISBN 0-292-73823-4 (paper)

This book is very respectfully dedicated to CLARENCE E. AYRES

Contents

Illustrations

Preface

THIS WORK is a survey of economics, done from the perspective of the institutional approach.

This approach centers on ongoing process. How did we get this way? What are the influences which guide or control the economy as it evolves from a vaguely known past to an uncertain future in a process where ideas as to what is desirable are continually changing? This institutional view of the primary role of economics differs greatly from a conception, such as that of price theory and general equilibrium analysis, oriented to demand and supply considerations in a context where it is assumed that the process to be analyzed is that by which the economy tends to a static (or steady-state growth) equilibrium and a welfare maximum and the motives of the participants are conceived to be a reflection of a personal psyche which is definitely given and oriented to monetary-gain maximization.

The implications of the institutional approach, viewed as an alternative to orthodox economics, are also contrasted with the implications of that better-known alternative: Marxism. There is also discussion of other nonorthodox, non-Marxist possibilities—such as underconsumption, the single tax, and Catholic economic doctrine—but justice is not done to such alternatives as "share the wealth," the Townsend Plan, or libertarianism.

The argument of part I is to a considerable degree critical of these other approaches to economics, at least to the extent that these are alleged by their proponents to provide a satisfactory general theory around which all economic analysis can be oriented. The possible value of the insights of various of these theories for dealing with certain situations and problems is not denied. But their sponsors frequently try to make these theories carry too heavy a load, try to use them to prove more than they are capable of proving and to describe more than they are capable of describing.

In part II, there is a discussion of the procedures and problems involved in trying to test for the validity of institutional theory as well as an effort to develop perspective as to how economic problems may be usefully analyzed in the institutional frame of reference. This does not mean that institutional theory provides analytical tools capable of rationally solving problems in the sense that price theory and national income theory purport to do. But the perspective of the institutional approach can help provide a setting in which civilized, understanding, and conciliatory people will be more likely to work out viable policies. A major difference between institutional and neoclassical economics is in terms of the types of questions which the methodology ostensibly permits answering.

Part III consists of a number of case studies in which economic problems are dealt with from an institutional perspective. Studies include the institution of property, the limited-liability corporation, government-business relations and regulation, the multinationals, the energy-ecology problem, the monetary system and inflation, and unemployment. In connection with quite a few of these studies, I make some allegations as to suitable policies for dealing with the problems. But the institutional theory, it should again be emphasized, does not provide a logical method which proves the desirability of these alleged answers. Rather, which policies will actually be adopted by society depends upon the appeal of the arguments advanced by the protagonists of different policies and upon the reaction of society to those arguments. Much of the institutional approach involves an effort to explain how these attitudes have come to be what they are and how they are changed. This is the process of self-correcting value judgments. I argue that (1) the dynamic of technical change, (2) the institutionalization of behavior norms, (3) the biology of the beast, and (4) the resource endowment of the universe interact to make and change these attitudes or values and to orient the decision-making process.

This book has been over ten years in the writing and rewriting. It has felt the influence of many people, and if I were to attempt a comprehensive list almost certainly some of the most genuinely helpful people would be omitted. That is a not entirely valid reason for not attempting such a list. At any rate, I owe a considerable debt to many people.

Wendell Gordon

Institutional Economics

1.
Introduction

DEVELOPING an understanding of how the economic institutions of society work and evolve ought to be the essence of the *methodology* of economics. The *concern* of the subject ought to be the welfare of people. And the *epistemology* of the subject involves, whether economists like it or not, the comprehension of what is knowable or understandable in economics. In particular, there is the implication here of the limit to knowledge involved in the circumstance that a unique welfare maximum is neither practically identifiable nor theoretically meaningful. The essence of what is going on is of a different nature than can be dealt with in the equilibrium-oriented, maximizing models now in vogue.

Certainly the problems to which economics ought to address itself are important. They involve the availability of jobs, the conditions of production, the standard of living, the meaning of welfare, the distribution of wealth, and the way to realize a better way of life.

These problems might be analyzed in the frame of reference of many different analytical models, many different methodologies and philosophical perspectives. In this book reference will chiefly be made to five concepts, and the implications of these five will rather frequently be compared.

One is the framework of neoclassical price theory and general equilibrium analysis. That frame of reference is oriented to static equilibrium. Usually concerned with a particular period of time, it studies how the forces assumed to be relevant (demand, supply, and so on) will or may interact during that period to produce an equilibrium price that equates demand to supply and that is part of a context which, this approach assumes, is capable of generating a welfare maximum. This timeless general equilibrium concept also contains the oft repeated allegation that value norms are given from outside. (Economists take them as given data, or like to say they do, and presumably do not question their validity or how they are arrived at.) The profit motive and the pattern of consumer preferences are thus taken as given. That means values are given data. The possibility that the workings of the economic system in fact may influence values is assumed away. The possibility that economists might well concern themselves with the role of value formation in the economic process is disregarded. And, although economists using this approach generally claim that they are "value-free" or "positive" economists, their approach has the by-product effect of sanctifying the status quo. They seem to say that Dr. Pangloss was right: "All is for the best in this best of all possible worlds." But this attitude itself is a value judgment. And it makes the role of the economist that of high priest, describing and defending the existing system.

The second analytical model is the national income (or business-cycle) theory of John Maynard Keynes. It does not assume full employment. In fact, it alleges that an (undesirable) underemployment equilibrium is possible. In general this approach assumes pure competition, much as does the price theory, general equilibrium approach. But it does question the assumption that the market works automatically and with reasonable speed to generate full employment and maximum welfare. This is business-cycle or "medium-run" theory. It is not *general* theory. The methodology in the hands of Keynes might be called comparative statics. The before and after of the policies for fighting depression are the matter of concern. This theory does not satisfactorily deal with the process of growth or change. And, when Roy Harrod and Evsey Domar tried to use it to this end, it spawned neoclassical (essentially static) growth theory.

The third frame of reference is the Marxist. Economists and reformers working in this frame generally do consciously make value judgments, frequently quite strong value judgments, to the effect that much is wrong in this world. But the scientific Marxist will allege that there are inevitable forces at work leading to the collapse of the capitalist system and the establishment of a better world order, forces which can be formulated into a change process adequately described by the syllogistic logic of thesis, antithesis, and synthesis. This is growth or change theory—insofar as this type of methodology or logic is capable of analyzing the process of growth or change.

The fourth possible frame of reference is heterogeneous: it is the various radical non-Marxist and noninstitutional proposals for dealing with economic problems.

The fifth possible frame of reference, the institutional, involves looking at social order as ongoing process. Conditions change. Human biology changes, technology accumulates, further knowledge of resource availability is acquired, and institutionalized behavior norms change. Individuals observe all these processes and are part of them; they adapt their values as an aspect of the ongoing process. And the value judgments which they self-correct as part of the process also influence the process. There is no identifiable utopia which people now can identify and mandate in terms of characteristics valid into the indefinite future. Life is an ongoing challenge. There will always be good works (and bad works and new works and new understandings) to be participated in by later generations. One generation cannot establish the norms for utopia and thus take the fun out of life for future generations. This is true because one generation cannot predetermine the values of the next, although it may powerfully influence those values. The most useful legacy that one generation can leave to the next is not knowledge of how to solve the welfare maximization problem, not the blueprint for the Garden of Eden, but an understanding of what ongoing social process is all about. This so-called institutional frame of reference is the only one of our approaches which comes to grips with growth or change or progress in terms that might be called post-Darwin.

The philosophy of this book, and of institutional economics, is pragmatic, in the tradition of the pragmatism of C. S. Peirce, William James, and John Dewey. In fact, this is what economic theory in the "American tradition" ought to be, because change and the effective handling of change are far nearer the heart of the "American way" than is the idolizing of pure competition or the sanctifying of the profit motive.

That this work is pragmatic is true despite the fact that many of the rather idealistic policy proposals of its last part no doubt will not be implemented tomorrow or, even, next week. People change their conception of what is good or desirable as conditions change. This is the essence of the value theory of institutional or instrumental economics. The approach will probably not appeal to those in search of "final truth," optima, maxima, perfection, or precision—and to those who believe that these goals are identifiable and obtainable as a result of the use of logical methods or the working of inexorable forces. It will not appeal to those who believe: "If we could just refine our methods a little and be a little more rational (if people would just listen to me), we could design paradise now—and woe to those who do not like the paradise thus generously provided."

A typical definition of economics has been that it is "the science which studies human behavior as a relationship between ends and scarce means which have alternative uses."[1] But this is scarcely sufficiently comprehensive. Allocation of effort is a problem in economics, certainly. But even in the area of resource allocation the problem is frequently institutional rather than logical. Efficient deployment of scarce resources is not so much the problem as is something else—forming a consensus as to what we want to do and effecting the institutional changes appropriate to that consensus.

NOTE

1. Lionel Robbins, *An Essay on the Nature and Significance of Economic Science*, 2d ed. (London: Macmillan, 1935 [1932]), p. 16.

PART I
Institutional Theory and Comparative Theory

2.
The Institutional Theory of Economic Progress: Technology and Institutions

A BRIEF SUMMARY of the meaning of institutional economics goes something like the following. The Theory of Economic Progress says that (1) the basic dynamic force in economics is technology. The process of accumulation of technical knowledge (or, more broadly, of all rational knowledge) has an internal dynamic of its own, and this process is *not* primarily controlled by such outside motivation as the profit motive or by outside need (such as a desperate need for a cure for cancer). (2) The institutions into which society is organized adjust slowly and reluctantly to assimilate and use new technical knowledge and to accommodate and adjust their own behavior norms the better to utilize this new knowledge. (3) How and where production will actually occur are conditioned also by the availability of the natural resources appropriate to the state of technology. (But, to the extent that many industries are not crucially dependent on nearby sources of raw materials, this latter influence is not a major factor in all cases.) Monitoring all these interrelations are individuals, who are what they are characterwise as a result of (4) their evolving biology and the impact of the evolving interaction of technology, institutions, and resources upon them. And, also, the institutions of society are monitoring the individuals. And technology and resources and individual biology are also limiting what individuals are capable of doing.

The other chief element in institutional theory is the Value Theory, which is itself dynamic rather than static. It is dynamic in the manner of the pragmatism and instrumentalism of C. S. Peirce and John Dewey. This concept alleges that what is valued by people changes with the passage of time as conditions and, in particular, technology (knowledge) change. Self-correcting value judgments are made by individuals (and by institutions), and re-evaluations of the appropriateness of a given technology for dealing with a given problem are made as technologies (and methods) are used and reused in dealing with problems.

One of the pioneering works in institutional economics is Clarence Ayres' 1944 *The Theory of Economic Progress*. And the numerous writings of Thorstein Veblen provide many of the varied insights which, beginning about 1899, formed the basis of the institutional approach.[1] Other writers in this tradition have included John R. Commons, Wesley C. Mitchell, Morris Copeland, John Dewey, Gardiner C. Means, Walton H. Hamilton, John Maurice Clark, C. Wright Mills, William F. Ogburn, Rexford Guy Tugwell, Allan G. Gruchy, Francis Stuart Chapin, Gunnar Myrdal, and even Kenneth E. Boulding and John Kenneth Galbraith. And in a larger context the approach includes Richard H. Tawney, Max Weber, and Adolf Berle. The Association for Evolutionary Economics and its *Journal of Economic Issues* have, in recent years, also fostered this orientation.

The Role of Technology

The institutional theory alleges that the accumulation of technical knowledge—defined in a very broad sense as involving all tools and all mental skills—is the dynamic force that controls in a major degree both what people have done with the look of the world and the nature of human progress and change.[2] Technology subsumes the capabilities that people possess for improving their material welfare and/or for performing tasks in ways that involve less effort or are more effective.

The basic difference between institutional and orthodox economic theory in this regard is the difference between an economic theory that gets its drive from the dynamism involved in ongoing technological change (and that is not primarily motivated by the profit motive) and an economic theory that gets its drive or motivation or direction from the desire of individuals for greater monetary gain. (In this connection, it should be noted that the institutional theory does not deny the existence and importance of profit motive considerations. It merely alleges that profit seeking is an institutionalized behavior norm that needs to be taken into account.)

Characteristics

Characteristics of the technological process are (1) its cumulative nature, (2) its dynamism, and (3) its continuity. Perhaps also it may be characterized by (4) an accelerated rate of accumulation over time. In fact, what is involved is an evolutionary process with its own built-in dynamism.

The first characteristic of the technological process is its cumulative nature, in the sense that knowledge grows on itself. Jacques Ellul has commented on this phenomenon: "Essentially the preceding technical situation alone is determinative. When a given technical discovery occurs, it has followed almost of necessity certain other discoveries."[3]

Roast pork followed the discovery of fire, the way Charles Lamb told the story. Iron weapons followed the discovery of processes for making iron. The horseless carriage followed the internal-combustion engine. (Note, however, that this is not technological determinism. I have not alleged that, with knowledge about fire, one could have forecast roast pork.)

Given the great importance of the phenomenon, a few other examples of the cumulative nature of the process of technological change may be useful. There is the sequence of events in architecture from the Greek pillars, via the Roman half-circle arches, to the Gothic pointed arches, and beyond. A. C. Drachmann has described a sequence of events involving the grinding of grain and the waterwheel:

> Like most technical problems in antiquity, these were solved ... through the slow accretion of craftsmen's skills.
>
> Grinding was originally done with a round stone that was rubbed along a hollow in another stone (the quern). Then the grinder (top stone) was made square and provided with a slit for feeding in the corn; the lower stone was flat and was placed upon a table, and the grinder was moved to and fro over it by means of a long wooden arm. ... By about 150 B.C. two other mills were widely used.
>
> The water mill was not introduced until about a century later, just before the end of the pre-Christian era. It probably had its origin in the water wheel of the period. ... At some point it must have occurred to someone that by adding paddles to the buckets, the wheel could be turned by the power of the flowing water itself and thus perform the work of the man.
>
> The next step was to put a gear wheel on the axle of the paddle-wheel and make it turn a vertical axle that carried a millstone. ... The water mill developed quickly.
>
> Mills now appeared throughout the Roman Empire, and were applied to several tools, including saws for cutting marble.[4]

Abbott Payson Usher has reported on the background of the revolution in textile machinery that was a feature of the inception of the Industrial Revolution: "The mechanical achievements of the 18th century in textile manufacturing were dependent on the great advances in light engineering at a craft level in clock- and watch-making, in lathe work in wood, and in the various crafts working with non-ferrous metals. The importance of clock- and watch-making is frequently underestimated. All the problems of the construction and control of geared mechanisms were involved."[5]

Another example of the cumulative nature of the process involves the role of the lathe. Invented in the sixteenth century, the lathe was necessary as a preliminary for making many scientific instruments (it was especially involved in the making of screws) and for the metal-cutting capability required in producing the machinery that caused the Industrial Revolution.

And the mind, having conceived the internal-combustion engine, by an internal dynamic of its own proceeds to consider the possible uses. And the automobile is hatched.

One discovery leads to another. The dissemination of one bit of new knowledge may provide the insight needed for solving another problem. In fact, a new scientific discovery generally occurs because it is the next natural step in a technological sequence, not because someone wants to solve such and such a problem and goes out and does it or because the profit motive called for a labor-saving rather than a capital-saving innovation. The cures for the common cold and for cancer will come at the appropriate stage in the evolution of our technology, not necessarily because we are desperate for cures for these ailments and a squad of scientists has been assigned the task of finding these cures. If wishing and conscious diverting of resources to the task could do the job, we would have had a cure for cancer long ago.

The second alleged characteristic of technology is its dynamism. To say that the process of accumulating rational knowledge and technology is dynamic is to say that essentially the process has an internal drive that is not primarily dependent on motivation from outside the process itself. Inventors do not obtain the insight that leads to a new discovery by watching a wad of money swaying back and forth and by jumping around trying to catch it. They are likely to get the insight after receiving or coming to understand some new discovery which they juxtapose in their mind's eye with problems and processes that they had been puzzling over. And, of a sudden, there is a connection made. And we have new knowledge. Whether some people have a more natural instinct for this sort of work because they have an urge to become millionaires is doubtful, but it is possible. However, it would be difficult to formulate an econometric test of the relation. We do know that some inventors have made great fortunes and some have been conned out of their possible fortunes by more adept entrepreneurs or innovators. But counting these two types of heads would still not reveal the extent to which the profit motive plays a causal role in technological accumulation.

Probably in few of these cases did society, ex ante, envisage the new technology that was desired, call on the inventor (with suitable promises of reward), and then get just the technology that was wanted. Things do not work that way, despite the fact that that is the basic conception of the modern theory of induced technical change.

Also, the temptation to assign a major causal role to the profit motive needs to be tempered by the circumstance that the profit motive works both ways—or perhaps three ways. (1) Conceivably, appropriate and desirable new inventions may be called forth by research workers primarily impelled by the profit motive. This is possible. (However, even in this case it seems likely that this will happen only if the stream of accumulating knowledge has arrived at the stage where it is more or less inevitable that this discovery would be made anyway.) (2) Frequently, techniques that have been discovered are lying dormant in what might be called a cookbook of unused available technologies. The role of Joseph Schumpeter's innovator-entrepreneurs is to leaf through this cookbook occasionally, and, if their profit-seeking instincts tell them that a given technique has possibilities, they may be expected to "innovate" the process, that is, to put it into production with the hope of realizing profitable sales. The profit motive is important in this case, although probably in a very rough-and-ready way. Precise comparisons of the profit rates associated with different possible innovations cannot actually be made at this stage. (3) Also significant in arguing the issue of the importance of the profit motive in relation to the process of accumulating technical knowledge is the circumstance that frequently the profit seeker is motivated to suppress, or not to use, or not to search for bits of knowledge which, if used, would render current plants and machinery "prematurely" obsolescent. Thus, the profit motive may call for discouraging as well as encouraging both research and innovation. But that the internal dynamic of the process of technical accumulation is important is unambiguous. People are stimulated by one idea to have another.

Again, it should be emphasized that this allegation regarding both the importance of the internal dynamic in the accumulation of technical knowledge and the denial that the profit motive plays a basic motivational role is not, at the same time, a denial of the importance of the profit motive. The profit motive is, or can be, fantastically important, especially in a capitalist society but also in a socialist one. However, the role it plays (either in encouraging or in retarding technical process) is largely institutionally determined. But more of that aspect of the matter later.

The third characteristic of the technological process is its continuity. In general, knowledge once acquired is not lost. And one can observe over the great sweep of history the process by which knowledge generates other knowledge in an ongoing, continuous process—for example, from arithmetic, to algebra, to calculus, and so on.

With regard to the controversial issue as to whether knowledge, once acquired, can be lost, I am afraid I shall cop out. Influential institutional economists (Ayres among them) have argued that in a certain basic sense knowledge, once acquired, cannot be lost. A steam engine was developed in Egypt by Hero of Alexandria about the time of Christ. Similarly, weaving machinery was invented but not exploited in Poland in the twelfth century. Much the same type of machinery five centuries later was basic to the Industrial Revolution. Was the knowledge found and lost or was it merely dormant?

A possible fourth item in the list of characteristics of the technological process is an accelerated rate of accumulation over time. But it seems unclear how the concept of accelerated rate of accumulation of technical knowledge could be quantified for purposes of statistical testing. And a process that involves, say, merely doubling knowledge every twenty years or forty years, or whatever, could certainly involve a major increase during the twentieth century without necessarily involving an accelerated *rate* of accumulation.

Also, it may be discreet to grant the possibility that the rate of accumulation may accelerate or decelerate or the quantity accumulated may even arrive at a stage where that is it: all is known that is knowable. This is conceivable, and no one can guess when such a slowing down might become observable. In any event, it is probably discreet not to allege the existence of any "natural law" to the effect that all knowledge is accumulating at an increasing rate.

Types

A somewhat more detailed classification of types of "all tools and all mental skills" may be helpful. In institutional economics what is subsumed under technology is very broad, including the range of pure science and even all rational knowledge, as well as technology in the narrower sense of technique. Technology includes much of managerial and administrative method and procedure, although aspects of these procedures show strong institutionalized, socially determined influences. It includes much of marketing and distribution technique, although many aspects of marketing and distribution pretty obviously also involve a strong element of habit and custom.

Some writers in this area like to emphasize a distinction between science and technology, and there may be contexts where this distinction has a usefulness. But, on the whole, I am inclined to agree with Ayres that this particular distinction is not significant for institutional theory. He writes: "Furthermore, as regards the nature of the process there is no difference between 'mechanical' invention and 'scientific' discovery."[6]

Classified in terms of nature of use (or specificity), the types of technologies may be identified as (1) specific to an individual plant or firm (firm-specific), such as the arrangement of machinery in a given plant of a certain shape. Or a technology may be (2) specific to an industry (industry-specific), a new process for making a known product, such as a procedure for making steel or aluminum pots. Or a technology may have (3) a general application in different firms or industries to common types of problems (function-specific), as, for example, a new system of bookkeeping that is usable in many industries. Most obvious of all is probably (4) the invention of a new product.

In some cases, technology may not be separable in any meaningful sense from the form and substance of the capital equipment in which it is embodied. The technology *is* the structure of the lathe, or the bulldozer. In other cases, technology may be almost entirely in the mind; it may be a way of doing things. It can be the knowledge that a little soap on the threads of a screw may facilitate turning the screw. This is technical knowledge, the essence of which is in the mind. Or "instinctive" knowledge as to which way to turn the steering wheel of a car when it begins to skid is technical knowledge. This distinction might be said to involve the *location* of the technology or knowledge: it may be in the mind, or it may be embodied in the structure of the equipment.

Behavior is technological behavior, it is functional, if it contributes effectively to human welfare and progress as welfare and progress are conceived by the individual and/or by society. It is institutional if it is practiced because it is the tradition to do things in that manner. Institutionalized behavior is not necessarily undesirable, but it is "institutionalized behavior." And it is not necessarily nontechnological or nonfunctional merely because it is institutionalized. So, we come to the matter of the nature of institutions.

The Nature of Institutions

To turn, then, to institutions and the implications of institutionalized or customary behavior: an institution is a grouping of people with some common behavior patterns, its members having an awareness of the grouping. But in this definition the emphasis is on the institutionalized behavior pattern. It is not especially helpful to reify institutions in the sense of thinking of them as buildings or groups of people. Individuals also play the role of custodians of the technical knowledge discussed earlier. So, the essence of the institution is the commonly held behavior pattern. John R. Commons has defined an institution as "Collective Action in Control of Individual Action."[7]

Examples of institutions include the family, the church, the social group, and, more specifically in the economic sphere, the corporation and the labor union—or, better said, the institutionalized behavior norms of those groupings.

Many years ago, William Graham Sumner said of institutionalized behavior norms or folkways:

> The folkways are habits of the individual and customs of the society which arise from efforts to satisfy needs; they are intertwined with goblinism and demonism and primitive notions of luck . . . , and so they win traditional authority. Then they become regulative for succeeding generations and take on the character of a social force. They arise no one knows whence or how. They grow as if by the play of

internal life energy. They can be modified, but only to a limited extent, by the purposeful efforts of men. In time they lose power, decline, and die, or are transformed. While they are in vigor they very largely control individual and social undertakings, and they produce and nourish ideas of world philosophy and life policy. Yet they are not organic or material. They belong to a superorganic system of relations, conventions, and institutional arrangements.[8]

Institutional theory does try to explain "whence or how" institutionalized behavior norms arise. But, aside from that, there is in Sumner's view much that is basic in the institutional theory regarding the nature of institutions.

Characteristics
The basic characteristics of institutions are that they are (1) static, (2) inherited from the past, (3) past-glorifying, (4) psychologically defensible, (5) dictatorial, and (6) creatures of habit.

An institution, as such, is static. Its behavior norms tend not to change, and institutions are resistant to change. John Maynard Keynes observed the phenomenon: "The difficulty lies, not in the new ideas, but in escaping from the old ones, which ramify, for those brought up as most of us have been, into every corner of our minds."[9]

An institution's behavior norms, its patterns of ways of doing things, are inherited from the past. This has to be because the setting involves ongoing process. And, in the nature of things, any behavior norm currently being applied has to have come into being at an earlier time. An institution is, then, an agency endorsing a complex of standardized behavior norms that continue to prevail until an outside power (technology or the pressure to modify exerted by other institutions) comes along to force their change.

A third characteristic of an institution is the past-glorifying, emotional nature of these behavior norms. Since the behavior patterns of the institution are inherited from the past, the individuals involved in some particular institution (as long as they continue the practices in question) tend to venerate the past that provided them with these traditions.

Similarly, much behavior is myth-based. This is to say that, at least as far as the present practitioners of the behavior know, there is no rational reason for their behavior. "Things have been done this way since time immemorial." "Way back when the great god Jupiter told us to do things this way." "It would rouse the ire of the gods if we changed our ways." When leadership has a vested interest in the status quo, and that is the standard situation, it is generally more convenient and more effective to defend the practices in this manner than by rational argument.

About three hundred years ago, John Locke, in "An Essay Concerning Human Understanding," was writing: "It is easy to imagine how, by these means, it comes to pass that men worship the idols that have been set up in their minds; . . . and stamp the characters of divinity upon absurdities and errors; become zealous votaries to bulls and monkeys, and contend too, fight, and die in defence of their opinions."[10]

Then there is the role of ritual. Traditions, every now and then, must be observed with appropriate ceremony and martial music so that people will get a thrill from doing the institutionally prescribed thing and thereby respect more fervently the institution itself. Soldiers on KP feel better (or used to feel better) about peeling the potatoes after an impressive flag-raising ceremony. We feel better (or used to feel better) about the state legislature and its goings-on after walking through the statehouse and being properly impressed by the majesty of the building, if not by the decorum of the proceedings.

Much of the strength and persistence of institutionalized behavior result from the fact that it has a basis in emotion. People obtain satisfaction from abiding by norms of behavior which they have been conditioned to respect or to consider appropriate. The army sergeant gets satisfaction from swearing, the bureaucrat from telling citizens that they cannot do something, the banker from higher interest rates, the fraternity member from paddling the pledge, the merchant from higher prices.

The acceptance and repetition of behavior are also conditioned by a sort of belief or faith that the behavior patterns that we have followed must be reasonable, psychologically defensible, even though the reasonableness of our behavior is not subject to scientific testing. Our self-respect requires that we feel that our behavior is reasonable and praiseworthy. We obtain self-respect by esteeming the source of our own behavior. If we lose respect for our inherited or acquired behavior patterns and yet find no new behavior pattern to respect, we lose respect for ourselves and may slip into a state of anomie. This is in fact a way of looking at the nature of the difficulty of western society in recent years.

On this point also Locke has something to say: "And had men leisure, parts, and will, who is there almost that dare shake the foundations of all his past thoughts and actions, and endure to bring upon himself the shame of having been a long time wholly in mistake and error?"[11]

An institution is also dictatorial. Its individual members are under powerful compulsion to conform, to behave in the manner that their institution "thinks" is proper. Any member of a fraternity or a sorority or a radical cell should appreciate what is involved here. Solomon Asch has commented rather strongly on the power of institutions to enforce conformity: "We have found the tendency to conformity in our society so strong that reasonably intelligent and well-meaning . . . people are willing to call white black."[12]

Those with most status in an institution have a very real interest in using its traditions to keep the membership in line. It will be argued that the rites of the lodge or the ceremonies of the temple or the fairness of the profit rate have been derived from a source the membership had better respect, or else. . . . The individual who breaks with the group's traditions is looking for trouble. By choosing to do things differently from parents or bank or trade association or labor union, she or he is in some sense disrespecting a higher authority. In some societies much older people have been viewed as respected authority, in others one looks to slightly older people and rejects the views of those substantially older. And there are other criteria for identifying the voice of authority: the largest biceps, most expensive clothes, the best gift of gab.

In addition, much, possibly most, behavior is performed out of pure force of habit, without our thinking at all about logic or reason, and habitual behavior of this sort is the most perfect example of institutionalized behavior.

Rationality, Habit, and Biology
The appreciation of the role of institutionalized habit and custom has basic implications for understanding human behavior. Much of the time a person is not behaving in response to an ongoing reappraisal of marginal utilities, whatever they are. One is not making an intelligent effort to weigh pleasure against pain in making choices. Rather, in connection with most actions, one is caught up in behavior patterns created by the institutions of the environment. William James has written:

> Important as is the influence of pleasures and pains upon our movements, they are far from being our only stimuli. With the manifestations of instinct and emotional expression, for example, they

have absolutely nothing to do. Who smiles for the pleasure of the smiling, or frowns for the pleasure of the frown? . . . However the actual impulsions may have arisen, they must now be described as they exist; and those persons obey a curiously narrow teleological superstition who think themselves bound to interpret them in every instance as effects of the secret solicitancy of pleasure and repugnancy of pain.[13]

There is no doubt that both heredity and environment influence the manner in which an individual responds to social or cultural pressures. There is interaction between biological and social influences. But the actual content of much behavior that is attributed to biological drives derives its particular form of expression from custom, habit, and institutionalized norms. Richard LaPiere and Paul Farnsworth have commented: "If motivational terms [such as organic hunger] are to be used to explain some complex patterns [such as entering a restaurant to order dinner], it must be clearly recognized that they do not refer to biological drives, but rather to complex social developments upon the original organic bases."[14]

We do have certain biological needs. And we will strive to satisfy those needs. Yet this information tells us very little about how we will do this. What we do, and how, and when are heavily conditioned by custom, habit, and social pressure. Muzafer Sherif has written:

Like other organisms, man is born with certain needs, such as the needs for nutrition, shelter, and later, mating. . . . Along with this, we note another fact. When we observe people in the search for food, shelter, or mates, we conclude that these activities run in certain prescribed channels. People do eat, mate and enjoy the security of shelter; but how and under what circumstances they will eat, mate and enjoy shelter are, to a great extent, regulated by customs, traditions, laws and social standards. This is true for every individual, living in every society we know, primitive or developed. If an individual does not come under this category to any important degree, he cannot be said to be a member of society.[15]

And Kurt Lewin has emphasized:

Social scientists agree that differences in conduct as they exist today among men, white, black, or yellow, are not innate; they are acquired. Divergences from the social norm are also acquired. Efforts to find an explanation of such divergences in "basic personality differences" have been unrewarding. It is probably correct to formulate the following, more precise hypothesis:

. . . The processes governing the acquisition of the normal and abnormal are fundamentally alike.

The nature of the processes by which the individual becomes a criminal, for instance, seems to be basically the same as the processes by which the nondiverging individual is led to conduct which is considered honest. What counts is the effect upon the individual of the circumstances of his life, the influence of the group in which he has grown up. . . .

In any field of conduct and beliefs, the group exercises strong pressure for compliance on its individual members. We are subject to this pressure in all areas—political, religious, social—including our beliefs of what is true or false, good or bad, right or wrong, real or unreal.[16]

Membership in Different Institutions

Before closing this discussion of the nature of institutions, an additional consideration or two should be noted. It is perhaps self-evident, but, then again, perhaps it is not. One person may play roles in, and have behavior conditioned by, various institutions: church, home, trade union, place of employment. And, in responding in one setting to the norms of one institution and in another setting to the norms of another, the nature of behavior (in response to the same issue) may be rather different in each setting. One may be genuinely full of concern for humanity while in church and genuinely concerned to increase profits at others' expense the rest of the week.

Also, institutions may be formal or informal. One institution may have formed its rules of behavior over many decades in a manner that never involved any effective group consideration of the rationale of its pattern, while another may have been established by law and endowed with a quite precise set of behavior rules by some legislative body.

The Need for Institutions
(Change vs. Order and the Role of Civilization)

Much of what has been said (and will be said) in this chapter with regard to institutions and their role may sound derogatory. That is regrettable. A society, to operate at all, has to have organization and, therefore, it has to have social and economic institutions. Behavior has to be controlled and regulated. Cars must observe the red and green lights at intersections. And, as our way of life gets technically more complicated, it will be increasingly important to have reasonable rules to control behavior. The necessity for standardization and simplifications (in a setting where things are tending to get all too complicated) thus means, in certain contexts, an arbitrariness that may seem unreasonable to a bright young woman with an IQ of 140 or repressive to a cute little boy. For example, you had better just sit there waiting for that light to change, even though you see no traffic coming from any direction, whether you are driving a car or riding a bicycle. And, as far as "keep off the grass" is concerned, it is true that the grass will not be killed if you are the only one who walks on it. But the advantaged, the intelligent, and the attractive have a special obligation to set a good example in the observance of reasonable rules. The "beautiful people" and the brilliant should not ipso facto be above the rules. They have more going for them than most people anyway.

I will argue in chapter 3 that civilization, as an alternative to chaos and bestiality, is possible only on the basis of social understandings that constrain people to act in a decent manner toward each other. These social understandings—for example, we will not call each other pigs, or kikes, or greasers, at least in a setting where the term is considered offensive, and we will show some concern for the sensibilities of others, both elder and younger—constitute that institution, that institutional order, which we call civilization.

It is interesting to note that the need for social institutions was recognized by the chief revolutionary of them all, Karl Marx, who wrote in his 1843 "On the Jewish Question":

> All emancipation is bringing back man's world and his relationships to man himself. Political emancipation is the reduction of man, on the one hand to a member of civil society, an egoistic and independent individual, on the other hand to a citizen, a moral person. The actual individual man must take the abstract citizen back into himself and, as an individual man in his empirical life, in his individual work and individual relationships become a species-being; man must recognize his own forces as social forces, organize them and thus no longer separate social forces from himself in the form of political forces. Only when this has been achieved will human emancipation be completed.[17]

Civilization has gotten where it is by imposing on individuals as they grow up behavior patterns which permit society to operate as a coordinated entity. The behavior of the maturing individual is conditioned by society as the infant becomes the child, the youth, and the adult. By the time individuals reach maturity, they have learned that there are some things society simply does not allow. And they will get along better if they conform. Even if an individual has a naturally rebellious instinct, he or she will have found out that it is better judgment to rebel in some ways rather than in others.

Individuals may have either of two quite different reactions when asked to behave in the institutionally prescribed manner: they may conform (and generally do) or they may rebel. Frequently they will rebel briefly and then conform. Or they may rebel against their own parents but, upon becoming parents, may force their own children to follow the precepts which they themselves had resisted. Make your bed; pick up your litter; speak civilly to your elders and to members of other racial groups; help with the dishes; get off the couch or at least get your shoes off the couch or off the edge of the coffee table or off the table in the library; get home from your date at a reasonable hour; do not make such a din with your rock'n'roll music; wipe your feet; wipe your nose; practice a little common courtesy. Making a halfway civilized citizen out of a baby *Homo sapiens* seems to take a considerable amount of doing and quite a period of time.

Some friction between children and parents seems a natural part of the growing-up process. Major rebellion is something else. Rebellion may reflect little more than a concern for self, or it may involve a reaction to a legitimate serious grievance. This makes a good deal of difference. Society improves as a result of successful rebellion in a good cause. It is in trouble if too many of its members spend too much of their time rebelling as an expression of self-indulgent insistence on having their own way in trivial matters. One type of rebellion may be the making of a society or culture. The other type, if there is a considerable amount of it, may well be that society's undoing.

Also, there is the problem of the moderately worthy cause which is overexploited by moderately aggrieved people with aggressive instincts or a compulsion to muscle their way into positions of leadership. A good deal of the present rebellion against the Establishment (whatever that is) probably, if implemented, would involve little more than a substitution of a new Establishment (meaning new institutions) for the old one. But the positive merit of such changes depends on the character of the new Establishment which is to replace the old. It is not enough to be told that the old Establishment must go, simply because it is the old Establishment, without regard to the desirability of the new institutional order.

If we conform to the little rules that are halfway reasonable, we are going to be in a lot better shape for protecting the greater freedom that really matters and for protesting the important unreasonable rules. Persons interested in being genuinely effective in changing some undesirable feature of society may be well advised to be pretty much of a conformist in most other aspects of their behavior. They will get a better reception when they present their arguments for changing what really needs changing.

We do have to have institutions (social organization and rules) in order to avoid chaos, in order to have civilization. The problem is to fix things so that we are masters of the rules instead of the rules (tradition and force of habit) being our masters. The society that is flexibly, continually, objectively, and intelligently reevaluating its rules and norms is going to assimilate technology more readily, offer a higher standard of living to its members, and be a more pleasant place in which to live than is the society which is rigidly frozen in its ways.

The objectionable institutional practice is the one which gets its sanction from habitual ways of thought, mores, and customs without being revalidated currently in terms of whether or not it facilitates the constructive use of worthwhile new technology. This is the test as to whether the practice is instrumental. However, if the habitual practice plays no significant role, there is no particular harm in its continuance. And if people enjoy it, get some emotional satisfaction out of it, fine.

Examples of Institutional Behavior

For the purpose of indicating what is involved, it may help to mention some of the characteristic behavior patterns of some institutions. The family, at least in the western world, is characterized by monogamy. The Catholic church has frowned upon the marriage of Catholics with non-Catholics. The pursuit of profit on the part of the corporation is considered to be respectable behavior. A landowner is entitled to enforce a no-trespassing rule. Bankers can create money against fractional reserves and charge interest when they lend the stuff. The government has the power to tax.

One must acquire some appreciation of the peculiar organizational structure of the corporation, of the relation between the corporation and the government, and of the relation between management and the profit motive before one can appreciate the role of the corporation in influencing all of our lives.

The Interaction between Technology and Institutions

Institutionally sanctioned behavior patterns control the tempo at which the institution will permit new technical knowledge to come into use. Institutions which are stubbornly resistant to change slow down the process. And the tempo at which new technical knowledge is disseminated and put to use influences the rate at which more technical knowledge is accumulated.

William F. Ogburn described the working of technology-institutions interrelations in these terms in 1922 or, perhaps, earlier:

A very common pattern is for the technological change to affect, first, an economic organization which, second, causes a change in some social institution, such as the family or government, and which finally causes a change in the social philosophy of a people. Thus technology brings the factors which take occupations away from the home; which cause a loss of other functions of the family, such as caring for the old; which causes the government to provide old-age pensions; which in turn tends to weaken the social philosophy of laissez faire. . . .

As the hoe evolved into the plough, food was raised from seeds of grasses—notably barley, oats, wheat, and rice—all of which could be preserved longer than fruits; and animal food, particularly milk, was produced from tamed animals. This increased food supply, based upon technology, made possible communities much larger than were possible in the hoe, or digging stick culture. . . .

Thus the first direct adjustment to the technology that increases the food supply and makes it more assured from season to season and from year to year is a larger population. But the adjustment in turn to a larger population may be a greater division of labor, a specialization of occupation, different religious ceremonies, a differentiation of age societies, or the creation of social classes. These are derivative adaptations to the original or direct adaptation to the technological innovation. . . .

Men adjust to the steam engine by letting it drive their tools for them. Consequently, they work away from home in factories. Then the family, a social institution, adjusts to the absence of workers and to the new production and to the additional source of income. The adjustments in the family are the decline in the authority of the husband and father, the removal of economic production from the home, the separation of husband and wife, and the different type of education for the children. These are not the direct adaptations to the steam engine but are adaptations to the uses of steam-driven tools away from the homestead. . . .

The most numerous adjustments to a technological environment are the derivative ones; for any one direct adaptation to a technological element creates a change in a custom or an institution to which several other customs or institutions will adjust. But commonly these derivative adjustments are not seen as adjustments to the technological element in the first instance.[18]

A Pole who, in the twelfth century, invented machinery for weaving cloth was hanged for his pains—"for threatening the established order. . . . The same invention in the 18th century triggered off the Industrial Revolution."[19]

The automobile permits the middle-income American family (an institution) to move to the suburbs. And the presence of large numbers of people (with automobiles) in the suburbs creates that remarkable institution, the suburban shopping center. It is easy to take interrelations like this much as a matter of course. We were brought up with them. And yet the mental effort involved in backing away and taking a second look may generate some impression that here are interrelations which have dominated our lives and which have economic as well as sociological content. They have made suburbia, for good or ill, what it is.

The behavior norms of the institution, to the extent that they are currently in existence, came into being at some earlier time, historically. There is therefore some basic presumption that these norms were probably to some significant degree more appropriate to the conditions of those earlier times, to the conditions that brought them into being, than to the conditions of the present.

The influential conditions of those earlier times may be classified as other institutions, technology, and nature. One institution can certainly influence another. One nation can influence another by defeating it in war. But, in an infinite regression, all the norms of all the institutions had to come from somewhere else, not just from other institutions. And the chief candidate for the role of major influence has to be the evolving technological or scientific knowledge. The social organization and the corresponding behavior norms appropriate to a hunting and fishing culture are going to be different from the norms appropriate to an automobile age. The rules controlling the right-of-way will be different, for one thing.

It is going to be and has been the nature of the evolving technology that has dictated the essential features of the behavior norms—not exactly but substantially. Technology qua technology probably does not much care whether drivers hold to the left or the right, but they had better get organized and all act consistently.

The Interaction of Institutions on Institutions (Indirect Adaptation)

Especially because there has been some confusion on this score, it is worth emphasizing that the whole interaction story is not told by a simple allegation that the utilization of new technology works directly to involve change in the behavior norms of certain affected institutions. The story is generally more complicated and more subtle. The norms of a certain institution may be affected directly by some new technology, and the changed comportment of that institution may be a subsequent influence forcing a change in the behavior norms of yet another institution. The quotation from Ogburn cited earlier is replete with examples of such interrelations.

Many women perhaps were freed for commercial employment because such household appliances as the vacuum cleaner and the washing machine and such food-processing practices as canning and freezing made the maintenance of the home a less time-consuming task. Many mothers then found it possible and desirable to work away from the home. As a result of more mothers working (an institutional change in one area occasioned by the vacuum cleaner, etc.), the institution of the day nursery increased in importance and exposed many young children to a rather different way of life. Even some fathers (but certainly not all) have assumed greater responsibility for the daytime care of their children.

Also, the possibility should not be denied, although it has been by some institutionalists, that the new institutions (or the old institutions featuring new behavior norms) may accelerate the process of generation of new technology or call forth new innovation from the available reservoir of unused techniques. Causation may run from institutions to technology.

But, for the record here, the claim should probably be made, in anticipation of what will be said later, that such influences can probably accelerate only slightly the rate of accumulation of new technology and can surely have virtually no effect on the timewise ordering of the new technical discoveries. However, the new needs of the reorganized institutions may have considerable effect in determining what of the already existing repertoire of technology will actually be innovated to commercial use in a given period. In the early 1960s, we already had the technology to get a man on the moon. But a considerable amount of innovation was required. And, no doubt, a considerable amount of genuine new technology was generated in the process of actually putting a man on the moon. The accumulation of technical knowledge was accelerated, but the technology so generated was not the basic essential technology for the space flight. That was already known.

In contrast, some indication of the reluctance of institutions to develop major new technology in their own area of competence may be seen in this quotation from Floyd Vaughan:

> The telegraph companies did not invent the cable. Neither the telegraph nor the cable companies invented the telephone. The telegraph, cable and telephone companies did not invent the wireless telegraph; they even declined to buy it. The telegraph, cable, telephone and wireless telegraph companies did not invent the wireless telephone. The gas companies did not invent the electric light. The horse-car street railways did not invent the electric railway. Again, steam companies did not invent the steam turbine and the internal combustion engine. Silk manufacturers did not invent rayon. Collar manufacturers did not invent the soft collar. Manufacturers of washing machines did not invent the continuous laundry. The entrenched shoe-machinery company did not develop the use of glue for attaching soles to shoes. Motion-picture producers did not invent television. Aviation pools and companies, either here or abroad, did not invent the jet engine. The basic concepts in electronics did not come from electric-equipment industries. The manufacturers of dynamite and other mild explosives did not invent the atom and hydrogen bombs.[20]

The Role of Resources

One more element, besides the roles of technology and institutions (and the biology of the beast, which will not be discussed here), needs to be added to the picture to complete the description of the core of the institutional theory of economic progress. This involves the role of resources. The location of particular industries will be oriented geographically by the location of the resources appropriate to the given state of the technology. In Zimmermann's terms, the raw materials of the earth, neutral stuff, become valuable resources because the given state of technology so decrees.[21] And, as technology evolves, the relative usefulness and value of different raw materials change. The manner and the place in which the technology-institutions interrelations work themselves out are conditioned by the geographical availability of that particular type of neutral stuff which becomes the most appropriate resource in implementing the use of the new technology. In the early 1700s, the substitution of coal for wood in steelmaking by Abraham Darby at Coalbrookdale in Shropshire, "thanks to Britain's exceptional resource endowment [in coal] . . . , changed a high cost industry [in Britain] into the most efficient in the world"[22] and made Britain the dominant industrial power of the nineteenth century.

Clarence Ayres commented on this situation:

> We know today that resources and uses are not independent variables. For many years Professor Erich Zimmermann, the leading authority on the subject of resources, developed the thesis that both the identity of resources and their relative scarcity or profusion are determined by the culture of the people in question. For example, even such a common material as aluminum, which exists (as we now know) in all parts of the world, can be identified as a resource only since its identification as a chemical element and, more specifically, since the discovery in 1886 of the electrolytic process for extracting the metal from bauxite.[23]

The identification of something as a resource is the result of an evolutionary process in much the same way that technology evolves, and human biology, and institutionalized behavior norms. Thinking along the lines of the technological influence on changing neutral stuff into resources suggests that one should be questioning the implication of the allegation by the gloom and doom prophets of our time that resources may be exhausted.

Around us is all the bulk of earth and air and universe and, especially, the sun. The earth is mainly something Erich Zimmermann has called neutral stuff. It is just there taking up space or creating dockage possibilities until such time as the state of technology makes some of it a valuable resource to feed into the machines. And, in any given state of the technical arts, that area of the world will be developing most rapidly which is well endowed with the raw materials appropriate to that state of the arts. And individuals will tend to go there.

Neutral stuff comes and goes as a valuable resource. There is not much point in speaking of the danger of exhausting our resources. The chemicals of which the earth is made are transformed, and they change in relative value, but they are not exhausted, although the process of entropy may diffuse them.

It may be that at some time in the indefinite future the improvement in welfare on planet earth will be held back by the lack of some particular resource or by the presence of too many people in relation to the area of the earth. One can hardly prove the contrary, but there is every reason to believe that this will not be the nature of our basic problem in the next hundred years, if we can survive the next ten.

We may want to limit population because it is our judgment that people are cluttering up the place, or are polluting it unduly, or are hard to live with, but it simply is not true that lack of raw materials is at present a significant factor holding down welfare—on the whole. The possibility, however, does exist that the institutional hindrances, which make difficult the increase in welfare in a country like India, may make population control a desirable development policy in such a country. Thus, population control may be opted for on the ground that it is easier to implement such a policy than it is to change certain other institutions. But that is a judgment which will be made by those in a position to make it (as part of the ongoing self-correcting value judgment process).

In addition, it should certainly be granted that at any given time particular shortages may create structural problems, or force institutional change, and may be a considerable cause of inconvenience until the the appropriate adjustments are made. In fact, the availability of resources plays a twofold role concerning which it is desirable to be explicit. (1) New technology creates new resources out of neutral stuff. And the location of the chief deposits of the new resources influences the location of the new industry. And (2) any particular resource may become exhausted. And its exhaustion may lead to a shift to other raw materials, for example, as sources of fuel, or to abandonment of some particular industry, or to a shift in the geographical location of an industry and a change in institutionalized norms in particular industries. The structural and geographical changes may cause great inconvenience to large numbers of people. And the difficulties will be enhanced as bureaucrats, industrialists, politicians, and labor unions resist making the appropriate changes. And any politician who wants to be reelected had better believe it.

The Deemphasis of Technological Progress

One final word of caution on the nature of technology and the appropriateness of planning to increase the tempo of accumulation of technical knowledge: the characteristics of new technology do play a powerful role in reshaping institutions. And technology is a powerful influence on the nature of the economy and of all society. But emphasis on the accumulation of *additional* technical knowledge is no longer of crucial importance for raising the standard of living, at least in the developed countries. This distinction is important. The world is already possessed of the technical knowledge required to provide everyone with decent physical comfort—food, clothing, and shelter. This is a general proposition, true for the world with anything like its present population, in the absence of a collision with a meteor.

Keynes wrote in 1931:

> It is the author's profound conviction that the economic problem, ... the problem of want and poverty and the economic struggle between classes and nations, is nothing but a frightful muddle, a transitory and an unnecessary muddle. For the western world already has the resources and the technique, if we could create the organisation to use them, capable of reducing the economic problem, which now absorbs our moral and material energies, to a position of secondary importance.[24]

And Ralph Nader alleged on "Face the Nation" on September 2, 1973: "We've got the answers; they're just on the shelf."

Of course, the comments of these two men do not prove that current knowledge is technically capable of providing decent welfare for all, but what is involved here is well worth mulling over. From one's own information about the state of knowledge, what might one infer for oneself? What would seem to be the production capability of the United States, of the world, with, or perhaps without, India and Bangladesh?

Certainly we still need to develop cures for the common cold and for cancer, as well as effective garbage disposal. And the energy crisis should not be taken lightly, nor should smog. But in the area of technology it is only specialized bits of technical knowledge that we need desperately. The massive further accumulation of additional technical knowledge on all fronts is a luxury, not a necessity. However, it is a luxury we can well afford; and life may be enriched by the new knowledge provided by new technology. It may also be debased.

Jacques Ellul goes further than this in an effort to downgrade technology. He appreciates its power, but he is not convinced that it is a good thing.[25] In fact, he probably goes astray, or too far, in denouncing technical progress for ruining civilizations. Contrary to his view, surely, technology is not to be condemned because it forces the modification of civilizations and institutions and cultures. A lot of them can stand some modifications, although this decision should be an aspect of the process of the self-correcting value judgments made by the people primarily involved. There is nothing sacrosanct about the cultures of the past—be they Hindu, or redneck, or Scotch Presbyterian.

The technology-institutions adjustment process does involve making some judgments as to what of the proliferating amount of technical knowledge is worth assimilating. If we are to be master, rather than slave, of this process, we must pick and choose with judgment. We do not want to assimilate all the technology that is available and anxious to be used (like germ warfare and nerve gas). But, whether we like it or not, the dynamism of technical accumulation is with us, shaping our lives and hammering on our institutions. However, society no longer needs especially to mollycoddle physicists and mathematicians on the grounds that their skills are of overwhelming importance for accumulating technical knowledge and that accumulating technical knowledge is all-important for raising standards of living.

The two problems of overriding importance that remain involve how to use the technology and knowledge that we have and will have in order to provide a decent living for all. This is primarily an institutional adjustment problem, not a technology accumulation problem, and it is such in both developed and underdeveloped countries. In addition, there is a technical assimilation problem of great importance in the underdeveloped countries. The relevant knowledge is generally already available in the developed countries, but in the underdeveloped countries it is up to the institutions to adjust, to pick and choose among available techniques, to use them, meanwhile adapting them to the circumstances of countries with relatively abundant supplies of labor.

Of general importance in both developed and underdeveloped countries is the problem of figuring out how affluent and naturally combative *Homo sapiens* can live together with other *Homines sapientes* in a degree of harmony and good-fellowship that will permit most people to truly enjoy life. We have the technology. But we have not yet worked out how to use it to make life a generally worthwhile experience.

Summary of the Theory of Economic Progress

For all events, the simplified schema of the aspect of institutional theory having to do with the process of change (the theory of economic progress) is as follows: (1) The important dynamic force is the accumulation of technical knowledge. (2) Institutionalized forms of behavior act as a brake on the assimilation and the constructive use of technical knowledge. Change in particular institutionalized practices is forced by technical progress. But the speed with which new technology will be introduced is controlled by the rigidity of institutionalized resistance to change. (3) How and where production will actually occur are conditioned also by the availability of the natural resources appropriate to the given state of technology. (4) Central to all these influences and interrelations is the individual as an evolving biological entity.

NOTES

1. C. E. Ayres, *The Theory of Economic Progress* (Chapel Hill: University of North Carolina Press, 1944); Thorstein Veblen, *The Theory of the Leisure Class* (New York: B. W. Huebsch, 1899).
2. C. E. Ayres, *The Industrial Economy* (Boston: Houghton Mifflin, 1952), p. 52. This is a broad definition of technical knowledge which includes as technology phenomena sometimes classified separately as science or technology (or techniques). Some of the terminological differences and problems are discussed in Francis R. Allen, *Social-Cultural Dynamics* (New York: Macmillan, 1971), and in Francis R. Allen et al., *Technology and Social Change* (New York: Appleton-Century-Crofts, 1957).
3. Jacques Ellul, *The Technological Society* (New York: Vintage Books, 1964 [1954]), p. 90.
4. In Melvin Kranzberg and Carroll W. Pursell, Jr., eds., *Technology in Western Civilization*, 2 vols. (New York: Oxford University Press, 1967), 1:57; for additional examples see J. Bronowski, *The Ascent of Man* (Boston: Little, Brown, 1973).
5. In Kranzberg and Pursell, eds., *Technology in Western Civilization*, p. 232.
6. Ayres, *Theory of Economic Progress*, p. 113.
7. John R. Commons, *Institutional Economics* (Madison: University of Wisconsin Press, 1961 [1934]), p. 69; see also Francis Stuart Chapin, *Cultural Change* (New York: Century, 1928), pp. 45, 48.

8. William Graham Sumner, *Folkways* (Boston: Ginn, 1906), p. iv.
9. John Maynard Keynes, *The General Theory of Employment, Interest and Money* (New York: Harcourt, Brace, 1936), p. viii.
10. John Locke, "An Essay Concerning Human Understanding," in *Great Books of the Western World*, vol. 35: *Locke, Berkeley, Hume* (Chicago: Encyclopaedia Britannica, 1952 [1690]), p. 112.
11. Ibid., p. 111.
12. Solomon E. Asch, "Opinions and Social Pressure," *Scientific American* 193 (November 1955): 31–35, especially p. 34; see also Kurt Lewin, *Resolving Social Conflicts* (New York: Harper, 1948), p. 58.
13. William James, *Principles of Psychology* (Chicago: Encyclopaedia Britannica, 1952 [1890]), pp. 808–890.
14. Richard T. LaPiere and Paul R. Farnsworth, *Social Psychology* (New York: McGraw-Hill, 1949), p. 39.
15. Muzafer Sherif, *The Psychology of Social Norms* (New York: Harper & Row, 1966 [1936]), p. 1.
16. Lewin, *Resolving Social Conflicts*, pp. 56–58.
17. Karl Marx, *Early Texts*, ed. and trans. David McLellan (Oxford: Basil Blackwell, 1971), p. 108.
18. William F. Ogburn, *On Culture and Social Change* (Chicago: University of Chicago Press, 1964), pp. 82–84, 134. In one of the essays, Ogburn indicates that he had this conception of the technology-institutions relation as early as about 1914.
19. Paul Streeten, *The Frontiers of Development Studies* (London: Macmillan, 1972), p. 68.
20. Floyd L. Vaughan, "Monopoly and Patents in the U.S.A.," *Cartel* (October 1957): 133.
21. See W. N. Peach and James A. Constantin, *Zimmermann's World Resources and Industries*, 3d ed. (New York: Harper & Row, 1972).
22. David S. Landes, *The Unbound Prometheus* (Cambridge, Eng.: Cambridge University Press, 1970 [1969]), p. 95.
23. C. E. Ayres, *Toward a Reasonable Society: The Values of Industrial Civilization* (Austin: University of Texas Press, 1961), p. 64.
24. John Maynard Keynes, *Essays in Persuasion* (New York: Norton, 1963 [1931]), p. vii.
25. Ellul, *Technological Society*, pp. 126, 130.

ADDITIONAL READINGS

Barnett, Homer G. *Innovation: The Basis of Cultural Change*. New York: McGraw-Hill, 1953.
Benedict, Ruth. *Patterns of Culture*. Boston: Houghton Mifflin, 1934.
Boulding, Kenneth E. *Ecodynamics*. Beverly Hills: Sage Publications, 1978.

————. "Toward the Development of a Cultural Economics." *Social Science Quarterly* 52 (September 1972):267–284.

Copeland, Morris A. *Fact and Theory in Economics: The Testament of an Institutionalist*. Ithaca: Cornell University Press, 1958.

Daumas, Maurice, ed. *A History of Technology and Invention*. New York: Crown Publishers, 1969.

David, Paul A. *Technical Choice, Innovation and Economic Growth*. Cambridge, Eng.: Cambridge University Press, 1974.

Dewey, John. *Intelligence in the Modern World: John Dewey's Philosophy*. New York: Modern Library, 1939.

Dorfman, Joseph. *Thorstein Veblen and His America*. New York: Viking, 1934.

————, et al. *Institutional Economics*. Berkeley and Los Angeles: University of California Press, 1963.

Dowd, Douglas F., ed. *Thorstein Veblen*. Ithaca: Cornell University Press, 1958.

Fusfeld, Daniel R. *The Age of the Economist*. Glenview, Ill.: Scott, Foresman, 1966.

Gambs, John S. *Economics and Man*. Homewood, Ill.: Irwin, 1968.

Gruchy, Allan G. *Contemporary Economic Thought*. Clifton, N.J.: Kelley, 1972.

————. *Modern Economic Thought*. New York: Prentice-Hall, 1947.

Hamilton, Walton H. *Industrial Policy and Institutionalism*. Clifton, N.J.: Kelley, 1974.

Jewkes, John, David Sawers, and Richard Stillerman. *The Sources of Invention*. 2d ed. New York: Norton, 1969.

LaPiere, Richard T. *Social Change*. New York: McGraw-Hill, 1965.

Malinowski, Bronislaw. *Dynamics of Culture Change*. New Haven: Yale University Press, 1945.

Martindale, Don. *Social Life and Cultural Change*. Princeton: Van Nostrand, 1962.

Mitchell, Wesley C. *Lecture Notes on Types of Economic Theory from Mercantilism to Institutionalism*. 2 vols. New York: Augustus M. Kelley, 1949.

Mumford, Lewis. *Technics and Civilization*. New York: Harcourt, Brace, 1934.

Myrdal, Gunnar. *Against the Stream*. London: Macmillan, 1974.

Nabseth, Lars, and G. F. Ray, eds. *Diffusion of New Technology*. London: Cambridge University Press, 1974.

Ogburn, William F. *Social Change with Respect to Culture and Original Nature*. New York: B. W. Huebsch, 1922.

Robinson, Joan. *Economic Philosophy*. Chicago: Aldine, 1962.

Rosenberg, Nathan. *Perspectives on Technology*. Cambridge, Mass.: Cambridge University Press, 1976.

Tawney, Richard H. *Religion and the Rise of Capitalism*. London: Murray, 1926.

Thompson, Carey C., ed. *Institutional Adjustment: A Challenge to a Changing Economy*. Austin: University of Texas Press, 1967.

Tool, Marc R. *The Discretionary Economy*. Santa Monica: Goodyear, 1979.

Veblen, Thorstein. *Imperial Germany and the Industrial Revolution*. New York: Augustus M. Kelley, 1964 [1915].

Wallas, Graham. *Our Social Heritage*. London: Allen & Unwin, 1921.

Weber, Max. *The Protestant Ethic and the Spirit of Capitalism*. New York: Scribner's, 1930 [1904].

Zimmermann, Erich W. *World Resources and Industries*. 2d ed. New York: Harper, 1951. A new edition was prepared by W. Nelson Peach in 1972.

3.
The Value Theory of Institutional Economics

The Concept of Value

"Value" is a judgment made by an individual (or, in some sense, by an institution or by technology) regarding what is desirable or esteemed. The conception that something has value involves the identification by one of these custodians of value (the individual, or the institution, or technology) that that something has desirability or is worthy of esteem. And value theory, or axiology, is the study of the process by which judgments about values are made and values are identified.

Essentially values are inherent in individuals, but there is a sense in which society as a whole and the particular institutions that make up society are the custodians of consensuses about values. And society and its constituent institutions play a role in imposing values on individuals. Also, the quality of the technology influences the degree to which the value goals can be realized.

Who is this individual who makes judgments about values? The answer would seem rather simple: it is any being biologically capable of having an opinion about the desirability or quality of something. Thus, all kinds of beings are capable of having values: smart people and morons, women and men, different races, monkeys, dogs, horses, the old as well as the young, and maybe the birds and the bees also, who knows?

The social and institutional structure of society, however, is going to influence which beings have more effect on determining the social consensus and on identifying the values which society imposes on individuals. (Who, or what species, is included varies as time passes and the process of self-correcting value judgments works itself out.)

It is the individual who matters, at least if individuals are the actors and they think so. But this does not mean that their values are unique, or permanent, or instinctive, or definitive, or clairvoyant. Quite the contrary: values are changeable results of changing circumstances and reflect attitudes not omniscience.

We choose to be concerned about the individual's stake in things because we are individuals. The concern of some individuals is pretty much concentrated on themselves. The concern of others may include other individuals or, at least, selected other individuals. Those with this extended concern may become involved with behavior interactions between and among other individuals, groups of individuals, and groups of individuals organized as institutions which are implementing certain behavior norms.

But before we become too enamored of the individual, it is worth speculating a little about what makes the beast tick.

Influences on the Individual's Values

The forces influencing the ever changing ideas about values of individuals are here alleged to be (1) the individual's biological heredity, (2) the force of technology, (3) the inhibitions of institutional norms, and (4) the natural setting (which involves resource availability).

The Individual's Biological Heredity

The biology of the individual beyond all doubt influences that individual's conception of what is desirable or estimable in the world. A being which did not drink water and a being which did would have different opinions of the value of water. Whether we value burbling in it as we drink is, however, probably more institutionally than biologically determined, except for babies. Also, it is biologically determined that we value eating, but whether we choose to hold a fork with our right or our left hand is institutionally determined.

We *are* our biological makeup, which is what it is because of a long-drawn-out process of mutation and natural selection and, perhaps, a few genetic accidents that explain some special differences between one individual and the next. (A benign, or not so benign, superior being may or may not have been influencing these processes.)

Technology

As a participant in the process of technological accumulation, the individual is continually reappraising the relative worth or usefulness of one or another of the available technologies for the purposes of getting a job done (which implements a value that the individual currently holds). The individual is also creating those new technologies or, at least, some people are. The merit or value inherent in the technology is appraised and reappraised in terms of its ability to produce desired results. This is the process of self-correcting value judgments. Is the technology which is used an effective instrument for producing a desired result or as effective an instrument as is available? If it is, or to the extent that it is, then value is inherent in that technology. It is a locus of value.

Such is instrumental value theory.

Ongoing value judgments are made continually, involving the reappraising of the merits of different tools or technologies for effecting desired ends. Meanwhile, the merits of the ends, the goals, the values subscribed to at the moment by the individual are also being continually reappraised. Thus, there is an ends-means-ends continuum in which both means and ends (tools, values, and behavior norms) are being reassessed by the individual. The appraisal of the tools as values and as means is changing in a process that also involves the appearance of new tools in a fairly erratic but ongoing process. The serviceability of the institutionalized behavior norms is also being reappraised both as a consequence of the changing attitudes of the individuals who make up the institutions and as a consequence of the qualitatively changing technology with which individuals and society are working.

Technology is the dynamic force which, over time, is overwhelmingly influential in determining the nature of society, the behavior norms of institutions, and the values of individuals. The institutions since the Industrial Revolution—the corporations, banks, and labor unions—came to have behavior norms very different from those of the dominant institutions of the Middle Ages—the guilds, feudal manors, chivalry, and slavery—precisely because the effective use of the steam engine and the open hearth and other new technologies required institutions different from those called forth by the three-field system and handicraft manufacturing. Thus, technology plays its influential role both because it has the capability for making the physical face of the world what it is and because in so doing it forces institutions to adapt and change their norms or values.

Institutions and Their Eternally Antiquated Norms

So, institutions acquire behavior norms or *values* in response to the exigencies of technology. A behavior pattern in existence as an aspect of the norms or values then held by an institution, however, tends to be continued until some positive new influence comes along to coerce a change. Consequently, at any given time, the behavior norms (or values) of institutions are characteristics which came into being at an earlier time and may be said to be, in all likelihood, more appropriate to the conditions, the technology, of that earlier time. But to say that behavior norms are antiquated does not preclude the possibility that they may represent values which individuals may wish to retain. The institutions of society do have norms or values in this sense, as Clarence Ayres points out.[1] And Ayres does use the term "values" to describe the behavior norms of institutions.

At all events, at a given time an institution has certain antiquated values or behavior norms. Bankers are more likely to consider would-be borrowers to be credit-worthy if they come from what the bankers consider to be good families. Labor union members may want their leaders to sound a bit uncouth and to wear dirty shirts or silk shirts—nothing in between will do. These currently held values may contribute little to the efficacy of either bank or labor union activities at the present time. But they are values: values from the viewpoint of the institution which endorses them and from the viewpoint of the individual who endorses such behavior.

Individuals brought up in the setting of certain institutions—the family and the church and their ethics, certain clubs and fraternities and their carryings-on, corporations and their profit seeking, politics and its lack of ethics—form their values in conformity with the exigencies of those institutions, as conditioned by the individual's biology, as influenced by the natural setting, and as constrained by technology.

The Role of Resources and the Natural Setting

The availability of more or less effective resources will make a difference in the evaluation of the relative merits of various techniques for making given products. The technique emphasizing the use of the more readily available raw material will be preferable—

more "valuable," as will be the more readily available, usable raw material.

The Values of Society and Its Institutions

The isolated values of individuals are only part of the economic story. Overshadowing these is the social consensus on values, the institutionalized behavior norms of society. As I said above, these behavior norms are inherited from the past and are imposed by society on individuals. However, they are modified by the influences at work in connection with the innovation of technology, and individuals are not entirely passive spectators of this situation. They have some awareness of the implications and the potential of the new technology, of the institutional modifications that seem appropriate, of the serviceability of the resources at hand, and even of the role of their own biological capabilities. So, in a context where individuals are massively influenced by the institutionalized behavior norms which have been their heritage, they are part of a process of self-correcting value judgments which is conditioning the whole interacting process.[2]

Technology as a Locus of Value

When some institutional economists speak of technology as the locus of value, they probably have either or both of two concepts in mind. First, the dynamic force which is technological accumulation plays a major role in reshaping institutions and the behavior norms of institutions. And institutions and their power to impose their behavior norms on individuals play a major role in conditioning individuals to appreciate the values fostered by the institutions. The values of individuals are not exempt from the impact of technology, either directly or via the effect of technology on institutions.

Regarding this, Ayres writes: "The values which emerge from this instrumental process derive their significance from that process." The technological value system is "one in which all tool activities are related to the continuum of means and ends and exhibit a mutual consistency of concertedness. . . . Technology is not 'things' but a form of human behavior." The "continuum of means and ends" defines "the general welfare."[3]

The other concept relevant to calling technology a locus of value is inherent in the wording when this type of value theory is called instrumental. Here emphasis is on the process involving continuously testing behavior. Technology is the instrument by which propositions or values are tested and desirable or valuable results are obtained. Values suggest that it is desirable to do something or that something is desirable. Effort is made to give effect to the values. The process involves the use of instruments, techniques, or methods, and the job is done more or less well. The result is judged. Have the desired results been obtained more or less satisfactorily? Has the technique functioned well as an instrument? Would some other available technique have served better? A technique has more or less value because it will accomplish more or less effectively the result desired. Technology *is* the instrument, and in this sense technology may be looked on as a locus of value.

Alfred Chalk seems to be taking this position when he writes: "When [Ayres] argues that the 'locus' of value is to be found in technology, I interpret him to mean that it is the continuity of the tool-using function which makes possible all human progress."[4] In an important sense this is a value theory distinct from orthodox economics, which is oriented to the proposition that it is the monetary profit motive that is primarily responsible for making the wheels go round.

We are feeling around in a quite different can of worms if the chief force influencing the nature (the form, the stench, the beauty) of the world and of our society is technology, since technology is accumulated in a manner that is very little influenced by the profit motive or by the social need for particular technological advances, such as a cure for cancer. The process is basically a self-contained continuum proceeding at varying speeds, depending on the effectiveness of institutional resistance to the assimilation of the new technology.

John Dewey says in *Reconstruction in Philosophy*: "The usefulness of a road . . . is measured by whether it actually functions *as* a road, as a means of easy and effective public transportation and communication [if it does, it is instrumental]. And so with the serviceableness of an idea or hypothesis as a measure of its truth."[5] And Ayres chooses to synthesize these influences thus in *The Theory of Economic Progress*: "To speak of value is to speak of the relation of any single act—choice, preference, decision, or judgment—to the whole life-process. . . . If economic value means anything at all, its meaning is that of a gradual and continuous realization of a more effective organization of the technological life-process."[6]

This way of looking at things makes the continuation of the life process an overwhelming concern and the technological continuum the instrument that orients the nature of the life process. Ergo, technology is the locus of value. If this strikes a chord with the reader, fine—if not, if the reader somehow gags at personalizing technology in this way, at thinking of technology as possessing values, as being a locus of value, that is quite all right, too. The reader can also gag at calling the behavior norms of institutions values and can revert to the simple position that it is basically individuals who have values. But for the individual's values to be socially acceptable there must be a consensus about them on the part of society.

The Self-Correcting Value Judgment

The value theory of institutional economics, which may also be called instrumental value theory (and is in the general tradition of C. S. Peirce, William James, and John Dewey), views value determination as a process involving continuously testing a technique (used in an effort to implement values) against the consequences of the use of that technique. It involves evaluating the technology against the results obtained when one uses that particular technology in an effort to implement a value. But, at the same time that the quality or the value of the technique is being tested, the value itself is subject to reappraisal in light of the consequences of the effort to implement it. Thus, values themselves are reappraised against the consequences of trying to give them effect. And the quality and changing nature of the dynamically accumulating technology dominate the whole process and the physical look of the world. This is the ends-means-ends continuum, which has no beginning and no end. This is not a teleological process. There is no paradise to be had at the end of the road or right after some revolution which is just around the corner, if we could just carry it off. Rather, this is a process which is ever ongoing. And in the course of this process individuals are continually reappraising. They are changing their opinion of which technologies work best, and they are discovering new technologies as a by-product of the internal dynamic of the technology accumulation process. They are rejecting some technologies and assimilating others. They are looking at the products of those efforts. And the innovation and use of the better and more desirable technologies force changes in the structure of institutions and their behavior norms. And those institutionalized behavior norms are the values of institutions and in their turn are affecting the values of individuals. And we have gone full circle and a half.

Wolfgang Friedmann has provided an example of this process:

> An enquiry into an ethical proposition may start with the formulation of a value hypothesis; but this value postulate is only provisional, and has to be tested by the means of its possible realization. A study of such means—which include the legal, social, and economic environment of a society—may influence and modify the value postulate. A convenient illustration of this approach might be the question of prohibition of alcohol, which deeply influenced American legal, economic, and social life for more than a decade after the First World War. Absolute prohibition could be stated as a value goal. Means of its execution consist in the appropriate Constitutional amendments, statutory prohibitions, administrative regulations, and the policing of the legal prohibitions [as well as the technology used in attempted enforcement—the speed of the Coast Guard ships, the investigatory techniques of the law enforcement officers, etc.]. An enquiry into the means of execution may show that the purported enforcement of prohibition leads—as in fact it did—to a vast increase in the consumption of illegal and often lethal alcohol, bootlegging, gang warfare, murder, and a general increase in criminality. The results of such enquiries may lead to an abandonment or the modification of the original value postulate. Abandonment of the ethical postulate, in the light of practical experience, is expressed in the repeal of the Constitutional amendment in the U.S. Constitution.[7]

The energy crisis of the 1970s has provided another example of the process of self-correcting value judgments at work, this time with respect to the serviceability of production techniques and the appropriateness of various raw-material sources. Coal has been one of the possibilities as a substitute for petroleum and natural gas. But there are better technologies for using coal than burning the large lumps which used to be standard. Alternatives include gasification, slurry, pellets, and so on. Much experimentation is going on with regard to the effectiveness of these different processes. And self-correcting, changing value judgments are being made and will continue to be made. Also with regard to the value of different alternative raw-material energy sources, judgments are being made and reappraised as to the relative desirability of emphasizing coal, shale oil, tar sand, hot (thermal) water, the sun, and so on.

The nature of our knowledge about alternative processes has been changing. This means that definitive (absolute, cost-specific) judgments cannot be made with once-and-for-all certainty. We have to back and fill, try and try again.

Another example of changing values is the value attributed to (the satisfaction obtained from) having a large number of children. Nomads have tended to restrict their number of children. Children apparently can be a lot of trouble to nomads, just as they may be to other parents who travel. But, in a society such as that of India in past centuries, large numbers of children apparently have been desired because they offered some sort of promise of security to their parents.

Truth and values evolve and are relative to the time, and place, and institutions, and technology (and heredity and the natural setting). Human nature and its scheme of values are being created and re-created every day. As Ayres says in *The Industrial Economy*: "The present nature of man—what human beings as we know them are—is a function of life in society."[8]

The test of behavior and/or technique is whether it gives desired results, whether it is effectively instrumental. The value theory, then, is that values are created and identified (instrumentally determined) in a process involving self-correcting (or self-adjusting) value judgments. One does things differently next time if a previous method did not work out satisfactorily: "the proof of the pudding is in the eating." A child who touches a hot skillet makes a self-correcting value judgment in a hurry. And the values, as to the desirable or the estimable, which the individual holds at any particular time are also determined in this process in the intermix with technology and institutions. And what can be done with all this at a given time is conditioned by the state of technology and the availability of appropriate resources.

The crucial ingredient in instrumental value theory is the ongoing nature of the process. The values of individuals change as individual attitudes change in a context of evolving heredity, changing institutional norms, evolving technology, and changing natural setting. No definitive judgment can be made now regarding what is best for all time. No master plan for a perfect state can be drawn up now, with the thought that this is the ideal social order for which we should all work and that, once we have arrived at this promised land, all will be for the best in this best of all possible worlds—permanently. This is simply not the name of the game, and life would be a big bore if it were.

The Cross-Cultural Nature of Institutional Value Theory

It should be noted that value theory, as stated above, is (if the approach is correct) common to all cultures. That is, it involves a principle that can be applied to all cultures. Certainly different cultures may value particular goods or circumstances differently, but that is not the crux of the matter. There is here a common principle, even though it may result in different evaluations of particular commodities in different cultures at a given time. Margaret Mead may be quoted in defense of something like this conception:

> In summary it may be said that world community seems most likely to be attained by working toward certain overall abstract and inclusive values, within which the different peoples of the world, who now see one another as separate, competitive, or unrelated, will be able to feel themselves a part, the cultures of each regularly related to the whole to which all give allegiance in different ways congruent with their own cultural values. Thus we would be working toward the type of multi-dimensional world culture, within which there would be interdependence of diverse values rather than a world in which any one interest or function so dominated the others that single value scales, competition, and destruction were the concomitants.[9]

The value theory methodology is general even though the concepts of what is valuable are not the same from culture to culture. For example, two cultures may have different views regarding the appropriateness of collecting interest on debts. Yet the value theory should be capable of explaining how both these conceptions were arrived at.

Also, values may be surprisingly similar in two societies with more or less similar technologies, two industrial economies, for example. Herbert Marcuse speaks of similarities in the values of western capitalism and Soviet communism—similarities that he says exist because of the similarities in the problems created by "the nature of the industrial society" in both places. And these similarities in value exist in spite of major protestations on both sides as to how different they are.[10]

Final Ends

All this implies that there are no values which people at a given time are entitled to claim will hold for all time or which it can be alleged certainly describe conditions in the ultimately desirable society. One cannot describe with confidence the characteristics of the perfect or most desirable society with assurance that those evaluations will hold into the indefinite future. The structure and behavior norms of the ideal commune, or of the Garden of Eden, or of utopia, or of heaven, or of Valhalla cannot be described or anticipated in any final sense.

To the extent that Christian ethics, and Marxist dogma, and the codes of various other religions and schools of thought try to describe definitively the ideal society, they are trying to do something that they have not been accredited as being competent to do. The future will insist on having its own say in the matter. And since the world of the future will belong to the people of the future, for better or worse, they will have their say and their way in the matter. James Buchanan has a conception of this when he writes:

> We do not "solve" the "problem" of social order by producing a unique "solution," regardless of the sophistication of empirical techniques. There is no objective "truth" to be established here. The "problem" of social order is faced eternally by persons who realize that they must live together and that to do so they must impose *upon themselves* social rules, social institutions. Economics and economists cannot evade their responsibility in the continuing discourse over such rules and institutions by shifting attention to trivialities.[11]

The Catalog of Current Commonly Held Values

To say that different individuals or different institutions or different cultures may value things differently does not mean that it is bootless at a given time and place to attempt to catalog the current commonly held values. Certain values may be quite generally held for long periods of time, maybe even forever. An attempt at a catalog of currently held values should be worthwhile even though it is both tentative and, even where confirmed at the moment, subject to change. Ayres has attempted such a catalog.[12] I now attempt a similar listing, alleging its applicability at least to western society in the 1970s.

The first value—the decent minimum—is the possession of a decent, minimum, material level of living for all, accompanied by the right on the part of the individual to pursue, not too obstreperously, an improved level of living. (This concept can have meaning as a right only if there is productive capability to meet it and an agency with the corresponding duty to implement it. I allege that the world does have the necessary productive capability to provide everyone with a decent minimum and that it is feasible to organize arrangements that can make the decent minimum available to all.) The second value—getting along pleasantly—is the conception that people have the right to expect other people to be pleasant and cooperative and have the obligation to behave so themselves. The third value—constructive self-expression—is the conception that the individual has a right to a degree of freedom of action that permits such constructive self-expression as will allow that individual to be proud of his or her own behavior. The fourth value—security—is the right to such security as is reasonably attainable, security of several kinds: employment, considerate care during illness, old age, and childhood. And there is also the matter of security against the ravages of war.

The realization or implementation of these values or goals or needs or desires for all people would seem to be the chief legitimate function of governments, at this time, provided there actually is consensus with regard to these values at this time.

The foregoing catalog represents an assertion. If the list seems reasonable to people in general, then now and here it is reasonable. If it does not seem reasonable, the human race will look elsewhere for criteria on goals and behavior, norms and values. It will not do without them, although there may not be agreement as to what they are. And, in line with the instrumental value theory, it will change them as it deems appropriate.

One other comment: rights exist only when there are corresponding duties—obligations on the part of others who have the power to act effectively to observe or implement the rights. The rights have to be implementable. I allege here that the rights indicated above meet these conditions: they are feasible for society to implement and there is meaningful consensus about them. They are therefore RIGHTS.

The Decent Minimum

It is appropriate to make an effort to justify, or at least to explain, the basis for this list of alleged values and rights.

At all events, the first in the list was the decent, minimum, material level of living. This should mean that everyone has a right to enough to live on in decent comfort. The presumption is that this is extremely important (and also quite feasible, given the current state of world technical knowledge). There is also a presumption that the usefulness (the marginal utility) of additional goods declines very rapidly after the decent minimum has been attained and that getting along on reasonably pleasant terms with one's fellows (the second right) rises very markedly in relative importance thereafter.

This psychological fact makes the use of rising average real national income a very suspect measure of increase in welfare, especially in a setting where substantial inequality and shifting degrees of inequality in income distribution are involved. Is rising income, if it is accompanied by increasing inequality, desirable?

The implementation of the decent minimum involves several things. For those able to work who live in a developed country, the crux of the matter is the implementation of the job guarantee. For the able-bodied poor of the underdeveloped countries, the job guarantee should also play a significant role. But in the underdeveloped countries there needs to be more emphasis on measures to increase production and productivity. Chapter 17 is concerned with these problems.

The implications are different when the question involves guaranteeing a decent minimum for those who are not able-bodied: the very young, the very old, the ill, and the handicapped. There is the black mother of ten who cannot possibly earn enough to maintain her family. There is the half-disabled, middle-aged father. There are large numbers of disadvantaged and infirm people in the ghettos, in the countryside, around the world. And the job guarantee does not solve their problem.

The problem of providing a decent minimum to the underprivileged, however, will be a less and less important part of the economic picture as time passes. *Homo sapiens* already has the technology to provide far more than a decent minimum for all, as well as the resources to do it, and increasingly will almost certainly so provide—unless we succeed in the neat trick of so contaminating our own environment that we wipe out the potential welfare gains from increased productivity. We may manage to accomplish this feat. But, for the general purposes of this book, it will be assumed that we will not. And it is also assumed that we are capable of structuring production in such wise that difficulties, such as the energy crisis, which need only be temporary, in fact only are temporary.

Many people in the United States are now living in comfortable affluence. And the same, in all reason, can be true anon for the world's population in general. The standard of living will be high and it will be rising. The momentum of improving technology and rising productivity will assure this unless human perverseness outdoes itself.

Getting Along Pleasantly

In the longer run, the more important and difficult problem is not going to be how to maximize the material welfare of those fat cats who inhabit the earth or even how to assure them a comfortable living. The affluent society is not necessarily the pleasant society. The problem is going to be how to cut down on the cat fights, after the tabbies get through stuffing themselves and napping, and how to cut down on the amount of tomcat yowling during the night. The problem is how to get along pleasantly together.

Our problem is to civilize ourselves, to create a society which is not characterized by the indecent telephone call, surliness, public and private gruffness and rudeness, inconsiderate behavior, bullying and violence, the mugging of the elderly, and the exploiting of the young (frequently by the young) with dope and otherwise. We need to pick up our own litter, control our own noise, know where our own cigarette smoke is going, drive with respect for the other driver, think about the implications of the things we do.

There is, for one thing, the syndrome of suburbia: "Won't somebody drive down to the all-night grocery and get a quart of milk for the scalloped potatoes?" (The cost of the trip will only slightly more than double the cost of the milk.) Daddy, who just came in dog-tired and griping, can go. Or Mary will be glad to go, only, if she does, it is pretty likely to be an hour and a half before she gets back. Sending Junior is out of the question. He is on the phone.

This is a way of life, and some of its participants are seething, others are being intentionally irritating, and others have the knack, it seems, of being utterly oblivious.

One may recall Thomas Hobbes and his view that humans naturally live out their lives in a state of war in which every being is against every other being, "and the life of man [is] solitary, poor, nasty, brutish, and short." For Hobbes, what was called for was a sort of covenant which would establish order, "justice, equity, modesty, mercy, and, in sum, doing to others as we would be done to." A king would enforce the rules of the covenant. For "covenants without the sword, are but words and of no strength to secure a man at all."[13] But, according to Hobbes, the king would be removable by the people if he failed to provide the protection which it was his function to provide.

There is probably good reason not to be as trusting of kings and dictators as was Hobbes and to, rather, place reliance in the long, slow democratic process of perfecting understanding among humans, an understanding of what must be involved in personal relations if we are to live together in a halfway pleasant manner. This is the problem of creating civilization. But Hobbes' idea that people need to get along would seem to be a simpleminded, basic truth.

It is probably possible to speak rather categorically concerning the obligation of society vis-à-vis humans and their behavior traits. Society is concerned for all people; it *is* all people. To the extent that individual self-indulgence is expressed in a manner that is harmful to the rest of society, society has an obligation to itself to inhibit this expression. The same is true of individual pursuit of power, wealth, or status. To the extent that individuals become obnoxious by the manner in which they pursue their goals, they can reasonably expect to be put in their place (perhaps by a sort of subtle ostracism). A distinction needs to be made between the desires of individuals and the goals which society can reasonably be expected to respect. There is a difference between freedom and license which seems difficult for the individual practicing license to appreciate. "All I did was . . . And, besides, nobody complained." But, if a society is to have self-respect, it needs to compel this appreciation of the distinction between individual desires and the values or goals which society can be expected to respect. The institutionalized attitude, which runs deep in our society, to the effect that the aggressive and the inconsiderate are to be given tacit approval is one of the real difficulties involved in evolving into a pleasantly livable society.[14] Camus has Caligula say in act 2: "On est toujours libre aux dépens de quelqu'un." And Veblen, speaking of the inception of civilization in the Baltic states, writes: "The common understanding that made group life practicable appears to have been in effect the rule of live and let live."[15]

Perhaps psychology has something useful to say on this problem. Mutually antagonistic people and groups may be more likely, spontaneously, to work out reconciliation if they are brought together, somehow, in a context that more or less forces them to work together toward common goals. Cooperative working in an effort to achieve goals in which all have an interest may be a way to eliminate bitternesses between groups. Muzafer Sherif speaks of "the effectiveness of superordinate goals in reducing intergroup conflict." [16] And he has worked extensively in trying to develop procedures by which this may be done.

The Self-Assertive/Social Animal and Civilization

We are both an aggressive and a social animal.[17] And we have some reconciling to do as we put those two characteristics together in the process of building a civilized society.

The meaning of civilization is the control of aggressiveness and nastiness so that people can live among their kin in a reasonably viable relationship. The essence of civilized behavior has to be that one will do, voluntarily, the things which it is obviously desirable that the average person should do in the process of making the community livable. Those suddenly active in the antipollution campaign should appreciate the appropriateness of picking up their own litter.

The reconciliation process cannot be worked out by hitting the other fellow over the head. It cannot be worked out by force, by the imposition of new norms and an autocratic enforcement of those norms thereafter—in Nazi Germany, perhaps, but not in a civilized society. Society, conceived as an institution, needs to rethink some of its ideas as to reasonable behavior and as to how reasonable behavior is enforced. Once there is social or group consensus, the bulk of the enforcement problem is automatically dealt with. People do conform to social or group pressure—although sometimes the group to whose pressures they are responding may impose antisocial behavior on its members. Society has a problem in determining how to deal with this kind of group. There is the trade association telling its members to lobby for a protective tariff. There is the fraternity fostering hazing, or the radical group fostering truculence and defiance, even on Gentle Thursday.

For several thousand years, civilization has kept the uncooperative and the mean in some sort of line by alleging that the human race has a purpose. This teleological approach states that there is a final cause, a great purpose in existence. You will go to heaven if you are good.

It has been intellectually satisfying for liberal intellectuals to refute this position. "Belief in God and heaven is not the solution," they say. These intellectuals may then be able to discipline themselves so that their behavior is a credit to civilization, in spite of the absence of the sanction of hell. But, once the sanction of hell is removed from the purview of most of the population, there seems some possibility that interpersonal aggressiveness will reassert itself and destroy civilization.

The degree of civilization that we have, the limited ability that we have cultivated during several thousand years to resolve difficulties by reconciliation rather than by fighting, is a priceless heritage—but a heritage that has been weakened rather than strengthened by the ethos of the Vietnam War ("search and destroy") and by the confrontation, challenge, and violence which have been cultivated by a significant segment of the population and fertilized by Watergate.

The idea that great problems can be solved by polarization of interests and violent revolution by the underprivileged against the Establishment, after which we automatically have the ideal society, is a prescription for chaos and for the destruction of what little civilization we have.

Family Life
Family life can be pure hell. It depends a good deal on whether the couple approaches the problems with a feeling of responsibility—or whether each is primarily concerned with what he or she can get out of it in a self-indulgent way. It would be nice if there were some sort of a test that could be given at the marriage license bureau which would determine whether the eager lovers have any real respect for the institution they are about to set up.

Children may make better citizens if they have the feeling that their parents have made good on their basic responsibilities to the family. Good-natured give-and-take in the family has to be a major part of a pleasantly livable world. There are responsibilities that result from a couple's presuming to set up a family, and making good on such responsibilities may provide much of the real satisfaction that makes life worth living.

With regard to the young and their discontent with their lot, something more may be said. The children of fine parents occasionally turn out badly. This is the first generation in the history of the human race to wax indignant on a major scale because it has not been handed a perfect world by its parents. Perhaps, in a way, this is the highest compliment that could be paid to the parents.

And, if this generation will get about the job, the race has now accumulated the knowledge and the technology which will permit it to create the world that youth is complaining about not having inherited.

Yet, in the nature of the beast, parents should not expect too much in the way of gratitude from their teenagers. It may well be much later, when rearing her or his own family, before these youths appreciate more fairly the circumstances of their own upbringing.

Enough of parents and children. They are an overworked subject these days and should be since, between them, they cause most of the trouble and make up 99.44 percent of the population.

Things Are Not So Bad
It may be well to speculate that the world may not be in such bad shape as a lot of people make out. Most people are not neurotic wrecks about to cop out. Dewey once wrote: "Never before in history has mankind been so much of two minds, so divided into two camps, as it is today."[18] But he was talking about the 1930s, not the 1970s. World War II, a horrible nightmare, when ruthless dictatorship almost conquered the world, is a thing of the past. Vietnam was a minor aberration by comparison with that holocaust. We have the technology to provide a decent living for all, if we will. We even have the technology and, bless us, the management skills necessary to dispose of the garbage, if we will. (We might just put it into six or eight really big piles in the six or eight states with the highest per capita incomes, let it season for a while, and sell it to Du Pont.)[19]

Constructive Self-Expression

Making Good on Responsibility (and Instinct Psychology)
The third commonly held value involves the desirability of constructive, self-fulfilling self-expression, the freedom permitting individuals to express themselves constructively.

We need to have a feeling of accomplishment if we are to respect ourselves, a feeling that we are doing constructive, worthwhile, even important work. If we do not, we are likely to go sour. An opulent society, even one which also provides a pleasant place in which to live, may not be quite enough for us. And this is to our credit.

This conception of human nature seems to have some psychological respectability. It is close to being the phenomenon A. H. Maslow calls self-actualization, which Erich Fromm says is a deeply rooted impulse, and which Thorstein Veblen calls the instinct of workmanship.[20] It may also be noted in this connection that behavior which, to the individual concerned, will satisfactorily represent self-actualization or pride in workmanship may be capable of fulfilling that role because of either hereditary or environmental influences. The implications of this proposition should not be made to depend on the outcome of the debate over the validity of instinct psychology.

Parenthetically, a word should perhaps be said about the psychology of instincts. The word "instinct" implies an attitude which is physiologically determined. Veblen, however, did not so define instinct. In fact, according to Ayres, Veblen purposely abstained from defining instinct at all. David Hamilton writes with regard to this question: "For instance, the instinct psychology, in explaining what is clearly cultural behavior by resort to some primordial genetic predisposition, is explaining cultural behavior in physiological terms. . . . It is just not true that cultural behavior is explainable in terms of psychological states, be these sensations, instincts, minute nerve synapses, or neuro-muscular-sensory articulations."[21]

Perhaps one can say that there is a physiological *instinct*, on the part of the individual, to do things which will earn praise. But the behavior patterns which will earn this praise are socially determined. And society in the interest of its own viability (and in the interest of creating the pleasantly livable environment) had better see that it is culturally determined that the behavior which will obtain this desired approval is behavior which is thought to be constructive by society.[22]

John Dewey writes with regard to human nature:

> Assured and integrated individuality is the product of definite social relationships and publicly acknowledged functions. . . .
>
> The unrest, impatience, irritation and hurry that are so marked in American life are inevitable accompaniments of a situation in which individuals do not find support and contentment in the fact that they are sustaining and sustained members of a social whole. . . .
>
> Since we live in a moving world and change with our interactions in it, every act produces a new perspective that demands a new exercise of preference. If, in the long run, an individual remains lost, it

is because he has chosen irresponsibility; and if he remains wholly depressed, it is because he has chosen the course of easy parasitism.[23]

Happiness is not enough. Nirvana is not enough. Being gentle on Gentle Thursday is not enough. The real trouble with smoking pot, as a solution, is this: we would not have solved our problem even if we could find a drug that, without harmful side effects, made us feel forever happy.

Making civilization work involves conditioning the young so that various of their primitive, aggressive instincts are suppressed. Society cannot afford to let all children have total freedom, regardless of what that freedom may involve, and hope that eventually they will adopt reasonable behavior patterns. Remolding human nature by cultural impact is the essence of the process. And it is tricky business: people can also be conditioned to the acceptance of slavery or to the role of mercenary or to the role of SS trooper. The process is too expensive and time-consuming, however, if all youths insist on learning the hard way everything the human race has learned since the Stone Age, instead of profiting a bit from experience. Ontogeny may recapitulate phylogeny but, perhaps, a little more efficiently. And we may save some grief by just getting on the horse on the left side, like we are told, without holding up the group while we argue as to whether the left or the right side makes any difference. Let us save the rebellion and the argument for worthier causes. It will be easier all around. And the horse will be a little less likely to buck you off.

In this old world, there are ten jillion learning experiences where humans have laboriously learned a reasonable way to do things. It may have taken ten thousand years in some cases, but finally the point got hammered in. There are many such situations. In some the rule is important; in others it is less so; and in a lot of cases the person asking the learner to do something in a certain way may not have, at the moment, the time or the inclination for an extended explanation.

The whole learning and civilizing process will be quicker and easier if people cultivate an attitude of quiet cooperation in most cases. Of course, on their own, they should think about the reason for each rule or constraint. And occasionally they should seriously question or even fail to conform, after they have given a responsible amount of thought to the matter, and that may well take *years*. But refusal to conform to almost all rules just because "rules are made by the Establishment and everything the Establishment does is self-serving and evil" is not a particularly enlightened response.

On the few issues that really matter in our lives, if we sincerely believe that something is genuinely wrong, we should make a production out of our resistance and should stick to our guns—for years, if need be. And, if it is an issue that matters much, it probably will take years.

Service
Another value involved in constructive expression and self-actualization may well be service to others. Strangely enough, in the setting of self-indulgence that seems to have characterized the more blatant aspects of the mores of the 1960s, the 1960s were also characterized by a very considerable amount of self-denying service to other people on the part of a whole lot of people, young and old. The Peace Corps was an example of willingness on the part of volunteers to try to help others at a very considerable cost in terms of self-sacrifice. That Congress did not make Peace Corps service an alternative to the military draft reflects little credit on Congress, on draft boards, or on General Hershey.

Self-Expression and Skill
Other vents for the need to have a feeling of accomplishment are the arts, crafts, hobbies, and sciences—and even bridge. Work in writing, painting, music, or drama can go a long way toward making life worthwhile for those with the appropriate talents, interests, or maybe just willingness to participate. Crafts, such as woodworking, boatbuilding, gardening, creating an attractive yard, working with textiles, with clay, and with ingenuity, can play a role. Sailing and nature study (if we can somehow manage to preserve a little nature) can be of consuming interest. And then there is golf. There are also cooking and sewing, two rather challenging and important activities.

It is easy to say that the solution for boredom is for Joe or Mabel to show a little responsibility and to cultivate a skill. It is not so easy to implement this (people seldom change their ways because somebody reads them a sermon), but this is a large part of the solution.

There is plenty that is worthwhile to do for those with eyes to see, or ears to hear, or hands to work; one does not even need to have all of the senses. In fact, some people who are at a disadvantage in this respect seem to react better than some of their more endowed fellows. At all events, constructive self-expression is the path to a life of which one can be proud, and only the individual can take the initiative that will lead to such expression. Even Marx said as much, at least according to Erich Fromm:

> Only in being productively active can man make sense of his life. For Spinoza, Goethe, Hegel, as well as for Marx, man is alive only inasmuch as he is productive, inasmuch as he grasps the world outside of himself in the act of expressing his own specific human powers, and of grasping the world with these powers. Inasmuch as man is not productive, inasmuch as he is receptive and passive, he is nothing, he is dead.[24]

Security

The fourth legitimate goal, security, is quite a hodgepodge of job security (which may be provided by the job guarantee), medical care during illness, care during old age and childhood, and security against the terrors of war. Some of these matters are discussed later. To others, justice is not done in this book. But, regarding the importance of the desire for security, John Dewey has written knowingly and well in what is perhaps his most important book, *The Quest for Certainty*.[25]

Rights and Duties

One may well say that, if society has the means (the productive capacity) to implement the above values (and if these values do represent a social consensus), they become rights. And society, that is, the government, has the duty or the obligation to implement them. A right in a meaningful sense cannot exist unless someone or some institution has a duty or an obligation to implement it. No one has a right to welfare, unless someone or something has the obligation to provide it. As goes the verse by Stephen Crane:

> A man said to the Universe:

> "Sir, I exist!"
> "However," replied the Universe,
> "The fact has not created in me
> A sense of obligation."[26]

But, if society has the productive capability to implement these values for all, people are certainly missing a bet if they do not require that their government assume the duty of providing for them. It is argued here and there in this book that (despite the energy crisis) the economy does have this productive capability. And it is about time that it was recognized that the government has the duty to make good in implementing these values.

Social Goals Are Not Unique, Addible, or Maximizable

There is the additional question—the aggregability question—as to whether the motivation and behavior of society can be explained as some sort of a sum of the motives and behavior patterns of the individuals making up society.

The above-alleged values are different in kind from one another, even though, in various ways, many of them are implemented (to the extent that they are implemented) by actions of the type we generally call economic.

That is, these human values are not homogeneous. There is no way that a common yardstick of value can be identified, the amounts of these different values be quantified in terms of a common unit of measure, and the whole thing added up to give a unique number for gross national welfare or value. This sort of addition (in an effort to get a unique total) cannot theoretically be done, because the ingredients are not homogeneous and they appear in continually changing proportions in the complete complex of welfare. Also, in the somewhat longer run, our judgments on *relative* values are or may be changing. That this addition in an effort to identify a unique total (and to check whether it is a possible maximum) cannot be performed is a point that needs to be emphasized in economics because a large percentage of the profession is spending an awful lot of time playing with econometric models based on a presumption that some such aggregation is meaningful. The difficulty is basic. It is not a case where, if we could just improve our data-gathering methods and the specification of our models, we could identify a blessed maximum of welfare. The point is that the concept of a welfare maximum cannot be derived from the theoretical premises.

Thus, the concepts of a decent minimum level of living, and pleasant interpersonal relations, and constructive self-expression,

and security are separately meaningful and "move-toward-able."
But the concept of a maximum combination of such ingredients is
without meaning. This distinction is important. The concept of a
social welfare maximum is without theoretical meaning and certainly without empirical verifiability.

This is the bread-and-butter concept that emerges when the
value theory of institutional economics is contrasted with the
value theory of the prevailing neoclassical, general equilibrium
economics. The concept of a competitive general equilibrium, as
representing a unique and desirable "best" situation, is without
meaning. And, as one backs down from the general equilibrium
level to the level of microeconomic price theory, this means that
such concepts as the equating of marginal products of factors
across industries and the equating of cost ratios and utility ratios
at the margin are not definitive guides to the desirability of certain
price and cost and production patterns.

This argument does not deny that it is presumptively good
judgment for a producer to cut costs and for a buyer to buy for less.
But it does mean that they are doing these things in a genuinely
micro setting involving a genuine *ceteris paribus* assumption, without a precise tie-in with any such concept as a general welfare
maximum. The conditions of overall welfare, on the other hand,
are dominated by quite different circumstances, by the processes
of valuation and change that actually exist in society, that institutional theory tries to identify, and that cannot be synthesized into
one homogeneous package.[27]

There are other circumstances that underline the theoretical
impossibility of conceptualizing a unique welfare maximum in a
halfway realistic world. There is the ambiguity as to what is the
"best" income distribution. There is the ambiguity as to what is
the "best" total population and rate of population growth. There is
the ambiguity that results from the fact that, as our per capita productive capabilities rise, our appreciation of the relative values of
things will change. There is the ambiguity that results from the
fact that efficiency cannot be identified (that is, the "best" practice
or technique cannot be identified) by knowledge about the comparative capabilities of techniques alone. The identification of relative efficiency of techniques is contingent on demand patterns. And
demand patterns are contingent on income distribution and tastes
and changing tastes. And the identification of the "best" income
distribution is itself a value judgment. (The logical argument in

connection with several of these allegations is worked out in the appendix to chapter 4: "The Possibility of Maximization.")

In the context of the institutional theory of value, society is ever changing its conception of what is desirable. We need to appreciate the nature of this process and the fact that it means there is no "best" income distribution or "best" population size that can be revealed to us either by logical positivism or by our instincts or by some clairvoyant idealist.

Something somewhat more precise should probably be inserted about the basic logic of the aggregation problem, a problem which needs to be solved if any unique total is to exist, much less a unique total that is also a maximum.

For example, lack of homogeneity among several items does not, per se, preclude the possibility of aggregation. In fact, no two items are ever exactly alike, and an exact likeness would be necessary for seriatim addition to be able to affirm that a certain composite is in fact a summation (according to any yardstick) of exactly similar items—a truism if ever there was one. However, on the contrary, homogeneity can also, conceptually, be obtained by mixing two different substances with a result that justifies speaking of the mixture as being in some meaningful sense uniform in composition. (Cream and milk blended into homogenized milk is an example.)

But these areas are not the ones in which the important issues occur in the value theory of economics. Perhaps the difficulty in that area, the aggregation problem, can be illustrated as simply as possible in a two-commodity world of necessities and luxuries, perhaps symbolized by a peck of turnips and an ounce of Chanel No. 5. In an economically meaningful sense, these are qualitatively different items. Can we add a hundred pecks of turnips and a hundred ounces of Chanel No. 5 and get a meaningful and consistent total? If the hundred pecks are selling for $5 a peck and the Chanel is selling for $5 an ounce, it looks like we can speak of the composite as being worth $1,000. And we can use this expression at this time and place to equate this composite selling for $1,000 to some other composite selling for $1,000.

For concepts of value to have much usefulness, however, they must generalize beyond equivalent money values at this time and place and beyond the micro, *ceteris paribus* assumption. Probably the demand for Chanel No. 5 is more income-elastic than the demand for turnips. Consequently, if income is redistributed from the rich to the poor, the demand for and the price of Chanel are going to fall relative to the demand for and the price of turnips. And comparison of the consequent total with the prior total money value is already slippery at best.

Conclusion

We are living in an ongoing scheme of things, and it behooves us to appraise and reappraise our goals and values as we go along. We had better be concerned about these values, and about our relation to others, and about the quality of our life.

The accumulation of technical knowledge is a dynamic process. This means that the drive, or the motivation, that makes the process go is inherent in the manner in which the assimilation of one bit of knowledge leads to another. In a meaningful sense, this is an automatic process not requiring outside motivation, although it is a process that may be speeded up or slowed down by factors (from outside the process itself) which influence the individuals involved.

It is appropriate for society as a whole to hold values in the manner of a consensus and to change them. It is important to try to understand the influences guiding these changes. And it seems reasonable to view individuals as the center of concern in this process.

Although values are ever changing, it does seem worthwhile to try to identify their current consensus (if such exists). The suggested value pattern is (1) bringing everyone up to a decent minimum standard of living and, beyond the decent minimum, (2) emphasizing the necessity of making society pleasantly livable, (3) permitting the constructive expression of the personality of individuals, and (4) implementing reasonable security. If the goals are stated this way, emphasis on the identification of a welfare maximum becomes no longer important, even if a maximum could be identified. And it cannot be, in theory or in practice.

I should add that the value theory of institutional economics offers the prospect of progress. We can improve ourselves and can make the meaningful judgments regarding how to do it. This is no picture of a utopia after revolution, which might seem pretty empty once we had it: it is a picture of ongoing struggle, improvement, and progress. We do have an ongoing, worthwhile, challenging, ever changing future.

The implication of these concepts that envisage values as changing with changing circumstances may perhaps not be what one might expect at first thought. The implication is probably not that there is a tendency toward a decline in ethical standards because there are no eternal verities to guide us in our quest for certainty.[28] Actually, the implication for the quality of individual ethics may well be quite the contrary and quite wholesome.

The individual is on her or his own and society is on its own. They can make something of themselves that they can be proud of, if they will. But people as a group have to do it for themselves. And they have to do it again and again every day. And people can only do it for themselves as a cooperative venture—not in a dog-eat-dog context. This way of thinking may well be conducive to the creation of improved ethics and relations among people. (Adam Smith's invisible hand contributed to putting economics on a wrong track.) It also implies that values are inherent in the means used to accomplish human purposes as well as in the transitory ends that may be envisaged as following from any given conduct.

A quotation from Ayres seems appropriate: "This naturalistic, instrumental, technological theory of value is not 'mere' theory. As I have already said and will continue to repeat, it is not a theory of how value judgments ought to be made. It is an account of how we do, now and always, actually evaluate the things we value."[29]

Yet, it is also a theory which permits us, even enjoins us, to have an opinion as to how things ought to be, even if there is nothing eternally definitive about this quality of oughtness. This is normative, not positive, economics. We do have values, and economists (as economists) should take an interest in understanding where they come from as well as how economics can contribute to their implementation.

Also, it is within the realm of reason to allege that this institutional value theory, in truth, is more nearly in the "United States tradition" than is demand and supply, static price theory. One may recall in support of this affirmation the picture painted by James Russell Lowell in "The Present Crisis":

New Occasions teach new duties; Time makes ancient good uncouth;
They must upward still, and onward, who would keep abreast of Truth:
Lo, before us gleam her camp-fires! we ourselves must Pilgrims be,
Launch our Mayflower, and steer boldly through the desperate winter sea,
Nor attempt the Future's portal with the Past's blood-rusted key.[30]

NOTES

1. C. E. Ayres, *The Industrial Economy* (Boston: Houghton Mifflin, 1952), pp. 300 et seq.
2. For somewhat similar concepts in psychology see, for example, Frederick H. Kanfer, "Personal Control, Social Control, and Altruism," *American Psychologist* 34 (March 1979): 231–239.
3. Ayres, *Industrial Economy*, pp. 310–319.
4. Alfred F. Chalk, "Ayres's Views on Moral Relativism," in William Breit and William Patton Culbertson, Jr., eds., *Science and Ceremony: The Institutional Economics of C. E. Ayres* (Austin: University of Texas Press, 1976), p. 156.
5. John Dewey, *Reconstruction in Philosophy* (New York: Holt, 1920), pp. 157–158.
6. C. E. Ayres, *The Theory of Economic Progress* (Chapel Hill: University of North Carolina Press, 1944), pp. 225, 228.
7. Wolfgang Friedmann, *Legal Theory*, 5th ed. (New York: Columbia, 1967 [1944]), pp. 31–32.
8. Ayres, *Industrial Economy*, p. 11.
9. Margaret Mead, *Anthropology: A Human Science* (New York: Van Nostrand, 1964), p. 144.
10. Herbert Marcuse, *El marxismo soviético* (Madrid: Alianza Editorial, 1969 [New York: Columbia University Press, 1958]), p. 269.
11. James M. Buchanan, "Methods and Morals in Economics: The Ayres-Knight Discussion," in Breit and Culbertson, eds., *Science and Ceremony*, p. 168.
12. C. E. Ayres, *Toward a Reasonable Society: The Values of Industrial Civilization* (Austin: University of Texas Press, 1961), pp. 165–273; see also Marc R. Tool, *The Discretionary Economy* (Santa Monica: Goodyear, 1979), p. 293.
13. Thomas Hobbes, *Leviathan* (1651), pt. 1, chap. 13; pt. 2, chap. 17.
14. See Thomas Moriarty, "A Nation of Willing Victims," *Psychology Today* 8 (April 1975): 43–50; Karl A. Menninger, *Whatever Became of Sin?* (New York: Hawthorn, 1973).
15. Albert Camus, *Caligula* (Paris: Gallimard, 1958), p. 68; Thorstein Veblen, *Imperial Germany and the Industrial Revolution* (New York: Augustus M. Kelley, 1964 [1915]), p. 166.
16. Muzafer Sherif, "Experiments in Group Conflict," *Scientific American* 195 (November 1956): 54–58.
17. See Wilbert E. Moore, "Social Structure and Behavior," in Gardner Lindzey and Elliot Aronson, eds., *The Handbook of Social Psychology*, 2d ed., 5 vols. (Reading, Mass.: Addison-Wesley, 1969), 4:283; Edward Zigler and Irvin L. Child, "Socialization," in Lindzey and Aronson, *Handbook of Social Psychology*, 3:521–533; Elliot Aronson, *The Social*

Animal (San Francisco: Freeman, 1972), p. 142; Sigmund Freud, *Civilization and Its Discontents* (New York: Norton, 1962 [1930]), p. 69; Erich Fromm, *The Anatomy of Human Destructiveness* (New York: Holt, Rinehart & Winston, 1973); Stanley Milgram, *Obedience to Authority* (New York: Harper & Row, 1973); Abraham H. Maslow, *Motivation and Personality* (New York: Harper & Row, 1954).

18. John Dewey, *Intelligence in the Modern World: John Dewey's Philosophy* (New York: Modern Library, 1939), p. 1003.

19. See L. C. Cole, "What to Do with Waste?" *New York Times Magazine*, April 2, 1972, pp. 30 et seq.

20. Abraham H. Maslow, "A Theory of Human Motivation," *Psychological Review* 50 (July 1943): 370–396, especially p. 382; Maslow, *Motivation and Personality*, especially chaps. 6, 11; Fromm, *Anatomy of Human Destructiveness*, p. 36; Thorstein Veblen, *The Instinct of Workmanship* (New York: Augustus M. Kelley, 1964 [1914]). A psychologist who questions this approach is Leonard Berkowitz, "Social Motivation," in Lindzey and Aronson, eds., *Handbook of Social Psychology*, 3:87.

21. David Hamilton, *The Consumer in Our Economy* (Boston: Houghton Mifflin, 1962), pp. 34–35.

22. See William F. Ogburn, *On Culture and Social Change* (Chicago: University of Chicago Press, 1964), pp. 3–32.

23. Dewey, *Intelligence in the Modern World*, pp. 407–411, 414–415.

24. Erich Fromm, *Marx's Concept of Man* (New York: Frederick Ungar, 1961), p. 29.

25. John Dewey, *The Quest for Certainty: A Study of the Relation of Knowledge and Action* (New York: Minton, Balch, 1929).

26. Stephen Crane, *The Collected Poems of Stephen Crane*, ed. Wilson Follett (New York: Knopf, 1930 [1895]), p. 101.

27. When Commons speaks of "reasonable value," he apparently has some such concept in mind (*The Legal Foundations of Capitalism* [Madison: University of Wisconsin Press, 1968 (1924)], pp. 107, 351). Jack Barbash synthesizes Commons' position: "Commons is not clear what reasonable value is. But when the diverse allusions are pieced together and viewed as part of his total framework, reasonable value appears to be, to begin with, the *method* of arriving at a result rather than any determinate result per se" ("'The Legal Foundations of Capitalism' and the Labor Problem," *Journal of Economic Issues* 10 [December 1976]: 801). Implementing values is to be understood as a meaningful process, not as a maximizing problem.

28. See Dewey, *The Quest for Certainty*.

29. Ayres, *Toward a Reasonable Society*, p. 34.

30. In Edwin Markham, comp., *The Book of American Poetry* (New York: Grosset & Dunlap, 1926), p. 115.

ADDITIONAL READINGS

Bandura, Albert. *Aggression*. Englewood Cliffs, N.J.: Prentice-Hall, 1973.

Commons, John R. *The Economics of Collective Action*. New York: Macmillan, 1950.

Dewey, John. *Human Nature and Conduct*. New York: Holt, 1922.

———. *Individualism Old and New*. New York: Capricorn Books (G. P. Putnam's Sons), 1962 [1929].

Diggins, John P. *The Bard of Savagery: Thorstein Veblen and Modern Social Theory*. New York: Seabury Press, 1978.

Dorfman, Joseph. *The Economic Mind in American Civilization*. New York: Augustus M. Kelley, 1966 [1946].

Dowd, Douglas F. *The Twisted Dream*. Cambridge, Mass.: Winthrop, 1974.

Geiger, George R. *Philosophy and the Social Order*. Boston: Houghton Mifflin, 1947.

Hamilton, David. *Evolutionary Economics*. Albuquerque: University of New Mexico Press, 1970.

James, William. *The Meaning of Truth*. New York: Greenwood, 1968 [1909].

Junker, Louis. "The Social and Economic Thought of Clarence Edwin Ayres." Ph.D. dissertation, University of Wisconsin, 1962.

Lutz, Mark A. *The Challenge of Humanistic Economics*. Menlo Park, Calif.: Benjamin/Cummings, 1979.

Mills, C. Wright. *The Sociological Imagination*. New York: Oxford University Press, 1959.

Peirce, Charles S. *Chance, Love, and Logic*. New York: Harcourt, Brace, 1923.

Sherif, Muzafer. *The Psychology of Social Norms*. New York: Harper & Row, 1966 [1936].

Sperry, R. W. "Bridging Science and Values." *American Psychologist* 32 (April 1977): 237–245.

4.
Other Concepts of Value

Values and Motivation in Orthodox Economics

The Historical Background

Economics has long been concerned with value, with the meaning of wealth, and with questions of desirability. For the mercantilists of 1500 to 1776, gold was wealth and people valued wealth. For John Locke in 1690, there was pleasure and pain both here and in the hereafter. Locke also had an embryo labor theory of value: the values of things may be examined by comparing the amounts of labor time that go into their production.

The concept of utilitarianism (the greatest good for the greatest number) evolved from Thomas Hobbes through Locke, Jeremy Bentham, John Stuart Mill, and Herbert Spencer. More or less involved was the solution of a maximization problem in which pleasure was offset against pain for the whole population in an effort to maximize the net result. Locke included pleasure in the hereafter as part of his netting operation; Bentham did not take into account possible compensation in the hereafter.

For Adam Smith in 1776, goods (rather than gold) were wealth and of value. He also distinguished between value in use and value in exchange. In the tradition of this distinction, economists have generally worried more about value in exchange (price) than value in use or usefulness to the consumer. And Smith, apparently with a maximization concept in the back of his mind similar to that of the utilitarians, alleged that the desired result could be accomplished in a setting where pure competition prevailed and each individual pursued only personal gain. Smith writes in *The Wealth of Nations*: "Every individual necessarily labours to render the annual revenue of the society as great as he can. . . . He intends only his gain, and he is in this case . . . led by an invisible hand to promote an end which was no part of his intention."[1] For Smith, the maximization problem was solved not by the use of the calculus of variations but by the invisible hand of pure competition.

David Ricardo in 1817 distinguished between "mass of commodities" and value and presented a labor theory of value in the tradition of Locke and Smith. For him, the relative labor time required to produce goods controlled their relative price or value in exchange. Karl Marx, in developing the meaning of value in exchange, which was the value concept with which he was also chiefly concerned, reworked Ricardo's labor theory of value. Vilfredo Pareto, around 1900, developed indifference curve analysis to describe the manner in which people assign relative values to different things and relate their various desires to what is attainable. (There is a bit of indifference curve analysis in the appendix to this chapter.) But the resultant for Pareto was not necessarily a value maximum—perhaps, rather, it was only a situation that would be as favorable as possible for one party without making somebody else worse off. Pareto's work, in a way, was the inception of the general equilibrium analysis which would seem to be the heart of modern, orthodox (general equilibrium) economic value theory.

Abram Bergson and Paul Samuelson, from 1938 to 1956, attempted to reformulate the Pareto approach using modified concepts: utility possibility frontiers, revealed preferences, and social welfare functions, with the implication that a welfare maximum can be identified. Kenneth Arrow and others have more recently tried to establish the conditions necessary for identifying a "general welfare" general equilibrium, but they seem to abstain from the effort to prove that such an equilibrium also corresponds with a maximum. It is also not entirely clear whether Arrow himself believes that the conditions necessary for equilibrium are a reasonably accurate description of the real world. At all events, those working in the framework of Arrow seem frequently content with arguing the issue of whether a unique equilibrium exists without actually insisting on trying to prove whether it corresponds with a maximum.

General Equilibrium Theory
Perhaps general equilibrium analysis in the manner of Bergson and Samuelson can be said to be the value theory of modern, orthodox, neoclassical economics. And perhaps it can also be said

that Milton Friedman and the other Chicago people also subscribe, despite some of the jousting and name-calling that go on between Chicago and Cambridge. But this is a strange value theory, one from which the protagonists have striven mightily to extract the value content.[2] Bergson and Samuelson accomplished this feat by way of the concept of revealed preference, Friedman by way of logical positivism.

Revealed preference: To discuss briefly first, however, the concepts of Bergson and Samuelson, the revealed preferences of individuals are the revelations involving how much people are willing to pay for things. Bergson and Samuelson seem to have thought that it was not possible to look behind such revealed preferences to identify the underlying values or to pass judgments on the manner in which those values are determined. They seem, nevertheless, to believe that it is crucial to maximize the sum total of those revealed preferences. Also, it should be added, they seem to have thought that they were analyzing in value theory terms, as witness the first sentence in Bergson's 1938 article: "The object of this paper is to state in a precise form the value judgments required for the derivation of the conditions of maximum economic welfare."[3]

Logical positivism: Logical positivism is a concept which may or may not be satisfactorily described as being derived from the positivism of the founder of sociology, Auguste Comte, or as being in the natural-law tradition, or as being in the inductive logic tradition, or is it the deductive tradition? The essence of the matter is surprisingly difficult to isolate, perhaps because the ingredients really are various, a not uncommon characteristic of ideas.

In the 1970s, however, it may be appropriate to say that logical positivism in economics is whatever the Chicago people say it is. Yet there is some disagreement among them. And an allegation by an outsider as to that position is bound not to be accepted unquestioningly. In fact, almost regardless of what is said, that outsider is going to be accused of "not really understanding." Nevertheless: "This common intellectual framework [of the Chicago people] is derived from three beliefs: first, that theory is of fundamental importance; second, that theory is irrelevant unless set in a definite empirical context; and third, that in the absence of evidence to the contrary, the market works."[4] It would be difficult to argue against the first two trite beliefs. The third is a bit hard to swallow.

Positivism and logical positivism reject metaphysics and speculation about ultimate causes or origins. Statements of fact are held to be meaningful only if they have verifiable consequences. Knowledge derives from experience. Milton Friedman says, quoting John Neville Keynes, that "a positive science [is] a body of systematized knowledge concerning what is"; he goes on to say that "its task is to provide a system of generalizations that can be used to make correct predictions about the consequences of any change in circumstances."[5] Observation, hypothesis, and experimentation are called for. And one might be tempted to say that this is all fine up to the point where it is given some special twists in economics.

It has become customary to quote Lionel Robbins at this point: "Economics takes all ends for granted. . . . Ends as such do not form part of the subject matter. Nor does the technical or social environment. . . . There is but one end of activity—the maximizing of satisfaction [utility]."[6] The question of whether this is good psychology seems to bother the economist very little.

It is assumed, though this position is scarcely really justified by scholarly experimentation using the analytic methods of logical positivism, that (1) economists are given their values from outside, (2) it is desirable to maximize these given values, (3) pure competition, if operative, would maximize the values, and (4) pure competition is really operative (even in a world apparently overrun with oligopoly, monopoly, and so on). This is the "the market works" and "there is no such thing as a free lunch" bit of wisdom frequently expressed at Chicago.

The first point, that economics is given its unquestioned values from outside, merits further comment. Frequently, in the first or second chapter in elementary economics texts, this is alleged to be the characteristic that distinguishes economics as a positive science from muddleheaded normative thinking. It is alleged that the job of economics is to take these externally given, unquestioned values and to do its scholarly research and investigation—on what? If it is also assumed that "the market works" to maximize welfare, the activity of economists becomes pretty much that of the intellectual dilettante spending hours leisurely describing, like Dr. Pangloss, how all things are for the best in this best of all possible worlds—while all kinds of terrible things are happening. But then Voltaire does leave Pangloss content in Constantinople. "Tous les événements sont enchaînés dans le meilleur des mondes possibles." And Candide is left with a mind to cultivate his garden.

One really would not think that all the proposals for negative income taxes, constant percentage-rate expansion in the money supply, indexation (monetary correction), and so on which have emanated from Chicago are really necessary in this best of all possible worlds.

Natural law and economics: Another common view, which may not be clearly differentiable from logical positivism, among contemporary orthodox economists as to the place of value theory in economics is in the natural-law tradition. In this tradition, there exist great eternal verities (timeless natural law) which establish what values are. The United States Declaration of Independence alleges that "all men are endowed by their Creator with certain inalienable Rights, that among these are Life, Liberty, and the pursuit of Happiness." And to this list Locke had already added the right to be protected in property ownership.

As far as the implication for economic analysis is concerned, there is not a great deal of difference between logical positivism and natural law. In both cases it is assumed that the name of the game is the maximization of profits or income. And the logical models involve an effort to explain how these results may be realized in production and marketing. Meanwhile, the values are given and unchanging for both the natural lawyers and the logical positivists.

Normative economics versus positive economics (logical positivism): Institutional economists maintain that economics, as such, has to concern itself with norms or values, where they come from and how they work, if economics is to be meaningful. Understanding the economic system requires understanding why as well as how.

This approach contrasts with the generally prevailing attitude that motivation is given from outside economics. However, this attitude leaves unanswered the question as to what determines which of all the possible assumptions from outside economists will choose to work with. In fact, economists generally assume that the entrepreneur wishes to maximize profits and the worker to maximize wages—and the economists have already made a normative judgment. On the basis of these psychological assumptions, the model of economic behavior for the economy is built—demand, supply, competition, general equilibrium, and all that. This is the value theory, or lack of it, of logical positivism, the Chicago economics department, and, actually, economics in general. That such an approach cannot tell very much about most of what really matters in the economy should be obvious—yet it does not seem to be so to most economists, wearing the blinders put on them by the graduate schools where they got their degrees.

An unquestioned assumption that competition prevails and that the motivation underlying behavior is to maximize profits and/or wages hardly provides enough basis for giving categorical answers to questions concerning such problems as cattle straying on another's land, divorce, capital punishment, marijuana, and education, but the preceding list of "economic" problems is actually only a small sample of problems recently dealt with by logical positivist (Chicago) methodologists in such journals as the *Journal of Political Economy*, the *American Economic Review*, and almost any other prestigious economics journal you care to name.

With this methodology, inherent in the assumptions and in the institutionalized state of mind of the economist is the conclusion that the practice of pure competition will solve the problem. And the formidable nature of the mathematics and the logical argument is calculated to discourage the average citizen from detecting that the conclusions are inherent in the questionable assumptions, which just happen to be normative.

The Possibility of Maximization
It is tempting and simple, and it reflects some credit on us, to assume that the maximization of human welfare is the prime goal of society and that such a maximum is identifiable or, at least, conceptually meaningful. Most people who conceive of themselves as reasonably idealistic may well think that, in some sense, they are trying to obtain the greatest possible welfare for their fellows. And it is probably the generally held conception that the duty of all officeholders, even the politician, is to try to obtain the greatest possible welfare for society, meaning by this perhaps the world or perhaps merely a single constituency. And the economist is the politician's strong right arm in this noble effort.

There are many other contexts in which the economist is interested in trying to solve maximization problems: executives are assumed to want to maximize profits, or it may seem desirable to maximize national income or per capita real income, or gross receipts, or the soybean crop. Are these efforts meaningful? Under what circumstances may they be, or not be, meaningful?

An economist's position with regard to maximizing has been stated by Samuelson: "It so happens that in a wide number of economic problems it is admissible and even mandatory to regard our equilibrium equations as maximizing (minimizing) conditions. A large part of entrepreneurial behavior is directed towards maximization of profits with certain implications for minimization of expenditure, etc. Moreover, it is possible to derive operationally meaningful restrictive hypotheses on consumers' demand functions from the assumption that consumers behave so as to maximize an ordinal preference scale of quantities of consumption goods and services."[7]

Samuelson comes close to saying that it does not matter whether people really behave this way or not. We have to have the maximization assumption, whether it is economically meaningful or not, or we cannot solve maximization problems. He says, for example, "Thus, we really argue backwards from maximizing economic behavior to the underlying physical data consistent with it."[8]

Definitions of optimum and maximum: Welfare economics, in the tradition of Vilfredo Pareto, is the branch of economics which theoretically addresses itself to the problem of conceptualizing the meaning of optimum (and maximum) welfare. That welfare economics, old-style, pre-1938 vintage, gave up on its efforts to identify a maximum and concentrated on the less definitive concept of optimum (how to make people better off without making anybody worse off) should provide some warning as to the tricky nature of the game. But the newer welfare economics of Bergson and Samuelson (but, it seems, not Arrow) has returned, undaunted, to maximizing. And solving maximization problems or dealing with problems in a way that presupposes the meaningfulness of a welfare maximum is the meat and drink of many, if not most, economists in the 1970s.

In the old-style jargon, an optimum was the best situation that could be worked out in a process that involved making people as well off as possible without making anyone else worse off. A typical optimizing model involved the swapping of goods among people who already had goods until there was no longer a possible swap which all swappers believed resulted in a gain for themselves. However, it should be noted that the optimizing procedure, so defined, was unable to handle the situation where a loss to one person might make possible a greater gain to someone else. A dollar loss to a rich person may mean more than a dollar gain to a poor one.

A maximum, on the other hand, would involve the greatest total, aggregate amount of welfare, a state of bliss which conceivably might be reached only by a process involving making some people worse off as other people are made relatively better off. In general, welfare economists, old-style, would have said that it is impossible to take the step from optimum to maximum because it is impossible to quantify the loss of the loser by comparison with the gain of the gainer. The realization of this impossibility is pretty good psychology, and it might have been better if economists had left things at that. But it is more fun if the game involves maximizing, and maximizing is also the game that politicians want the economists to play. And economists can go farther in Washington if they are willing to provide answers that allege maximums or quantify net gain and loss. So, optimizing, new-style, seems to carry pretty much the same implication as does maximizing, any style. And a lot of economists are spending a lot of time trying to solve maximization problems, which are now frequently called optimization problems or control theory problems.

Conditions for optimum resource allocation: Welfare economics, new-style, in its effort to do the best it can by society, specifies three conditions for optimal (maximizing) resource allocation. (1) In order to have "optimal allocation of commodities among consumers . . . the marginal rate of substitution between any two commodities must be the same for any two consumers." (2) In order to have "optimal allocation of inputs among producers . . . the marginal rate of technical substitution between any two inputs must be the same for any pair of producers." (3) In order to have "both the optimal allocation of inputs among industries and the optimal allocation of commodities among consumers . . . the marginal rate of substitution between any two commodities must be the same as the marginal rate of substitution between these commodities for any producer."[9] If these conditions are met, all is for the best . . . (This is alleged to be true even though Mansfield's graphs representing these relations are frequently poorly drawn.) The theory also laboriously proves the possible existence (even the necessary existence) of a general equilibrium which can encompass these characteristics—at least if we only had pure competition, if we could disregard the income distribution problem, if growth and change were nonexistent, if everybody's tastes were alike, and if we had a few other things like full employment, a whole mare's nest of nonexistent conditions.

In the context of the difficulties involved in identifying a maximum, one may recall the contradictions demonstrated by Immanuel Kant in his *Critique of Pure Reason*. The antinomies (or contradictions) of Kant are examples of "proofs" of the existence of quite contradictory relations. Some of the mutually contradictory proofs include "whether the world has existed from all eternity or had a beginning—whether it is infinitely extended, or enclosed within certain limits—whether anything in the world is simple, or whether everything must be capable of infinite divisibility—whether freedom can originate phenomena, or whether everything is absolutely dependent on the laws and order of nature—and, finally, whether there exists a being that is completely unconditioned and necessary, or whether the existence of everything is conditioned and consequently dependent on something external to itself, and therefore in its own nature contingent."[10] Kant "proves" each of these contradictory possibilities. And who is to say, even now, that in one or another of the cases one of the proofs is correct and the proof of the contradiction is false.

An allegation: In the appendix to this chapter, several of the standard situations where economists try to maximize something are looked at. The conclusion is that in these cases a unique, meaningful maximum does not exist. Or, much too restrictive assumptions are required to create the possibility of a unique, identifiable maximum. The real world is not made that way. The cases where meaningful maximums seem not to exist include (1) the case of a general welfare maximum, if the possibility of different income distributions is permitted, (2) the case of a consistent measure of the real value of an increase in production, and (3) the case of a maximum growth rate, on any but the most artificial, linear assumptions.

There are other problems, even with the concept of Pareto optima. In the real world, even in the beginning of the adjustment process, you cannot avoid dealing with the problem of setting one person's gain against another's loss. The human beast insists on fighting the battle in those terms and has yet to see an adjustment process that an economy could slip along that would not disadvantage somebody or at least give somebody a chance to feel disadvantaged.

True, it is good tactics to proceed in a way that will hurt relatively few people. Progress and improvement will occur more expeditiously the smaller the numbers of people imagining themselves injured by the process. But value theory cannot avoid the responsibility of weighing loss against gain: judgments are made all the time that involve appraising one person's loss against another's gain. The judgments frequently may not be well made, but they are made, they have to be made, and they will be made. And welfare economics, in the tradition of Pareto, has been a quite sterile sidetrack which had a first-glance appeal in offering the prospect of resolving conflicts of interest without ever having a conflict—or, rather, resolving them up to the point where the conflict became overt, and then of a sudden saying that such a judgment cannot be made. Actually, trust the welfare economists to be a degree more devious than this and develop a concept that says: let the big winners throw a few crumbs to the losers (the compensation principle), and this procedure can resolve the difficulty. To some extent, we practice this approach when we raise money by means of the progressive income tax to use in programs to benefit the poor, but there is no operational method for identifying the best distance to go down this road. Nothing is gained by kidding ourselves on this point.

Of course, all this is well known to the leading welfare economists, so well known that they are likely to express some irritation when the matter is called to their attention. And yet, in general, they have refused to implement the appropriate conclusion—the methods of welfare economics are not capable, even theoretically, of identifying most desirable policies and procedures.

Little wonder that welfare economics has been of virtually no help in formulating policies for dealing with the problems of the real world.

Proponents of welfare economics, when criticized, are prone to say that everybody (that is, all the theoreticians, all the priests in the temple) is well aware of these weaknesses in the theory. But criticisms of the approach are rarely published by them in legible English, and sophisticated articles using welfare economics concepts in sterile ways (frequently with profuse apologies for the indeterminateness of the results) are commonplace in the professional journals. An article is likely to close with an expression of the modest hope that the author may have opened up a new line of inquiry. And the profession goes on complacently hoodwinking a public that wants to be hoodwinked, wants to believe that the practice of competition and the workings of the law of supply and demand, if we could just implement them, really would operate to maximize welfare—and economics can prove it.

Despite the awareness, on the part of the high priests of the system, of the theoretical weaknesses of welfare economics, probably most economists have not really bothered to understand what is involved. And, in general, people, including other economists, tend to assume that such a sophisticated logical structure must have something to it.

Some people, who may not be convinced of much of anything by the preceding esoteric argument, may be convinced by more earthy examples. Let us say that you have the job of determining whether one situation or another represents a greater amount of welfare. Which contributes more to social welfare: the exhilaration someone gets from reckless driving or the pleasure somebody else gets from spending a quiet evening at home reading a good book. Add up the utilities if you can. Where is the yardstick?

Welfare economics is a failure as value theory. Why has it hung around? Perhaps one reason it enjoys such durable intellectual prestige has been due to the fact that it could not be tested with data from the real world. In the context of untestability, it represents an impressive intellectual tour de force which is bound to impress the outsider with the intellectual prowess of economists, provided the outsider is not from Missouri.

Neither economists nor other people are smart enough to identify a general welfare maximum or to quantify alternative claimants to the title. If we smarten up, realize that we cannot identify a maximum (or an optimum), where do we go from there? Is all hope lost? Should we go out and drown ourselves? Or, bless us, is the basic problem of establishing and identifying reasonable social goals simplified? Perhaps the latter is the case. We do not need Hamiltonians or Pontryagin maximizing methods or control theory in order to be able to say a good deal that is useful about policy. We need a little common sense, a desire to assure that all people have a decent minimum, that beyond that they get along pleasantly, have and make use of the opportunity for self-expression (reasonably used), and enjoy security against hardships, in such wise as the race is capable of creating such security.

Law and Economics

The law, especially the common law in the English tradition, involves a mixture of logical positivist, natural law, and pragmatic influences.[11] The manner in which the law evolves as conditions change and judges interpret and reinterpret precedent in an effort to make current decisions seem reasonable in light of current problems is a reflection of the application of pragmatism in the manner of Peirce and Dewey. It is an example of the process of self-correcting value judgments.

On the other hand, the "respect for precedent" aspect of the common law (perhaps with natural-law overtones) is an example of an influence which tends to resist the change of institutionalized behavior norms.

This mixture of ability to change combined with stability and respect for tradition has made the common law an institution to be reckoned with. It is probably even a major aspect of the explanation of the substantial development of the English-speaking countries in recent centuries.

Recently, however, the common law and the legal system in the United States have been wooed by a new influence. Economists and lawyers at the University of Chicago have mounted a major effort to indoctrinate the law with the idea that legal decisions, especially those having to do with economic matters, should be made on the basis of logical positivist–type thinking.[12] Some Chicago professors (Posner, Ehrlich, Becker, Coase, Stigler) seem to believe that, if they do a thorough hard-sell job on the lawyers, logical positivism can take over as a new and dominating doctrine in the law and that courses in this tenor should be featured in all law schools.

Perhaps a version of economics with a simplistic value theory, assumed given from outside (as well as an assumption that pure competition and the desire for gain provide a base on which logical positivist–type logic may be used to resolve legal problems), may have a certain usefulness in countries whose legal systems feature fully formulated codes such as the Code Napoleon. But it hardly seems conceivable that anyone could believe that such a theory and such economic dogma could have a wholesome place in the English common-law tradition, with its built-in but nonformalized ability to respond to ever changing conditions.

If there is to be "an economics and the law," it might, at least in the common-law countries, be better couched in terms of an economic theory geared to responsiveness to ever changing conditions, in a setting of respect for tradition.

The Position of the Psychologist

The Attitude toward Economics

Economists and psychologists have not interacted to any marked extent, despite the obvious fact that the motivations that underlie economic behavior must be rooted in psychological considerations. Some psychologists, however, have had enough awareness of what is involved in economics to have formed some opinions as to the defensibility of the psychological bases underlying economics, its value theory and its methodology.

Abraham H. Maslow, for example, writes: "We must say harshly of the 'science' of economics that it is generally the skilled, exact, technological application of a totally false theory of human needs and values, a theory which recognizes only the existence of lower needs or material needs."[13]

Some passages from *The Handbook of Social Psychology* run as follows:

> Classical economics minimized its dependence on motivational theory in psychology by taking utility maximization (for the consumer) and profit maximization (for the entrepreneur) as the sole motives of economic man. . . .

> In extreme cases, the result has been to change economics from an empirical science to a vast tautology in which entrepreneurs maximize profit by definition—for profit is defined as "that which entrepreneurs maximize"—and consumers maximize utility by definition—for the same reason. . . .

> *Economics* can be defined as the discipline which purports to describe, predict, and explain behavior in the marketplace. The *a priori* assumption that each human being behaves like "economic man" underlies both the descriptive and predictive aspects of economic analysis, and raises questions of how far economics, in its present state, conforms to the norms of science.[14]

Satisfying versus Maximizing

James March has written of the economist's explanation of the behavior of executives:

> What happens once a problem is identified? The textbook answer is that the executive obtains all relevant information and chooses the

alternative which maximizes profits (or other objective). Such a theory seems implausible.

An alternative theory, proposed by H. A. Simon and others, draws heavily on the early work of a group of German psychologists, particularly Kurt Lewin. It rests on these very simple propositions.

1. Individuals do not attempt to maximize utility but seek to achieve alternatives that are "satisfactory." A satisfactory alternative is one that is better than the "level of aspiration."

2. The level of aspiration changes over time, going up when achievement goes up, coming down when achievement comes down. It adjusts upward faster than downward.

3. If the individual sees an alternative that is satisfactory, he will not search very vigorously for additional alternatives.

For the first two of these propositions there has been considerable evidence for at least twenty years. It is the combination of these two with the third, however, that makes the system an interesting and dynamic one.[15]

Richard Cyert and March, jointly, have described a somewhat different concept—the possibility of "coalition goals"—of what the executives may be about.[16] They say, as others have said, that there is evidence that the level of profit maximization is not the overriding goal of the firm. Rather, some set of coalition goals, usually including commitments in the areas of production, inventory maintenance, sales volume, market shares, and profit (taken together), makes up a hodgepodge of goals. Also, the goal or aspiration level changes over time as a result of feedback from experience. (This comes close to being the self-correcting value judgment concept.)

Maslow's Basic Human Needs

Maslow has described an alleged hierarchy of basic human motives and their relationship.[17] There are (1) the physiological needs such as food, clothing, and shelter. But, since "a satisfied need" will no longer motivate behavior, if we already enjoy adequate food, clothing, and shelter, our behavior thereafter is going to be motivated by other considerations.

If the basic physiological needs are satisfied, but those are the only needs that are satisfied, the prime human concern will probably be for (2) safety—security against danger, threat, and deprivation. The organism may well be almost wholly dominated by these considerations if it lacks security. It may hunger for order, routine, and normality if it believes existence is unreliable, unsafe, or unpredictable. (Children with quarrelsome parents usually wish for an organized, peaceful family and world.) But, just as was the case when the physiological needs were met, the person who enjoys security may be almost entirely unconcerned about security needs.

The person satisfied in the need for safety, as most people in our culture are to a degree, may experience a prime need for (3) love and affection. If that need is satisfied, the prime concern may then be (4) ego-gratification. The person may wish esteem and recognition. If this need is met and the individual, in consequence, feels self-confident, strong, and capable, the highest level of basic need and motive may be expressed as (5) self-actualization. But the emergence of self-actualization as the central motive—a concept which seems rather closely akin to Veblen's instinct of workmanship, and a rather far cry from the profit motive—rests on the prior satisfaction of the physiological, safety, love, and esteem needs.

Of the values alleged, in chapter 3, to be currently held, Maslow's physiological needs roughly parallel the right to a decent, minimum standard of living. It is not clear whether the right to a pleasant environment has any clear parallel in his scheme. The right to self-expression, in ways that permit people to be proud of their own behavior, has a parallel in Maslow's self-actualization. And the right to security has a clear parallel in his security need. Maslow's needs for love and for ego-gratification were not cataloged in chapter 3, perhaps because they cannot represent *values* that society has an obligation to fulfill. Perhaps they are and always will be privileges rather than rights—as far as society is concerned.

Induced Character Change or Behavior Modification

John R. Commons, in his discussion of the meaning of institutional economics, says:

> In the stage of Pragmatism, a return is made to a world of uncertain change, without foreordination or metaphysics, whether benevolent or non-benevolent, where we ourselves and the world about us are continually in a changing conflict of interests. And, like Locke, we investigate how our own minds and the world about us actually behave in a society of human beings whose future is frankly recognized as unpredictable but which can be controlled somewhat by insight and collective action.
>
> This we conceive to be the problem of Institutional Economics.

Institutional economics is not something new—it always has been the obvious accompaniment of all economic theories. For this reason it may often seem to be superficial, since it is so commonplace and familiar. But this may be the very reason why it needs investigating and why it is most difficult to investigate. The whole progress of all the sciences has been from the most remote objects—even thousands of light-years away—to the most intimate, which are our own wills in action." [18]

At any given time, each individual is entitled to have his or her own views about what is desirable and to try to convince others of their appropriateness. That is, people are entitled to try to get other people to change their attitudes, provided the listener is also entitled to hang up the phone. In some settings this might be called induced character change or behavior modification. And in some quarters the very thought of such meddling with the psyches of others is anathema.

In economics, one issue might be put in terms of whether it is appropriate or desirable to try to get people to be more public-spirited in their behavior and less oriented toward selfish gain. Would such a policy be desirable, possible, ethical, unethical?

Thinking along these lines would seem to be the essence of the approach of the behaviorism school in psychology from John B. Watson shortly after the turn of the century to B. F. Skinner at the present time. [19] Why not finagle to make human behavior correspond more nearly to the heart's desire—of the dominant social group? In fact, behaviorism proper in psychology seems to go a good deal farther than this and, as in the *Random House Dictionary*, may be defined as "the theory or doctrine that regards objective and accessible facts of behavior or activity of man and animals as the only proper subject of psychological study." Introspective data or references to consciousness, or mind, or subjective values are excluded from consideration. Behaviorists conceive that "motivation" is a concept that cannot be gotten hold of. So the domain of psychology, according to them, is the explanation of human behavior entirely in terms of overt physiological activity, behavior caused by the working of the nervous system in response to identifiable stimuli. Behavior is merely a physiological reaction to environmental stimuli. The value of introspection is denied. Thinking is merely subvocal speech. Emotions, except perhaps for rage, fear, and love, are conditioned by habit and can be learned and unlearned.

So, the behaviorists run rats through mazes to condition their behavior and are intrigued by the possibility of doing the same thing with people. What is one to think of such activity?

In a modest way, people are doing this to each other all the time. Wives are trying to make their husbands shape up. Parents are trying to mold the character of their children and their dogs. Certainly a good deal of this sort of thing can be done, is being done, and should be done.

A somewhat different question is whether one major social group might appropriately try to condition in a major way, or under certain circumstances, the behavior of another social group. Here again, it seems, a lot of this is going on. In fact, in some sense, this is what formal education is all about. And perhaps one should say that society as a whole does and should oversee the education of its children. There is a reasonable presumption that over millions of years the human race has learned a little, which youth could absorb through the educational process instead of having to learn the hard way. However, to say that education is desirable and that the process has to have some socially determined order is not to say that everything done in the educational process is sound, well-meaning, and disinterested. Plenty of individuals and groups are grinding plenty of private axes, and dealing with this situation involves the process of ongoing, self-correcting value judgments.

There are further varying conditions and problems. Should psychologists, such as B. F. Skinner, be allowed to use people as guinea pigs in behavior modification experiments? Again, I suppose the answer is, for better or worse, that they are doing it all the time. If some criminals may thereby be induced to mend their ways, the results may be desirable. At the same time, society has an obligation to itself to ride herd pretty observantly on the manner in which such things are done.

To try again: should certain groups (such as scholarly psychologists or the hatchet men of the political party in power) be allowed to do this sort of thing to large groups of the ordinary population and of school-age youths? What were the implications of Hitler's doing it to the German people?

Maybe it makes a difference whether the character or behavior modification is attempted by the use of drugs and brain surgery, mass hysteria, or group intimidation of other groups or whether the modification is attempted by logical, reasonable persuasion (either education-type or Madison Avenue–type). (Advertising may be looked on as studied effort at behavior modification on a grand scale.) Whether the use of drugs and brain surgery to effect behavior modification should be entirely ruled out, let me leave that as an issue for others to argue about. But surely we can say that, in the present state of our civilization and attitudes, the accepted and acceptable view is that the use of high-handed behavior modification procedures should be extremely circumscribed.

In a slightly different slant at behavior modification, it may be observed again that people are practicing behavior modification on themselves all the time by the use of medicinal drugs, aspirin, whiskey, marijuana, cigarettes, heroin, or coffee, generally without quite understanding what they are doing. But surely there is a difference between the voluntary private use of heroin and the public spectacle often made by the heroin addict. Also, the voluntary taking of drugs by more or less conscious and intelligent individuals may be viewed as morally different from the administration of LSD to unknowing subjects, if society chooses to view the matter differently. However, all these acts have certain consequences and in no case can the actors expect to be entirely excused from answering for the consequences, if society chooses to hold them accountable. This is not a world in which society is going to allow everyone total freedom, without regard to what that freedom may involve. In any event, society has the potential for making decisions in these matters and taking various coercive measures—with heaven knows what ultimate effects.

Perhaps, at least for now, given our presently conceived values, we would want to reject Skinner's proposal that implies setting up psychological commissars to control behavior in terms of the judgment of the behaviorists as to what is appropriate behavior. Nevertheless, we would want to allow for the possibility that changes in attitudes or values may be brought about in various ways and by various means. It is most desirable, however, to have a general ongoing awareness of what those ways and means are and of what influences are operating. Society, meaning people, had better know what it is about and be in a position to prevent procedures that it considers objectionable: only in this way will behavior modification be our servant rather than our master. And there will be a lot of self-correcting value judgments going on in this process.

Various behavior modification possibilities may be identified: (1) Changing technology causes changes in institutions (values, attitudes, and behavior) as society adjusts to the use of the new technology. This is behavior modification, affecting both institutions and individuals. (2) An institutionalized motive, such as the profit motive, as individuals act to implement it, may result in character modification in other aspects of behavior. For example, the implementation of the profit motive (and what it implies for self-seeking competition) may imply less generosity in terms of one's attitude toward one's fellows. (3) The demonstration (or emulation) effect may operate: people may behave better because they see other people behaving better. There are other permutations and combinations in this syndrome, for example, a corrupt administration in the manner of Grant's or Harding's presidency no doubt stimulates others to crime in both low and high places. (4) Cajoling, arguing, and Madison Avenue–type advertising may influence the attitudes of people. (5) Force and power (à la the Nazis), drugs and coercion may modify the character of the people affected. Such programs may come into being in all sorts of ways and for all sorts of reasons and may involve voluntary and involuntary participation, psychological commissars and other behaviorists.

How can society achieve reasonable, decent behavior of all its members? Basically, the situation seems to involve the continual appraising and reappraising by society and its members of its/their own behavior and attitudes as well as the influencing, in a million subtle ways, of individuals who have unfortunate behavior characteristics. (This view would correspond to instrumental value theory.) Or is something more in terms of controlled behavior change called for?

Perhaps about all one can or should say, by way of conclusion, on this touchy subject is that peoplekind, as it goes along, will be modifying its views as to what is appropriate in the area of behavior modification. Such are the workings of instrumental value theory. This is an area where perhaps one can say that it will be good judgment to move slowly and double-check the consensus as society evolves. Especially, it would seem very dubious to attempt to develop an overt policy of general behavior modification involving the formulation of national policy and the establishment of agencies to implement that policy on the general run of adults.

Conclusion

It is not necessary to pass judgment on the relative merits of different psychological approaches to have a basis for saying things significant for economics. The starting point of economics is, or ought to be, an understanding of how people behave. Psychological and other studies of human behavior do not seem to support the commonly held economics position that human goals are simple and, in general, involve some unique, aggregable, and maximizable concept of gain (individual and/or collective). Human motives seem to be more complex than that. They are diverse, they are not susceptible to aggregation, and, in general, they are not maximizable, at least not in any measurable way.

The significance of this for economics is that in many micro, industry-level, firm-level, individual-level situations it is useful to estimate the procedure that will maximize gain (perhaps monetary profit in a given time period on some assumption or other as to what prices, etc., will be). This procedure can provide a sort of first approximation of a meaningful picture of the situation and can be a useful indication of what is reasonable production or pricing policy. But where economics has really gone astray is in alleging that there is a useful way in which this sort of behavior at the microlevel can be aggregated into a concept of maximum general welfare.

Of course, in fact, all of us are mixtures of many characteristics, in varying degrees, and the composition of the mixture is likely to change at different periods in our lives. Much depends on the accident of the personality of the person one marries, the personalities of one's immediate associates at work, the personalities of one's neighbors, and health. The composition depends on the institutional environment in which one lives and on the way one's personal biological makeup reacts to that environment. And it depends a lot on luck.

In their analysis, many economists have tried to keep the economic frame of reference apart from the frames of reference of the other social sciences and to separate the nature of the problems dealt with by the economist from other aspects of problems that the decision maker must take into account—and these efforts have done no service to economics or to decision making on the broader scene.

Of course, there is a lot of literature on decision making and on motivation and on values. Management courses in colleges of business are full of it, for one thing. And what has been said above scarcely scratches the surface of the arguments of Freud, and Jung, and Talcott Parsons, and C. Wright Mills, and J. B. Watson, and B. F. Skinner, and Abraham Maslow, and legions of others, largely unread, or at least unassimilated, by most economists.

Part of the problem with arguing issues of this sort with economists is that reasonably competent economists are quite likely to agree that motivation and behavior are not completely explained by the rational, economic man, maximizer syndrome. They will probably express some incredulity that you could possibly be so simpleminded as to believe that they are so simpleminded. They may say: the rational, economic man, maximizer syndrome is merely a useful first approximation; anyone with a grain of sense knows this and can modify the results of the economic analysis to fit a conception of the broader realities. They may even say modestly that this is the way decision makers should use and discount economic analysis.

Yet there remains the point that the use of one first approximation precludes the use of another, perhaps more useful, first approximation and may distort thinking about alternatives so that the decision makers, although ostensibly free to opt for alternatives, may not have the mental attitude that will permit them to do so. They have been brainwashed by the first approximation and by the intellectual prestige of the brainwashers.

It is important to note that we are talking about values and the relevance of one theory of value by comparison with another. And the point economists need to understand is that the concept of self-correcting value judgments substitutes for price theory as value theory. This does not mean that it is unimportant whether a *given* price is higher or lower. What it does mean is that prices and the whole package of information going with the analysis of the purely competitive market do not aggregate to a meaningful optimal (maximal) general equilibrium, for at least two reasons: (1) the analytical process, in the setting of halfway reasonable assumptions, cannot produce a unique solution, and (2), even if it could, the alleged behavior patterns are not an adequate description of how people act in this world.

By contrast, the self-correcting value judgment concept provides a frame of reference in which influences more sophisticated than profit maximization can be taken into account. And it is not committed to finding a unique solution that represents a welfare maximum, such as does not exist.

This is as far as the institutional theory goes. It is no criticism of the concept of self-correcting value judgments and of the value theory of institutional economics that it fails to go farther and offer pseudosolutions to what in fact are unanswerable questions. A theory is not required to provide eternally valid logical positivist–

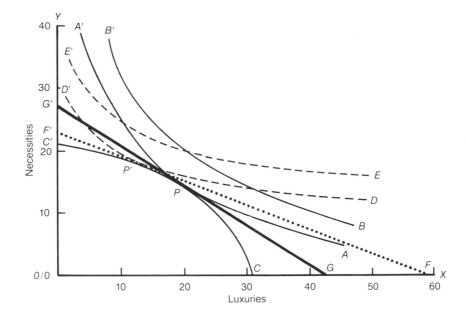

Figure 4-1. Maximization: the income distribution case

type answers to questions that do not have such answers or to find
eternal verities of the natural-law variety where none exist.

APPENDIX. THE POSSIBILITY OF MAXIMIZATION

In this appendix, several of the standard situations in which economists
attempt to solve maximization problems are looked at.

The Income Distribution Case
In figure 4–1, $C'C$ is a so-called production block (or production possibility
curve, or opportunity-cost curve). It says that, if all of a country's productive resources are devoted to producing luxuries, then Oc of luxuries can
be produced. If all are devoted to producing necessities, then Oc' of necessities
can be produced. And, if the productive resources are divided between the
production of luxuries and necessities in various proportions, the output

mixture possibilities are represented by the various points on the *C'C* curve. *C'C* is drawn concave with respect to the origin to represent the likely situation of increasing costs. That is, to produce more and more of one commodity (say, luxuries) requires giving up increasing amounts of the product whose production is being curtailed (necessities) in order to produce each additional unit.

Curves *A'A* and *B'B* are only two of innumerable, so-called community (or consumer) indifference curves. Along any one of these curves the various combinations of luxuries and necessities are alleged to be equally desirable in the opinion of the community of consumers conceiving the curve. The further outlying (from the origin) the consumer indifference curve, the greater the welfare that it represents.

Parenthetically, the social welfare functions of Bergson and Samuelson try to allow for the fact that a community's concept of welfare may not really be susceptible of representation quite so simply or so naïvely. Whether their refinement adds anything to the picture but complexity may well be debatable. At all events, for the moment, let us work with community indifference curves. This might not be defensible if determinate results were going to be alleged as a conclusion. But, if much the same sort of indeterminateness arises in both the community indifference curve procedure and the Bergson-Samuelson procedure, there are some grounds for working with the simpler procedure.

In figure 4–1, the possible maximum welfare is represented by the tangency of the production possibility curve *C'C* with the furthest outlying indifference curve that it can reach. In this case, welfare is maximized at point *P* on indifference curve *A'A*. The production possibilities do not permit reaching the more desirable *B'B* indifference curve.

And so, all is well—we have an unambiguous maximum. But . . .

Perhaps income is redistributed to give relatively more to the relatively poor. Or, perhaps, in different cultures people like slightly different things. Or, in the same culture, tastes change from one generation to the next—people like pot more and whiskey less. The result should be, to use the income redistribution case as an example, with the poor getting a somewhat larger share of the total income, that total spending is oriented more toward necessities and away from luxuries. Community indifference curves *D'D* and *E'E* (in contrast to *A'A* and *B'B*) represent this possibility and, perhaps, represent the community's indifference curve preference pattern after the income shift has taken place.

P' is the new welfare maximum, representing the tangency of the production possibility curve with the furthest outlying of the new set of consumer indifference curves that it can reach. But it represents a mix of necessities and luxuries different from that of *P*. Who is to say whether *P* or *P'* represents the greater general welfare? Economics has no methodology that permits it to answer this question.

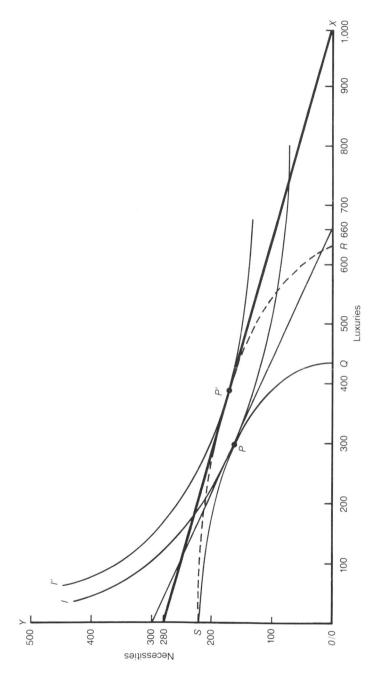

Figure 4-2. Maximization: the case of increased production

Let me beat this dead horse a bit more. The exchange ratios (prices) between luxuries and necessities in the two cases may be represented by the slopes of the tangents *G'G* through *P* and *F'F* through *P'*. If units of luxuries are used as the measure of value, common denominator, or monetary unit, then, in the production-consumption pattern corresponding to *P*, national income (that is, gross national product) is represented by the distance *Og*. It is the greater quantity *Of* if *P'* represents equilibrium. So, using luxuries as the measure of value, *P'* represents a higher income (or production or welfare) than does *P*.

If necessities are used as the measure of value, however, then the GNP is *Og'* if *P* is equilibrium and the lesser quantity *Of'* if *P'* represents equilibrium.

Thus, depending on the income distribution and the identity of the commodity chosen as a yardstick, *P'* represents either more or less GNP than does *P*, and which point represents the greater community welfare is indeterminate.

The Production Increase Possibility

On the production side, a somewhat analogous line of argument can be used to demonstrate that an unambiguous increase in production potential (see figure 4–2) as represented by a movement from production possibility *SQ* to *SR* may ostensibly represent a rise or a fall in the gross national product, depending on where we produce along the production possibility curves and on which commodity we use as a yardstick of value. This expansion in production may give this ambiguous result without regard to the income redistribution possibilities. Let income distribution remain as it was. In this example, fairly reasonable community indifference curves are rigged to show the possibility of a result that exhibits the production increase as a national product decrease when necessities are used as the yardstick. If we use commodity *Y* (necessities) as the yardstick and produce at point *P* first, then expand production to point *P'* as a result of expanded production capability, represented by the new production curve *SR*, the yardstick tells us that the GNP has fallen from 300 to 280, despite the facts that production has surely expanded since we are operating on a further outlying production possibility curve and that the consumer indifference curves tell us welfare has increased because we have managed to reach a further outlying consumer indifference curve. If luxuries are the yardstick, the GNP increases from 660 to 1,000. (Bear in mind that the slope of the tangents through *P* and *P'* have to represent price—or the exchange ratios between *Y* and *X*—which must exist if pure competition is to clear the market at points *P* or *P'*.)

So, here is the possibility of an inconsistent evaluation of a change, a possibility which arises in a somewhat different manner than does the difficulty arising as a result of changes in income distribution. This is a

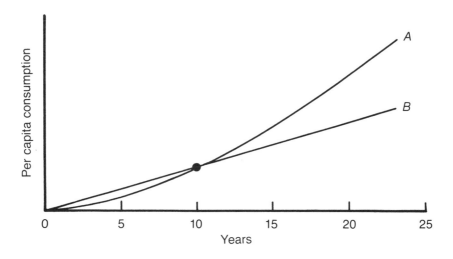

Figure 4-3. Maximization of the rate of growth

variation of the so-called index number problem—a problem economists often call attention to before they sweep it under the rug.

Growth Rates
Then there is the problem of growth. In growth models, the identification of the most desirable path along which the economy may expand is a special case (or perhaps it is the general case) illustrating the difficulty involved in making a precise distinction between more and less desirable. The difficulty involved in pinning down the meaning of a rate of growth, let us say in per capita average consumption, is indicated in figure 4–3. Does growth path 0A or growth path 0B represent the more desirable rate of growth initially? Perhaps path A corresponds with an especially high rate of saving during the early years of development—and higher per capita income after the tenth year is the payoff. If we evaluate the situation before the tenth year, however, we may conclude that path 0B represents the more desirable, or at least the more rapid, growth path. A possible way to deal with this problem is to identify some particular year as the terminal year of concern or to say that we have some certain goal, such as a certain amount of capital stock (or as much capital stock as possible, or "in what proportions it would be nice to possess capital stocks at the end of the planning period," or some such), in some particular future year.[20] If this is

done, it is then possible to pass judgment on the relative merits of two development strategies. But the price paid in order to be able to pass this judgment is high—we have prejudged that we are more concerned with the welfare of our children than with the welfare of our grandchildren (or vice versa).

Meaningful Maximums

The preceding discussion has been generally critical of the meaningfulness of maximization concepts in general equilibrium analysis and in economics as a whole. The implication is that the concept of maximizing the general welfare is without precise meaning. And equating marginal this and thats in an effort to maximize the gross national product or the general welfare is, as a rule, not a meaningful operation. In particular, equality between the technical rate of transformation in production and the marginal rate of substitution in consumption does not assure a welfare maximum on any reasonable set of assumptions.

These arguments, however, should not be taken as alleging that maximization exercises are always a useless operation in economics. On the contrary, it may be of considerable use in business, especially in connection with short-run planning, to make assumptions about costs and prices and to check out what procedure seems likely to yield the largest profits during the next six months. Working out the most effective mathematical procedures for making such calculations is a worthwhile activity, for which the practitioners should be paid the going wage rate, but it is a world away from the frame of reference involved in the effort to maximize the general welfare.

General Appraisal

Perhaps the preceding presentation, instead of being set up in terms of community indifference curves, should have been presented in terms of the social welfare functions and utility possibility frontiers of Samuelson and Bergson. The result would have been more elegant, more complicated, and more up-to-date, but the analysis would have led to quite similar indeterminate results. As long as Samuelson has no procedure (beside consensus by magic or dictatorial fiat) for ascertaining the appropriate income distribution, he has really not improved the content of the analysis, by comparison with the analysis in terms of community indifference curves.

In either event, the general conclusion would seem to be that, even in the framework of its own assumptions, the methodology of general equilibrium analysis has trouble identifying a unique maximum without simplifying the assumptions beyond reason. And, whether economists interested in working with the real world are well advised to straitjacket themselves into the setting of pure competition, general equilibrium economics is open to question.

NOTES

1. Adam Smith, *An Inquiry into the Nature and Causes of the Wealth of Nations* (Chicago: Encyclopaedia Britannica, 1952 [1776]), p. 194.
2. Abram Bergson [Burk], "A Reformulation of Certain Aspects of Welfare Economics," *Quarterly Journal of Economics* 52 (February 1938): 310–334; Paul A. Samuelson, "Social Indifference Curves," *Quarterly Journal of Economics* 70 (February 1956): 1–22; Milton Friedman, *Essays in Positive Economics* (Chicago: University of Chicago Press, 1953).
3. Bergson, "Reformulation," p. 310.
4. David Wall, ed., *Chicago Essays in Economic Development* (Chicago: University of Chicago Press, 1972), p. vii.
5. Friedman, *Essays in Positive Economics*, p. 3.
6. Lionel Robbins, *An Essay on the Nature and Significance of Economic Science*, 2d ed. (London: Macmillan, 1935 [1932]), pp. 15, 31.
7. Paul A. Samuelson, *Foundations of Economic Analysis* (Cambridge, Mass.: Harvard University Press, 1955 [1947]), pp. 21–23.
8. Ibid., p. 23.
9. Edwin Mansfield, *Microeconomics* (New York: Norton, 1970), pp. 414–416.
10. Immanuel Kant, *Critique of Pure Reason* (1781), vol. 1, second part, second division, book 2, chap. 2, sec. 4 (p. 151 in the Britannica Great Books edition).
11. See H. H. Liebhafsky, *American Government and Business* (New York: Wiley, 1971), especially chaps. 1–4; Wolfgang Friedmann, *Legal Theory*, 5th ed. (New York: Columbia, 1967 [1944]).
12. See Richard A. Posner, *Economic Analysis of Law* (Boston: Little, Brown, 1972); Ronald H. Coase, "The Problem of Social Cost," *Journal of Law and Economics* 3 (October 1960): 1–44.
13. Abraham H. Maslow, *The Farther Reaches of Human Nature* (New York: Viking, 1971), p. 321.
14. Herbert A. Simon and Andrew C. Stedry, "Psychology and Economics," in Gardner Lindzey and Elliot Aronson, eds., *The Handbook of Social Psychology*, 2d ed., 5 vols. (Reading, Mass.: Addison-Wesley, 1969), 5: 297, 270, 271.
15. James G. March, "Business Decision Making," *Industrial Research* 1 (Spring 1959); reprinted in Harold J. Leavitt and Louis R. Pondy, eds., *Readings in Managerial Psychology* (Chicago: University of Chicago Press, 1964), p. 449.
16. Richard Cyert and James March, *A Behavioral Theory of the Firm* (Englewood Cliffs, N.J.: Prentice-Hall, 1963).
17. Abraham H. Maslow, "A Theory of Human Motivation," *Psychological Review* 50 (July 1943): 370–396.

18. John R. Commons, *Institutional Economics* (Madison: University of Wisconsin Press, 1961 [1934]), pp. 107–108.
19. J. B. Watson, *Behaviorism* (New York: Norton, 1925); B. F. Skinner, *Beyond Freedom and Dignity* (New York: Knopf, 1971).
20. This is done, for example, by Robert Dorfman, Paul A. Samuelson, and Robert M. Solow, *Linear Programming and Economic Analysis* (New York: McGraw-Hill, 1958), p. 330.

ADDITIONAL READINGS

Barber, Bernard, and Alex Inkeles, eds. *Stability and Social Change*. Boston: Little, Brown, 1971. See especially the Robin M. Williams, Jr., essay: "Change and Stability in Values and Value Systems."

Commons, John R. *The Legal Foundations of Capitalism*. Madison: University of Wisconsin Press, 1968 [1924].

Debreu, Gerard. *Theory of Value*. New Haven: Yale University Press, 1972.

Dobb, Maurice. *Welfare Economics and the Economics of Socialism*. London: Cambridge University Press, 1969.

Dukes, W. F. "Psychological Study of Values." *Psychological Bulletin* 52 (January 1955):24–50.

Kahl, Joseph A. *The Measurement of Modernism: A Study of Values in Brazil and Mexico*. Austin: University of Texas Press, 1968.

Kunkel, John H. *Society and Economic Growth*. New York: Oxford University Press, 1970.

LaPiere, Richard T., and Paul R. Farnsworth. *Social Psychology*. New York: McGraw-Hill, 1949.

Lewin, Kurt. *Resolving Social Conflicts*. New York: Harper, 1948.

Lindzey, Gardner and Elliot Aronson, eds. *The Handbook of Social Psychology*. 2d ed. 5 vols. Reading, Mass.: Addison-Wesley, 1969.

Locke, John. "An Essay Concerning Human Understanding." In *Great Books of the Western World*, vol. 35: *Locke, Berkeley, Hume*. Chicago: Encyclopaedia Britannica, 1952 [1690].

McDougall, William. *An Introduction to Social Psychology*. London: Methuen, 1960 [1908].

Maslow, Abraham H. *Motivation and Personality*. New York: Harper & Row, 1954.

Merton, Robert K. *Social Theory and Social Structure*. Glencoe, Ill.: Free Press, 1957 [1949].

Mills, C. Wright. *The Sociological Imagination*. New York: Oxford, 1959.

Mishan, Edward J. "A Survey of Welfare Economics." In *Surveys of Economic Theory*, vol. 1, pp. 154–222. Prepared for the American Economic Association and the Royal Economic Society. 3 vols. New York: St. Martin's Press, 1967.

Parsons, Talcott, ed. *Theories of Society*. New York: Free Press, 1961. See especially part 2 of the General Introduction, pp. 30–79.

Restack, Richard M. *Pre-Meditated Man*. New York: Viking, 1972.

Rokeach, Milton. *Beliefs, Attitudes, and Values*. San Francisco: Josey-Bass, 1968.

Unger, Roberto M. *Law in Modern Society*. New York: Free Press, 1976.

Veblen, Thorstein. *The Instinct of Workmanship*. New York: Augustus M. Kelley, 1964 [1914].

Wilson, Edward O. *On Human Nature*. Cambridge, Mass.: Harvard University Press, 1978.

5.
Microeconomics and Decision Making

MUCH ECONOMIC THEORY is couched in terms of the decision-making problems of the citizen, business executive, or economic planner. Whether in the individual, firm, or governmental context, the decision maker uses certain information and value judgments mixed into a certain analytical methodology as a basis for making decisions as to how much to buy, produce, sell, or what-have-you.

Price theory and national income theory are the chief analytical methodologies available to orthodox economics for guiding decision making. To be operationally useful, they have to involve (1) behavior assumptions, such as the profit motive (or the desire for gain), and (2) assumptions as to the stability of relationships among the economic variables involved in the methodology of the analysis. This latter generally is the constancy assumption (or the "unchanged pattern" assumption), an essential ingredient in virtually all econometric model building in both the price theory and the national income theory bailiwicks. And it is a key consideration whether the theorizing is at the price theory level, where the constancy of price elasticities may be the crux of the matter, or at the national income theory level, where the constancy of the marginal propensities to consume, save, and import is likely to be the crux of the matter.

This chapter is concerned with decision making by individuals, industries, and firms—microeconomics. And chapter 6 is concerned with decision making and planning at the level that affects the whole economy—macroeconomics. For economists, price theory is the chief analytical tool at the microlevel. And price theory generally begins with an assumption that business enterprises are trying to maximize their profits and individuals are trying to maximize their incomes. Much of the analysis is conducted on an assumption of pure competition, but oligopoly and monopoly may be considered.

The Pure Competition Assumption

A standard statement of the pure competition assumption might run as follows. The participants are (1) all-knowing or economic men, (2) desirous of maximizing gain, and (3) present in such large numbers that no one of them can perceptibly influence price or total production, but (4) each can move freely, and immediate-ly, and costlessly to other, more remunerative activities. Also (5) all the items produced in the industry under discussion must be exactly alike. And (6) these influences interact to create full employment.

The University of Chicago School would seem to hold that these assumptions are in fact reasonably descriptive of this world. It is said: "The market works." Proponents of this approach do not necessarily argue that the assumptions accurately describe the real world. They may merely argue that the real world operates pretty much as though these assumptions hold. But, since nobody can prove anything conclusively to the satisfaction of all discus-sants on this point, all go their own merry way. And by some quirk of fate much, if not most, economic analysis does presuppose that the purely competitive market really works. Yet, to myself and many other writers, the use of such a frame of reference disregards plain common sense. The market by and large is not purely com-petitive. In that sense, it does *not* work. However, it may work like blue blazes in a lot of imperfect senses, meanwhile taking a lot of demand and supply into account.

Homeostasis and Behavior Reinforcement

The Equilibrium Concept

Price theory is generally oriented to the proposition that there is some kind of equilibrating force at work which, when things get out of order (when demand exceeds supply or supply exceeds demand), tends to bring the economy or the industry or the firm back to equilibrium and full employment. This is the condition of homeostasis—the tendency toward equilibrium. The concept is the essence of the work of Alfred Marshall, of most price theory texts, and of the view of the general public on demand and supply.

(Keynes' *General Theory* is also equilibrium economics, however with the additional feature that there can be equilibrium in a setting involving something less than full employment.)

The competitive assumptions are thought to be basic in creating the setting that makes a natural tendency toward equilibrium an operationally meaningful concept. Whether such a tendency is in fact generally operational is one of the most important questions with which economists ought to be concerned.

The Tendency away from Equilibrium and Behavior Reinforcement

It would seem, however, that many economic problems are better understood in a context where a tendency toward equilibrium is not considered to be the theme. Human behavior may just as well be tending in all kinds of other directions. And economic process may be better understood in a context where an effort is made to understand the whys and wherefores of ongoing behavior, without any presumptions about the tendency to settle into stable equilibrium or to tend toward equilibrium.

Behavior is ongoing. Certain things that happen earlier influence later behavior, and the prevailing institutionalized behavior patterns are eternally operating to influence this process. The failure of the current economic orthodoxy to effectively handle such major recent problems as inflation, the balance of payments, the decline of the railroads, and the energy crisis is probably in considerable part due to the nature of its assumption of the tendency toward static equilibrium, when in fact powerful influences are leading us away from equilibrium.

The decline of the railroads, leading to results that were probably undesirable from almost all points of view, may have resulted from a process somewhat like this. People were using autos and airplanes more; so the railroads cut back on the quantity and the quality of their service; and, as a result, people used the railroads less, and so on. This is a sort of self-fortifying or self-reinforcing process that leads to an end result quite different in kind from that visualized in equilibrium analysis.

Once an inflationary process has gotten underway, the labor unions want higher pay to offset the effects of inflation, the executives want higher profits to offset inflation, the teachers want higher salaries, and so on. These higher costs then serve as justification on the part of business for further increases in prices. And spiraling inflation, self-reinforcing inflation, is underway. Individuals are under strong pressure not to fall behind in this race. This is not a situation where a few business or labor leaders can stem the tide by moderating their own demands. They just get left behind if they do, like the New England farmer who generously did not pasture his own cattle on the village commons.[1]

In John Platt's terminology, one may be trapped into a behavior pattern that leads to long-run results that are both contrary to the social interest and contrary to one's own interest. The "tendency toward equilibrium" analysis fails to get hold of the nature of such processes. But understanding the prevailing behavior patterns and institutional arrangements of the society has a whole lot to do with society's ability to intelligently come to grips with such situations.

In the face of a general inflation, it is important to understand that no single social group is the villain of the piece, certainly not the farmers or the butchers or even the gas company officials (although perhaps not all). At all events, inflation should be viewed as an exercise in social behavior and social understanding much more than as a study in leads and lags in a process thought to lead naturally to equilibrium.

The temptation is strong for economists with mathematical backgrounds, when they see the implications of the behavior reinforcement phenomenon feeding back to fortify the inflation or the decline in the railroads, to believe that the situation is made to order for analysis with the sophisticated mathematics of closed-loop control systems, of feedback transfers, and such like.[2] The use of mathematics in this area, however, requires the ability to quantify the magnitude of the feedback, and this is exactly where a major amount of the trouble lies. In the inflation example and the railroad example and many similar cases, the magnitude of the feedback is simply not ex ante quantifiable. And mathematizing the relations tends to obfuscate some reasonably simple, and obvious, and crude, and important phenomena.

At all events many, if not most, short-run or middle-run or business-cycle-run economic problems are probably best dealt with as problems in understanding or trying to understand how self-reinforcing, interacting human behavior is expressed in a given (individual or group) institutional setting involving ongoing process rather than as an exercise in equilibrium analysis.

Influences on Choice

The Range of Influences

It will probably be helpful at this stage to try to develop a coherent picture of the *range* of influences (not just the gain-maximizing motive) on choice, although some repetition of the discussion in chapters 3 and 4 is involved.

It was alleged in chapter 3 that there are these values: the decent minimum, getting along pleasantly, constructive self-expression, and security. However, even if individuals hold these values, or some others, to recite them does not explain how they make a decision. What is the basis for individual decision making?

We may ask certain individuals: why did you do that? On what basis can they give an answer? How reasonable and definitive an answer are we entitled to expect?

Several things may be said, some with fair certainty.

For one, except in a fairly clear-cut, simple, and nontraumatic circumstance, we cannot expect to get a correct answer. We cannot find out why persons did something by asking them. If they know, they may not tell us. Why should they? But, even more likely, each individual probably does not have a clear-cut, simple reason.

We may be trying to get a vice-president in charge of personnel to say why somebody was not promoted. The reaction might be quite different from what it would have been before HEW. In other days it might have been: "By God, I don't like the way he combs his hair. What's it to you?"

Now, however, . . .

Stopping at a red light is an almost pure case of an institutionally dictated choice. A choice made to spite one's spouse is an almost pure example of an irrational choice. Taking a drink of water after working in the sun on a hot day is an almost pure biologically dictated choice. The operations of varying degrees of rationality are somewhat more difficult to visualize clearly.

One may experiment with the following fourfold classification of influences in individual decision making: (1) habitual, customary, institutionalized, more or less automatic (instinctive or spontaneous) nonrational reactions, (2) accidental, nonrational reactions, (3) rational, thoughtful (albeit institutionalized) behavior designed to further (or conceivably to retard) general or social interests, and (4) rational, thoughtful (albeit institutionalized) behavior in the individual selfish interest (or, conceivably, disinterest). I will allege later that institutionalized influences play a large role in connection with all but the accidental, nonrational reactions, which are nonetheless important in the decision-making process.

The first influence alleged was habitual, customary, institutionalized, more or less automatic (instinctive or spontaneous) reaction. We jam on the brakes when something runs across the road in front of our car. Some people gallop off spontaneously to take advantage of a bargain. Later in life we may scream spontaneously under certain circumstances because of some unpleasant experience as a small child. (We do not need to argue out with Freud whether or not everything is sexually motivated, or even what that would mean, for this to be true.) We may go to the grocery store every Tuesday and Friday on our way home from work. Or we may blink if an object is coming in our direction.

There are many factors in the background creating this predisposition to various automatic reactions: our biology (the result of mutation and natural selection), circumstances à la Freud in our upbringing, institutional and social pressures, habit, and custom.

In terms of the economics of all this, probably the influence most important to emphasize is the institutionalized basis for much of this behavior. The nature of the behavioral reaction in a given situation is determined to a large degree by the social, cultural, mores-type influences in the individual's background. We may buy bonds instead of stock in "arranging our portfolio balance" because bonds are less risky (provided they are not Big Mac bonds) and we were brought up to do the less risky thing—or vice versa. Or we may buy railroad bonds because we were enthralled by railroads as a child.

The institutions are what they are and exert the influence they exert because of the circumstances under which they were created. All institutions, and the behavior norms they involve, have a history. Important as an influence, in this context, is the nature of the evolution of the (technical) knowledge available to a society. As knowledge is accumulated as a continuing, ongoing process, its nature impacts on institutions and on social and economic behavior norms, influencing what those norms become. Change in those institutional norms occurs as society adjusts to use (as effectively as may be) the ever changing knowledge at its disposal. The self-correcting value judgment (as conditions and knowledge change) is the essence of the institutional or instrumental value theory of William James, John Dewey, and Clarence Ayres. But, also, the nature of the institutional changes is conditioned by the biology of people and by the influences of the process of mutation and natural selection. And it is also inhibited by the norms of the institutional order already in existence.

Out of this sort of background come the controlling influences on the *spontaneous* reaction of the individual to many, and perhaps most, outside disturbances. In the area of economics, when I buy that brand of peas because it is cheaper than the brand beside it, this may be an automatic, spontaneous reaction that does not involve thinking about why I want to buy something because it is cheaper. Or I'll buy this quart of ice cream because the sign says that it is absolutely the most expensive ice cream in the whole world, but I do not really think about why I am moved to buy something because it is the most expensive thing of its kind. Or I may buy the small but expensive Cadillac Seville. I may spontaneously make that choice because it shows I'm modest, without thinking about the implications of modesty. Or, in the back of my mind, there may be the consideration that everyone really knows I could have bought the bigger car, which cost no more. And the thought of being "free" to make such a decision warms the cockles of my heart. I probably do not slow down to rationalize the whys and wherefores of these reactions, or I may slow down to do some rationalizing before I buy the Seville. In this latter case, my decision will probably be of the type considered later, the rational but selfish decision.

The second possible influence was accidental—perhaps random, perhaps not—nonrational reaction. Perhaps after carefully considering but being unable to make an important decision, a person flips a coin. This would be a nonrational decision based on an influence that does have a probability distribution.

Another possibility would be that, after carefully considering an important (or not so important) decision, a spouse does what he or she does because it is what he or she believes the mate desires, or because it is the reverse of what the mate desires, or because someone says: "Never buy a car on a Friday," or "My Uncle Jack always said . . ." Decision making as a result of nonrational or irrational reactions means that happenstance controlled the outcome. There might well be no predictable regularity of pattern. The outcome would not have a probability distribution in any useful, usable, or statistically meaningful sense. And it would seem to be important to understand (especially in economics) that a goodly proportion of *de novo* major decisions are probably made in a context involving no clear-cut basis for choice, where happenstance determines the outcome. However, once the particular choice is made, it will call forth innumerable additional acts that will follow more or less automatically, as in the first situation, or rationally, as in the third and fourth situations.

But the person was hung up on the basic decision. And the influence that tipped the balance, even on important decisions, was frequently trivial, even irrelevant, or irrationally spontaneous. Some impulse jumped a synapse. And away we go, with implications for ourselves and others. How much irrational accident will be involved in the energy policy (or lack of it) that emerges in the United States?

There are two types of "rational" decisions. One, the third item in the list of influences, was a rational, thoughtful (albeit institutionalized) behavior designed to further (or conceivably to retard) some general or social interest. The individual may have all kinds of "reasons" for coming to a conclusion. The logic may or may not be very good, and a maximizing-type calculation may or may not actually be attempted. Also, the social values—the decent minimum, getting along pleasantly, and so on—may be taken into account in all sorts of ways and with all sorts of weights being given to the various factors as the individual reflects upon these factors and their relative importance.

The individual's opinion as to what is more or less important in this more or less "rational" decision-making process is very largely institutionally determined (by upbringing, employment, social position, etc.), much as is the situation with the customary, automatic decision discussed earlier. The individual is putting together institutionalized considerations in a more or less thoughtful and rational way. Also, as mentioned in connection with customary, automatic decisions, the institutions and their influence on the individual are what they are primarily because of the role of technology and biology in shaping institutions.

Then, fourth, there is the rational, thoughtful (albeit institutionalized) behavior in the individual selfish interest (or, conceivably, disinterest or disservice). Again the individual may or may not be consciously trying to maximize something or other or believe that she or he is so trying. The object under consideration may be salary, or income, or profits, or personal welfare, or various other things—measured in either monetary or real terms or in some more amorphous terms.

With regard to the attitudes that condition the rational decision-making process when the individual is trying to further personal interests, I will repeat the comment made in connection with the rational effort to further social interests: the individual's opinion as to what is more or less important is very largely institutionally determined, and the norms of institutions have the origins already mentioned.

This is the aspect of the decision-making process where, if anywhere, the standard economic assumption of the economic man trying to maximize personal gain has its role to play. But even here one must qualify any endorsement of the meaningfulness of the concept of the rational maximizer. Some people are more intelligently rational than others, but probably most of us, in connection with most ostensibly rational decision making, just give rationality a lick and a promise. We may be quite thoughtfully and intelligently rational without approaching the economic decision-making problem as a problem in maximization. And as long as this is the case much economic analysis loses its relevance.

At the level of the individual, trying to serve some personal interest in the *very* short run, there may be some genuine usefulness or relevance to an economic man assumption and a gain maximization methodology. And here, for example, an effort to set prices at a level that will maximize profits in the next planning period may well be a useful first approximation of reasonable behavior.

Or it may not. The individual making the decision that will render up the gain needs to be the person who will receive the gain, or it is a little difficult to have confidence in the allegation as to motivation. And, just at this point, the process of corporate decision making conjures up some problems.

The Profit Motive in Corporations
To be practically meaningful, the profit motive must involve the assumption that decision makers in corporations are basically interested in profits, increasing profits, and maximizing profits. If they are not, the multitudinous economic models based on this assumption are fanciful.

That corporate executives speak with warmth about their concern for profits seems to provide some justification for the profit motive assumption. And the sign-wavers at Republican conventions with placards extolling the virtues of free enterprise certainly generally, sincerely believe in the meaningfulness and healing properties of the profit motive. Here is a genuine deeply ingrained attitude.

And yet . . .

When one gets down to the nitty-gritty, this attitude is probably pseudo. It is a façade. The executives had better allege (and in some sense convince themselves that they believe) that corporate profits are the name of the game. If they do not speak this language with convincing sincerity, the anonymous stockholders might just rise in righteous wrath and evict them from office. All that the executives really have to do is speak the language and seem to believe it, and the stockholders will leave them alone and continue to sing the praises of the free enterprise system. Also, by this time, the executives may genuinely believe it.

If, on the other hand, one makes the additional assumption that the executives are chiefly interested in their personal gain, the possibility of a conflict of aims is suggested. The executives may not be making decisions on corporate policy in a context where maximizing profits is an overriding consideration. Higher salaries for executives reduce corporate profits. Generous expense accounts and fifty-cent filets mignons in executive dining rooms reduce profits. And stock options and generous executive retirement plans cut into the equity interest of the ordinary stockholders.

It is quite easy (human psychology being what it is) for the executives to be generous to themselves in these various respects and at the same time more or less genuinely believe that they are working for a better deal on profits—to the greater good of the stockholders.

Also, the executives may well be interested more in plowing back profits in order to have the pleasure of dominating ever larger empires than in distributing profits to stockholders as dividends. Some stockholders may approve of such use of their "profits," others may not, but neither group has an effective say in decision making on the matter.

Another possibility is that, in some cases, the corporate executives may be a little old and a little tired and quite content if the corporation rocks along protected in its share of the market by a network of restrictive practices. During the 1930s, such a behavior pattern was called rationalization.

Corporate executives may also make decisions on patriotic or "good citizenship" grounds that will have the effect of reducing profits. In fact, executives on the average may be about as likely to be patriotic as the next fellow.

All in all, it is not clear that the corporation, as an entity, is working to maximize profits (a good deal of neoclassical and Marxist theory to the contrary notwithstanding). And, if it is not, a lot of price theory becomes a pretty bootless logical exercise and a lot of the paeans to the "enterprise system" lose their underlying rationale, as does the logical structure of price theory and general equilibrium analysis. The logical difficulties with general equilibrium theory which were discussed in the appendix to chapter 4 become of mere academic interest. The relevant frame of reference does not exist.

Yet, it is worth repeating: sellers will nevertheless still have an interest in selling at higher prices and buyers in buying at lower prices. Substantial individual freedom (from government harassment) may still be a major aspect of the better life. And freedom to go into the line of work one prefers is an aspect of individual freedom that probably contributes to the productivity and standard of living, as well as the morale, of an economy.

Commodity Market Decisions

The Meaning of Market Prices

Neoclassical price theory alleges that demand and supply (at the industry level) interact to determine price at the point where they are equal. Demand curves slope down to the right, supply curves up (see figure 5–1), and initial equilibrium is at P. A fall in demand involves a movement of the whole demand curve to the left and a lower price, because the intersection with the supply curve will perforce be at a lower price at P'', since the supply curve is rising to the right. At least, that is what the geometry says. And the allegation is that demand and supply interact in this way, and the market is assumed to work. The chief tools of analysis are demand and supply (represented by curves on graphs alleging how much will be demanded or supplied at various possible prices) and cost

Figure 5-1. Demand and supply

curves (describing how much it costs to produce varying quantities of goods). If the analysis is to be at all exact, it must be possible to identify the shape of these curves with some precision.

The Constancy Assumption
One may even use somewhat stronger language. If demand and supply patterns are to be manipulated with any readiness in working out relations, it is convenient if the curves have a property called *constant* elasticity along their length. (The nature of the elasticity concept is discussed in the appendix to this chapter.) The possible shapes that economists are disposed to permit the curves

to assume are, therefore, rather powerfully limited. Then we use statistical techniques that force raw data about production and prices to say that the curves have these convenient shapes, whether they really do or not. And then, more readily than we should, we blithely answer questions as to how much a firm will produce in order to maximize profits or as to what the price will be when demand equals supply.

The Nature of the Usefulness of Price Theory

Almost any problem can be analyzed in the context of price theory: the drug habit (Miller), capital punishment (Ehrlich), pornography, the chewing gum market, the abortion market, prostitution, marriage, advertising, the all-volunteer army, pollution, zero population growth, the multinationals, the property rights of trespassing cattle (Coase), the behavior of administrative agencies (Posner), the bail system (Landes), the optimum enforcement of laws (Stigler), crime and punishment (Becker), the brain drain (Myint). Or one can allege some other worthwhile relations: if the revenuers become more effective, the price of bootleg whiskey will rise (Miller); if potential murderers are rewarded for not committing murder, there will be fewer murders (Ehrlich); if crime is made less economical, there will be less crime (Stigler); if a person's cows graze on another's land, the free market is ready, willing, and able to deal with the problem (Coase).

Ayres has written: ". . . to question whether the operations of the market—that is, the whole apparatus of buying and selling— mean what they have been traditionally alleged to mean is not to argue against buying and selling. . . . The whole point to the Veblenian criticism of the classical tradition is that the economy is not regulated by the price system. It is regulated by the institutional structure of Western society, of which the market is at most only a manifestation."[3]

There are many situations where the solution of maximizing problems may be useful at the microlevel in helping with decision making by firms or industries. The firm, appropriately, may try to maximize profit in the next planning period as effectively as it can, given the prevailing ground rules. In this setting, to solve the maximization problem, executives may appropriately make some simplifying assumptions. They may well assume some "constant" parameters: certain prices and costs will remain the same, tax rates will remain the same, and so on, at least for a while. On the basis of this information, they decide how much to produce in the next planning period and at which prices to sell, probably influenced also to a considerable degree by some rules laid down by the government. These calculations might well involve the methodology of linear programming, but generally they do not. They usually involve some rules of thumb, some rough calculations relating guesses about costs and receipts in the event that various possible alternative policies are followed, hoping they have taken into account the factors which will in fact be important and opting for one of the policies (sometimes after flipping a coin), as well as a short prayer to whatever god they happen to believe in.

Price comparisons are meaningful. A lower price is more desirable from the viewpoint of a buyer; a higher price is more desirable from the viewpoint of a seller. What does not stand up, out of price theory and general equilibrium analysis, is the allegation that market price—or perhaps, better said, consumer surplus— can be equated to social value. Nor does the conclusion that the government should not ever intervene or regulate stand up.

Similarly, there is something to be said for competition. Competition, in the sense of two companies competing for sales, may result in lower prices and better merchandise. Two companies competing may create a situation in which consumers get more courteous service, lower prices, and a better product than some government enterprise might provide. But this is not exactly the economist's concept of (pure) competition involving a setting where there are so many sellers and buyers that no one can affect price.

H. H. Liebhafsky says of market prices:

> Instead of being an ultimate standard of valuation to which the social order *ought* to conform, *actual* market prices are in reality a reflection of that social order which does exist. To accept *actual* market prices as a measure of social valuations is thus to accept the *status quo* in markets; and to argue that a particular configuration of prices *should* exist is tantamount to arguing that the social order which will produce that configuration *should* exist.
>
>   . . . Practicing economists (especially those in government service) have always operated within a pragmatic context of self-correcting value judgments to make policy recommendations relating to goals which are instrumentally defined but never final.[4]

Similarly, Alfred Marshall wrote long ago:

> The Statical theory of equilibrium is only an introduction to economic studies. . . . Its limitations are so constantly overlooked, especially by those who approach it from an abstract point of view, that there is a danger in throwing it into definite form at all.[5]

In any event, demand, supply, and price considerations work through the system in such highly institutionalized ways that it stands to reason that individuals concerned about prices had better bestir themselves to understand what those behavior norms are. Price *theory* is not enough.

APPENDIX. DECISION MAKING AND PRICE THEORY

In this appendix, the standard microeconomic models, which ostensibly ought to be able to describe and guide decision making at the firm and industry levels, are discussed in a somewhat more technical manner than was done in the body of this chapter.

Industry Demand, Supply, and Price

Figure 5–2 illustrates the concepts of demand and supply and of consumer and producer surplus. The ordinary argument is that competition works to determine quantities demanded and supplied and to determine price at P, where demand equals supply. The demand curve sloping downward to the right allegedly represents the larger and larger quantities of the product which people are presumed to buy at lower and lower prices. The supply curve, rising to the right, implies that producers are presumed to produce and supply larger and larger quantities subject to the lure of higher and higher prices. At P demand would seem to equal supply at a price of about $2.80 and a quantity of about 3,300. The market would be cleared; all that was produced would be sold: no surpluses, no shortages.

The area DEP, labeled consumer surplus, would seem to represent about $4,455 [($5.50 − $2.80) × 3,300 ÷ 2], and the area FEP, marked producer surplus or economic rent, would seem to represent about $3,960 [($2.80 − $.40) × 3,300 ÷ 2]. It is a standard price theory argument that the consumer surplus area, in a value theory sense, represents utility or value that the consumer has received over and above what has been paid for. And the producer surplus area represents utility or value that the producer receives over and above costs, when selling at the price corresponding to P. The amount of each, consumer and producer surplus, is measurable in money. The area is a sum of money describing a quantity of value or utility. And, in many exercises designed to prove or disprove the desirability of

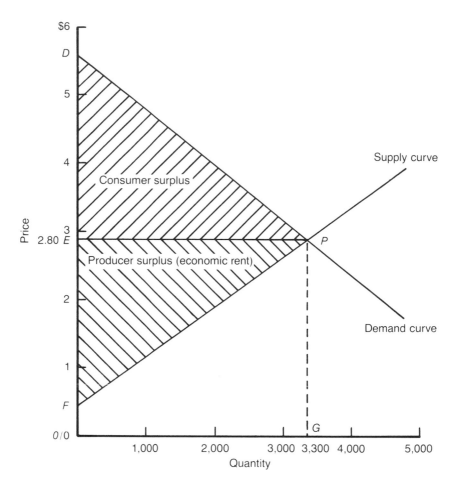

Figure 5-2. Industry demand and supply: consumer and producer surplus

some decision, the logical positivist–type proof as to whether there is gain or loss hinges on whether these areas are increased or decreased in size.

If real life problems are to be dealt with using these analytical tools, it needs, at the least, to be possible to estimate the location of these demand and supply curves from actual data. But, in fact, all that can actually be observed is how much is bought and sold at a given price during a given time period, and that is only the point *P*, which is common to the demand curve and the supply curve, not the rest of the curves. (Or conceivably, if at

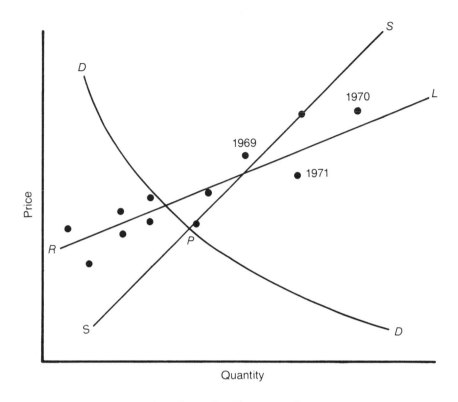

Figure 5-3. Quantities bought and sold: scatter diagram

the prevailing price the market is not cleared, the price and quantity corresponding to what actually happened may not be on either the demand or the supply curve.)

Where, however, assuming identification is possible, do we get the additional information to complete the demand and supply curves? We may get price-quantity information for successive time periods (time-series data), as is illustrated in figure 5–3, and locate the corresponding points. Or we might get the data on price and quantity for a given product during a given time period in several markets (cross-section data).

We could then run a line (regression analysis) through the pattern of points in a way that seems to strike a reasonable average among them. We thus have a line such as *RL* in figure 5–3, representing how much has been bought and sold at various possible prices. But is *RL* a demand curve or a supply curve? Pretty clearly it is neither. In econometrics, however, a great deal of ingenuity goes into rationalizing the slopes of demand *DD* and supply *SS* curves, starting from this sort of raw data and using additional information on related circumstances to justify pinning down the curves. This is a tricky game. And, as the demand and supply curves so derived are used as a basis for extended additional analysis, we would do well to remember occasionally the extremely shaky basis on which the original demand and supply curves were constructed.

So, various artifices, and subterfuges, and proxy variables, and questionnaires are used as a basis for making the estimates. For example, we may use data (so-called time-series data) regarding how much of a commodity is bought and sold in successive periods of time and at what prices, when what we really need to know is how much would be bought and sold at various possible prices at a given time. Or we may use data (so-called cross-section data) as to how much is bought and sold at various prices in different markets at a given time, when, again, what we really need to know is how much would be bought and sold at various possible prices at a given time in one market in particular.

Also, since the only definite information available (in either cross-section or time-series data) states how much was demanded *and* supplied at a price, there is no way to separate demand behavior from supply behavior with precision. This is the identification problem. There are a lot of gimmicks for separating demand forces from supply forces. You may do a multiple regression using as additional independent variables the weather, which allegedly affects only supply, or some other factor which allegedly affects only demand. This will separate demand influences from supply influences after a fashion. But you still do not really know whether the demand (or supply) curve, so derived, is located in a way to represent with any precision the variable in which you are interested—even though the resulting curve probably does represent more, say, demand influence than supply influence.

Perhaps the most important implication of this identification problem is that it is substantial and real. The concepts of demand and supply are not theoretically independent. A change in demand may well affect supply— perhaps via national income changes. Or an increase in demand may lead to a nonreversible increase in production capacity; but once the increase is installed it is there; it is irreversible even though the demand curve moves back to its former position. Thus, the commonly assumed independence of demand and supply curves is dubious.

This leads us to two key concepts in price theory—elasticity and marginality.

The Elasticity Concept and the Identification Problem
A demand elasticity is a (pure but not particularly precise, or perhaps it is pseudoprecise) number that ostensibly describes, in a neat capsule, what

will be the difference during a given period of time in the quantity demanded (purchased) by buyers if there is a price change. For example:

$$\begin{array}{c}\text{The elasticity of demand} \\ \text{with respect to price}\end{array} = \dfrac{\begin{array}{c}\text{The percentage change} \\ \text{in the quantity demanded}\end{array}}{\begin{array}{c}\text{The percentage change in} \\ \text{the price}\end{array}}$$

Presumably the figure for salt is close to zero, and the figure for a durable consumer item such as a television set ought to be considerably larger than one. Similar elasticities may be computed to describe the supply situation. If these elasticities are knowable, it would be helpful from the viewpoint of the producer to know what they actually are.

Graphs of demand curves representing the standard elasticity possibilities from zero to infinity are freely presented in most undergraduate texts. The demand curve in figure 5–1 probably has an elasticity close to a constant of one along its length. A vertical demand curve would have an elasticity of zero, a horizontal line of infinity. The demand curve of figure 5–2 has an elasticity varying from much greater than one to much less as we read from left to right. Graphs of the standard supply curve possibilities are seen more seldom. Figure 5–4 illustrates some of the possibilities. In the case of a simple parabola based on the origin, the exponent on the independent variable is the elasticity. (Readers might be intrigued to see whether they can write a formula for a constant elasticity supply curve that is not based on the origin.) A curve rising ever more steeply to the right, such as DE, is elastic in the range where the tangents (for example, at P) cut the vertical axis, is inelastic in the range where the tangents cut the horizontal axis (the P'' case), and has unit elasticity at the point (P') where the tangent is also a ray out of the origin. Curve DE illustrates these possibilities for changing elasticity along a curve. For the curve $Q = aP^{b'}$, the elasticity, b', is constant along the curve and is greater than one. For $Q = aP^{b''}$ the elasticity, b'', is also a constant along the curve but is less than one.

Since demand and supply price elasticities are among the more basic concepts in economics, and since it is essential to be able to identify them if many price theory relations are to be mathematized in formulas of any reasonable degree of simplicity, it is fairly revealing of the state of the "science" that the values of the elasticities cannot be computed in a *theoretically* satisfactory manner by the methods presently at the disposal of the profession. (And, if they could be, it would probably turn out that they would not have the desirable property of constancy along their length.)

The relevant information as to how much would be demanded or supplied at a given time and place at various possible prices is literally unobtainable, because all we ever really know about the shape of demand and supply curves, if that, is the location of their intersection. (This point was

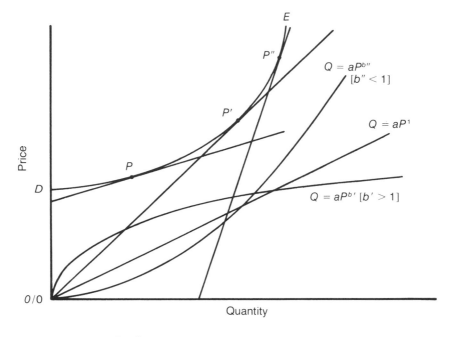

Figure 5-4. Supply elasticities

made in the preceding section in connection with the discussion of efforts to produce demand and supply curves.) We do not know the shape of the rest of the curves and consequently do not know the elasticities or whether they are constant along the curves. Even if we ask people what their elasticities of supply and demand are, we cannot be sure that what they tell us represents in fact what they would do. In reality, the chance that they would understand the question would be slight. Nevertheless, in spite of this uncertainty, we sometimes do ask them.

Cost Curves and the Marginality Concept
Cost curves (total, fixed, variable, marginal, and submarginal) are the other basic price theory concept (see figure 5–5). The cost curves, when put together with information about the demand for a company's product (it is generally assumed that the demand for the product of a given company under competition is infinitely elastic—much or little can be sold at the prevailing unchanging price—marginal and average revenue being the

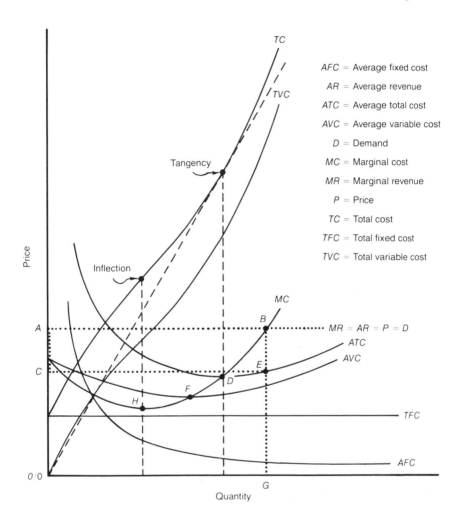

Figure 5-5. Short-run equilibrium of a firm under competition

same), reveal the most profitable level of production for the firm—which is at the point where nonconstant marginal cost equals constant marginal revenue, point B, and maximum possible profits are the $ABEC$ area delimited by the vertical distance between B and the average total cost curve.

In figure 5–5, price or cost (P) and quantity of production (Q) for the product of some particular small firm are represented on the axes. Total cost (TC) is the total of all costs involved in producing various amounts (Q) of the product. Average total cost (ATC) is total cost divided by the number of units of the product. Total fixed cost (TFC) is the amount of cost the firm must meet (such as interest on bonds and office rent) regardless of how much it produces; it does not vary in the short run and so is represented on the graph by a horizontal straight line. However, as more and more units are produced, average fixed cost (AFC) falls. Total variable cost (TVC) is total cost less total fixed cost. And average variable cost (AVC) is the averages of the total variable cost which depend on the level of production. The chief variables in the variable-cost part of the picture are (1) labor, more or less of which will be hired depending on the level of production (Q), and (2) raw materials, more or less of which . . . etc. At least this is the short-run story.

In long-run equilibrium the fixed-cost curves and the variable-cost curves would not exist; only the total-cost curves would exist. Equilibrium would be at demand (D), the point where a horizontal line is tangent to the lowest point on the ATC curve. Profits would be zero. And marginal revenue (MR)—average revenue (AR), price, and demand—would be brought down to the D level by the entry of more firms into the industry.

The marginal-cost (MC) curve represents the change in total cost (and also in total variable cost, the two magnitudes being the same) as the quantity of production is expanded. The logic of these interrelations happens to require that (1) the marginal-cost curve intersects from below both AVC and ATC at their lowest points and (2) AFC is always the same height as the vertical distance between the ATC and the AVC curves.

Much of the curvature pattern derives from the underlying argument as to the shape of the total-cost curve. It is argued that, at low levels of production, total costs rise ever more slowly up to an inflection point. Beyond that they rise ever more rapidly as the difficulty of expanding production, after the inflection, mounts. The level of production at the inflection point corresponds with the minimum on the marginal-cost line.

At some stage in the process, average total cost reaches a low, and that level of production corresponds with the tangency of a ray out of the origin with the total-cost line. This is also the level of production where the marginal-cost curve cuts the average total-cost curve from below.

All this is to some degree black magic. But involved are internally consistent relations that must hold, given the definitions of terms and the argument (which may not be entirely correct) as to the shape of the total-cost curve and the argument as to how much of the cost is fixed cost.

We have George Leland Bach saying in his elementary text: "The problem of economizing scarce resources so as to maximize wanted production for consumption is the core of the study of economics."[6] And George Stigler says: "The entrepreneur is combining two variable productive services in the most efficient proportion if no redistribution of expenditure between them will increase the total product. This efficient proportion is achieved when

$$\frac{\text{Marginal product of A}}{\text{Price of A}} = \frac{\text{Marginal product of B}}{\text{Price of B}}.\text{"}[7]$$

All this is just so much misleading mumbo jumbo. These gentlemen cannot possibly identify efficiency unless they can identify a maximum in the combination of the products which are being produced. The difficulty is not just that borderlines get fuzzy. The ranking of the desirability of different market baskets filled with different combinations of goods changes depending on income distribution, or on the identity of the yardstick used, or on differences in tastes. The maximum of one moment is something less the next.

Now, of course, in many situations the difference between efficiency and bumbling ineptitude is recognizable. And it is desirable that there be efficiency instead of bumbling in the productive process. But it is doubtful that economists are any great experts at identifying or implementing efficiency at the technological level.

These are areas where the failure is a theoretical one. It is not that, if we would just sharpen our tools, we could solve the problem. There is no solution. The allegation that welfare is maximized where all the appropriate marginality equalities occur is simply not a description of the real world. (For several demonstrations of the way these logical arguments break down, even in their own frame of reference, see the appendix to chapter 4.)

In this life, on important issues, one may have few options. For example, in the selection of a lifetime helpmate, in the meaningful sense, one may have only four or five options. Under the wire, the option may just be Henrietta and Dorothy or Dick and Joe. Which one you pick is going to make all the difference in the world as to whether your future life is pleasant or not. And this principle—marginal cost equals marginal revenue—is supposed to tell you which to pick.

In spite of everything, we have Everett Hagen writing in 1968, as have a hundred economists before him, that "the criterion for optimum allocation of resources is . . . [that] output is maximized if the social marginal productivity of each input is maximized."[8]

Monopoly, Monopolistic Competition, and Oligopoly

A slightly more (but still not particularly) realistic model might assume laissez faire (the government does not interfere with business) but cease to adhere to all the precepts of pure competition. Such models are those of monopolistic competition, oligopoly, and monopoly. They continue to assume that all the parties involved in the productive process are trying to maximize their own gain. But they drop one or another of the assumptions of pure competition—frequently, the assumption that no one of the parties can influence price or, less frequently, the assumption that productive resources can move freely and instantaneously from one employment to another. Joan Robinson, Edward Chamberlin, and John Kenneth Galbraith have toiled in this vineyard.

Such theories may well describe particular aspects of real world behavior better than do the applicable aspects of general equilibrium/pure competition theory. The difficulty is that they do not and cannot add up to a defensible whole. They may more accurately describe the world (although they probably are not completely accurate in their description of the limited segment to which they address themselves). But in no event can they either justify or explain the economy as a whole. They cannot describe an income distribution pattern that has any claim to represent theoretical equity. But those working in this area generally do not claim that the basic industry-level models add up to a description of an ethically defensible economy.

Figure 5–6 is a standard monopoly pricing model. The marginal cost (MC) and the average total cost (ATC) curves have the same meaning as in figure 5–5. But in the monopoly case it is argued that the firm is looking at a downward-sloping demand (= average revenue) curve, unlike the horizontal demand ($D = AR = MR$) curve of figure 5–5, where it is assumed that the small firm, in effect, confronts a given market price which it cannot influence and which will be the same however much or little it produces.

Since, under monopoly, the demand curve for a firm's product probably does fall (lower prices calling forth greater demand), the marginal revenue (MR) curve is below the demand curve and is falling more steeply. It is stating how much revenue will be increased by one more sale (and, since average price is falling, that means the increase in revenue resulting from selling one more unit is less than the average revenue).

Then we apply the same rule of thumb as the one that identified the level of production in figure 5–5: the profit-maximizing executives will produce that level of output at which marginal cost equals marginal revenue. They will produce no more because, to the right of that point, additions to cost are greater than additions to revenue. And they will produce up to that point because, for any place to the left, marginal revenue is greater than marginal cost, and they can consequently increase net profit by moving to the right till they get to the $MC = MR$ intersection. At that level of production, the price they can get away with is Oa (greater than Oc). They charge accordingly and collect a so-called monopoly profit corresponding to the area $ABDC$.

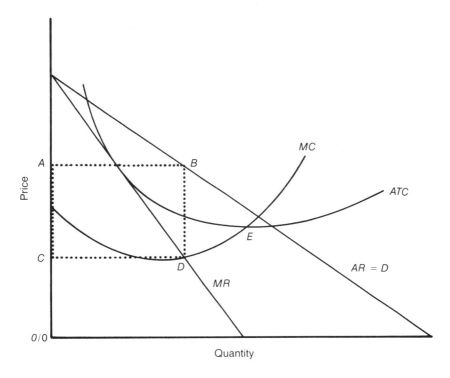

Figure 5-6. Monopoly pricing

It is a neat trick if you can do it. And this story indicates why regulating public utilities (which are generally monopolies) is desirable in the interest of keeping the public from being robbed by these monopoly profits.

Conclusion

Whether any or all of these decision-making methods, and many more such as linear programming, input-output, and shadow pricing, generously made available by economists to business executives and planners with decisions to make, are much help seems debatable. In fact, executives rarely seem to use these economic methods to help with their decision making.

Certainly none of this price theory analysis helps the owner of a little bookstore to decide whether to order a few more copies of the current best seller for the Christmas trade. It does not help the owner of a shoe store to decide whether to order many shoes of a certain design. And certainly no one has ever accused the manager of the nearest supermarket of computing the elasticity of the demand for bananas.

And when we try to describe various firms and industries this way and then add them up to get a Walras-type description of the whole economy and then determine whether the country is optimizing or maximizing, we are trying to get blood out of a turnip.[9]

The foregoing does not deny the possibility that there may be some sort of method in the decision-making madness of business. There certainly are rules of thumb, and criteria, and standard methods, but these methods just may not have much to do with the optimizing procedures of price theory. In *The Handbook of Social Psychology*, Cyert and March are cited as reporting the prevalence of "pricing decisions that are clearly made by programmed decision rules whose relation to marginalist principles of economic behavior are, at best, remote."[10]

In spite of all the foregoing, let us defend the proposition that policy makers should put as few shackles on the economy as possible and try to make prices and price comparisons as meaningful as possible, not because equality among marginal product/price ratios insures economic efficiency and welfare optima or maximums but because it is generally desirable, in decision making, to have as much halfway accurate information as possible.

Decision-making problems involving maximization may be solvable with results that have some economic content if the problem is delimited narrowly enough. But certainly there is no such thing as a meaningful general social welfare maximum or an optimum growth path for society as a whole. However, there may well be patterns for putting together raw-material prices and factor costs and quantities in the short run in a way that will provide information that is useful for certain limited purposes, for example, to maximize the profits of a single enterprise in the short term.

The border line between situations where meaningful maximums can be identified and situations where they cannot be is a question of fact in which problems of both economic significance and mathematical logic play a role. In general, probably long-run equilibrium for the firm is not a concept which can be gotten hold of theoretically in a meaningful manner; however, in certain types of situations, meaningful microeconomic, short-run relations may be gotten hold of.

NOTES

1. See John Platt, "Social Traps," *American Psychologist* 28 (August 1973):641–651; B. F. Skinner, *Contingencies of Reinforcement: A The-

oretical Analysis (New York: Appleton, 1969); Thomas C. Schelling, "The Economy of Micromotives," *Public Interest*, no. 25 (Fall 1971): 61–98.

2. See, for example, the models developed in R. G. D. Allen, *Mathematical Economics* (London: Macmillan, 1956), chap. 9.
3. C. E. Ayres, *Toward a Reasonable Society: The Values of Industrial Civilization* (Austin: University of Texas Press, 1961), pp. 27–28.
4. H. H. Liebhafsky, *American Government and Business* (New York: Wiley, 1971), pp. 15, 18.
5. Alfred Marshall, *Principles of Economics*, 6th ed. (London: Macmillan, 1910 [1890]), pp. 460–461.
6. George Leland Bach, *Economics*, 3d ed. (Englewood Cliffs, N.J.: Prentice-Hall, 1960), p. 23.
7. George J. Stigler, *The Theory of Price*, rev. ed. (New York: Macmillan, 1952 [1942]), p. 127.
8. Everett E. Hagen, *The Economics of Development* (Homewood, Ill.: Irwin, 1968), p. 406.
9. See Maurice Dobb, *Welfare Economics and the Economics of Socialism* (London: Cambridge University Press, 1969), p. 135.
10. Herbert A. Simon and Andrew C. Stedry, "Psychology and Economics," in Gardner Lindzey and Elliot Aronson, eds., *The Handbook of Social Psychology*, 2d ed., 5 vols. (Reading, Mass.: Addison-Wesley, 1969), 5: 288.

ADDITIONAL READINGS

Boulding, Kenneth E. *Economics as a Science*. New York: McGraw-Hill, 1970.

Chamberlin, Edward H. *The Theory of Monopolistic Competition*. 8th ed. Cambridge, Mass.: Harvard University Press, 1965.

Clark, John Maurice. *Studies in the Economics of Overhead Costs*. Chicago: University of Chicago Press, 1923.

Friedman, Milton. *Price Theory*. Chicago: Aldine, 1962.

Gambs, John S. *Beyond Supply and Demand*. New York: Columbia University Press, 1946.

Leftwich, Richard H., and Ansel M. Sharp, eds. *Economics of Social Issues*. Rev. ed. Dallas: Business Publications, 1976 [1974].

Liebhafsky, H. H. *The Nature of Price Theory*. Rev. ed. Homewood, Ill.: Dorsey, 1968 [1963].

Maccoby, Michael. *The Gamesman*. New York: Simon & Schuster, 1977.

Robinson, Joan. *Economics of Imperfect Competition*. London: Macmillan, 1933.

Ward, Benjamin. *What's Wrong with Economics?* New York: Basic Books, 1972.

6.
Macroeconomics
and Decision Making

MACROECONOMICS uses as its basic analytical ingredients national income as a whole and national investment as a whole or the total saving of the economy, total employment in the economy, and so on. It does not aggregate from micro beginnings.

The Insights of Keynesian Theory

National income, or Keynesian, macroeconomic theory acquired prominence as an alternative to price theory and general equilibrium analysis during the Great Depression of the 1930s. The chief influence was the 1936 *The General Theory of Employment, Interest and Money*, written by John Maynard Keynes. The theory was, at least initially, a fine, healthy antidote to some of the stereotypes of price theory, especially the one that pure competition (and free enterprise), if let alone, can be counted on to deal to best advantage with the business-cycle problem.

One of the useful alternative perspectives provided by Keynesian theory was that the saving-investment process does not need to start with prior, voluntary, personal saving. The inception of the process is not dependent on individual decisions in an assumed pure competition setting. In particular, investment may occur first, in a sense before saving, and the necessary equivalent saving may then be drawn out as a result of the process. So, a government may do something about depression unemployment by throwing additional "investment" funds into the spending stream or by creating devices which will induce business enterprise to (borrow and) invest more.

These created funds can put the unemployed to work during a

depression, and production and employment can improve at the same time that the process is having little if any inflationary impact.

However, the theory was depression theory, and its chief useful insights had to do with depression and depression unemployment. It is perhaps not hard to understand that the use of such a theory in the economic development theorizing of the post–World War II period did not work out very well. The theory does not have much to say for dealing with full employment, overfull employment, and economic development problems, despite its very considerable use in efforts to deal with these situations.

Also, pretty clearly, this is not a process that can be fine-tuned. One cannot say that a $351 million increase in government spending will increase the gross national product by $843 million and create 2,437,000 jobs.

Yet, it has been exactly this sort of pseudoprecision that neo-Keynesian economists have tried in subsequent years to superimpose on the basic Keynesian argument. And they have tried to play the game during periods of more or less full employment and inflation with results not particularly useful. This sort of thing, practiced rather unimaginatively but with much calculation of econometric models, has been the chief bag of tricks of the president's Council of Economic Advisers.

The Macrotheory Approach

National Income Theory and Constancy
National income (or macroeconomic) theory, using information about saving, investment, and consumption tendencies (called propensities in the jargon), tries to answer such questions as, How much new investment or increased government spending need occur in order to obtain full employment or to raise the gross national product to such and such a level? Just as is the case in price theory, for these relations to be worked out with any degree of mathematical pseudoprecision it must be possible to stylize the basic relations into such concepts as a *constant* marginal propensity to save, a *constant* marginal propensity to consume, or a *constant* marginal propensity to import. And, again, statistical estimating techniques are applied to raw data that involve assuming these relations are constants, whether they are so in fact.

Forecasting, Decision Making, and Planning

Once the magnitudes of the constant parameters, which it is assumed control the relations among the economic variables, have been determined, it is possible to use the model to do various things. The future can be forecast. Or various possible forecasts can be made on the basis of various different assumptions as to the possible magnitudes of the independent variables. The future may be simulated.

Decision makers and planners can use this information to determine what they should do about the independent variables which they are in a position to do anything about. That methodology of this sort is pretty much the heart of present-day economics can be readily confirmed in almost any elementary textbook.[1]

For all such activity to be legitimate, however, the constants must be constant, or at least more or less so, when they are called upon.

The Validity of the Constancy Assumption

It may make a good deal of difference, when a crisis comes along, whether these constants accurately describe real relations that remain the same after the beginning of the crisis. If the constants hold, the econometric model involved can be used to tell the planners how much to cut taxes, or raise tariffs, or increase investments in order to deal with the difficulty, which may well be unemployment or a run on the dollar. But if the "constants" change in value after the inception of the difficulty, and the planners assume they have not, their planning may not be particularly helpful.

If economists (on a light teaching load with a large grant) can find one of these constants and establish that the constancy really holds through thick and thin (that is, after the storm clouds have gathered) and can, in consequence, do some reliable predicting or responsible planning, their professional reputation is made and they have done something worthwhile. Such work is important, the work should be done, it is desirable to find these constant relations if they exist—but only if they exist. Moreover, the foundations (the National Science Foundation, the Ford Foundation, and so on) love to finance activity of this sort. The grant request can be pretty specific, and the grantors think they know what they are going to get for their money; so, an utterly disproportionate amount of the research funds available to economists have gone for research of this type. A fantastic amount of data manipulation goes on. Fancy equations and precise-looking coefficients are presented to describe relations among the variables. Frequently the researchers acknowledge at the end of their articles describing their machinations that their results do not seem entirely conclusive and suggest that they may need another sizable grant to pursue the matter further. This is sometimes called sending good money after bad, and it is a rather common practice.

A trouble with the approach centered on the search for constant parameters is not that it is entirely invalid: it is that it represents a half truth. Some of these economic relationships are probably more or less constant for substantial periods of time, and it is worthwhile to have some conception of their likely accuracy. In the context of institutional theory, one would say that during the period that a social institution is more or less set in its ways certain of its behavioral relationships will be quite constant. People of a certain income level in suburbia in 1969 will probably, on the average, save such and such a percentage of their salaries during the boom phase of the business cycle. It is useful to be able to identify such a constant, and it is not entirely fruitless to be able to plan intelligently during periods of institutional stability. And the identification of the constants is a help in this regard.

The trouble, however, is that it is usually during times of crisis, when the really important economic decisions are made, that the constants will not hold. This is just the time when the institutions and their "fixed" relations are subject to flux. And, although it is important to plan adequately during periods of stability, and the constant coefficients may be a help then, it is even more important to be able to adopt appropriate policies during times of crisis.

All this suggests that a major fault with present-day mathematized economics is its emphasis on identifying constants, which turn out not to be constants when they are needed most. Maybe the trouble is, as Coleridge wrote in *Christabel*, that "constancy lives in realms above" instead of on terra firma. It is not really that economics as a whole is one big fraud. However, one might wish that, at least at the undergraduate level, economics majors received a genuine social science orientation instead of the group of required courses in micro- and macrotheory that reek of relationships which hardly hold in this world but which the students had better master if they are going on to graduate school (which they are probably not going to do).

Choice as Either-Or (and without a Probability Distribution— Again)

It is possible that order in the universe does not require smooth demand and supply curves and consumption functions of a proper shape. There may be a reason for behavior; yet that reason may not be gotten at by looking for the appropriate point on a curve assumed to have hyperbolic form. In fact, there may be no curve, hyperbolic or otherwise. Much decision making, perhaps most, is a one-shot proposition. You do the thing or you do not. And no range of choices, represented by a smooth curve, was ever involved.

The big decisions may be just as much one-time shots in the dark as the little decisions. Should the atom bomb be dropped on a Japanese city? Should the United States try to put a man on the moon? Should the country opt for some particular new development in mass urban transit, such as rapid transit along densely populated but narrow feeder routes in a process that involves trying to concentrate population along the spokes of a wheel?

The choice between Sabin and Salk polio vaccines is a example of an either-or decision where, from the perspective of hindsight, one can say that the wrong decision was probably made. Salk should have been used and Sabin rejected, because the presence of the live virus in the Sabin vaccine has perpetuated the disease, which, it seems, has been completely eliminated in countries using the Salk vaccine, which does not contain the live virus.

It should be added, in the general run of such either-or choices as we actually make, that there exists no knowable probability distribution to tell us how likely we are to be satisfied with our choice. There is a level of judgment involved but not a choice with a probability distribution.

The Decision-Making Process: Another Approach

Society has goals which are more or less well formulated and consistent. It also has decision-making processes that may or may not implement the goals with any precision. And economics has various models which describe how all this may work itself out, most of them predicated on an assumption that economic magnitudes can be measured, or at least ordered, and compared in ways which are generally controlled by constant interrelations. However, things frequently do not work out as these models allege, and consequently decisions made on the basis of such models may be in error.

A different perspective on the macrolevel decision-making process may be helpful.

Majority-Rule Voting

The possibility of inconsistent results: Can a democratic voting process, regardless of how gerrymandered it may be and how much of the population is involved, generate an "acceptable" result on a question of policy—any question? There is also the question as to whether society is willing to live with the results of the democratic decision-making process once those decisions have been made by the agreed-on procedures.

Kenneth Arrow has been at considerable pains to point out some of the difficulties involved in getting a consistent set of decisions out of a process that involves making decisions on a series of interrelated matters by a succession of majority votes:

> Let A, B, and C be the three alternatives, and 1, 2, and 3 the three individuals. Suppose individual 1 prefers A to B and B to C (and therefore A to C), individual 2 prefers B to C and C to A (and therefore B to A), and individual 3 prefers C to A and A to B (and therefore C to B). Then a majority prefer A to B, and a majority prefer B to C. We may therefore say that the community prefers A to B and B to C. If the community is to be regarded as behaving rationally, we are forced to say that A is preferred to C. But in fact a majority of the community prefer C to A. So the method just outlined for passing from individual to collective tastes fails to satisfy the condition of rationality, as we ordinarily understand it.[2]

Does this mean that the situation is hopeless and that we must abandon the democratic process as the basic decision-making method—in much the same sense that we are forced by our inability to identify a welfare maximum to back away from the attempt to maximize welfare as an operational goal?

Arrow lists the types of possible procedures for making social choices as (1) voting, (2) the market mechanism, (3) dictatorship, and (4) convention. Perhaps readers are already convinced that the market mechanism, although it may play a useful role, is not a desirable final arbiter. Perhaps also they are willing to rule out dictatorship. And perhaps we are left with a mixture of democratic voting process and convention, that is, democratic process plus habit and tradition (which is to say institutionalized behavior). We are not going to improve anything by following the precepts of habit and tradition; so we are pretty much thrown back on the democratic voting process, or some version of it, as the best alternative in an imperfect world when we wish to make an effort to improve matters.

We may agree with Arrow about the possibility of getting inconsistent results out of a succession of majority votes on a group of interrelated issues. Probably most of us have participated in public assemblies working under Robert's rules of order and have seen the parliamentary procedures work out in a sequence of events that makes it impossible for the group ever to vote on some issue in the form in which we would really like to see the vote taken. We vote on an alternative choice. We make our choice by a majority vote, and we go home and grumble.

Perhaps we find that, after all, we can live with the imperfect result of the majority vote. It turns out not to have mattered too much. Or perhaps it does matter, and we try again, perhaps even effecting a change in the procedural rules (doing something about the congressional seniority system, for example) in the meantime. And the result after the next hassle is better. (There are a lot of contexts where we can confidently separate better from worse, even though we cannot pinpoint a maximum.)

There are more important difficulties with the democratic decision-making process than are shown by Arrow's demonstration of the possibility of inconsistent results flowing from the process. Especially there is the frequency of erratic, capricious, and arbitrary action. Dictatorship also frequently generates erratic, capricious, and arbitrary action, but democracy is not exonerated because dictatorship is a sorry arrangement.

The problem with the democratic process is to make it work in a manner that the people can halfway respect—not to make it always regurgitate consistent results or theoretically precise maximums or optimal growth paths.

The capricious nature of the legislative process: That a certain bill (perhaps calling for the expenditure of $9.5 billion dollars during the next year) is or is not passed in December of some year may make a fantastic amount of difference in the lives of a great many people. The result may almost literally be unpredictable up to the day of the vote or the veto, and that vote or veto may not occur until the time period to be covered by the expenditure has already begun. If the bill becomes law, the administrators, who were not able to plan ahead confidently on the assumption of passage, will suddenly have to hire several new bureau chiefs and a lot of staff. They are likely to try to hire professors in the middle of a semester, to the greater confusion of the universities and the students. (Some professors respond spontaneously to such calls; some do not.) Or they will hire some dollar-a-year (or higher-priced) executives whom the corporations can spare, sometimes with pleasure.

At any rate, it is little wonder that the new program (any new program) in its formative years is disorganized, lacking in clear-cut focus, and perhaps even a mite corrupt—just as the congressional investigating committee may later point out.

If at the last minute the bill is defeated or vetoed, the administrators, who had been trying to do some advance planning on the assumption that the bill would pass, will have, with profuse apologies, to tell the ever available professors or executives that they cannot hire them after all, or give them that subsidy, or the money for that research project.

Legislative bodies do have a certain obligation to develop procedures that will make their actions somewhat more reliably predictable. They need to pass laws that have built into them some characteristics permitting the people affected by the laws to plan ahead better. Phasing-in and phasing-out programs should be planned for. The feast-or-famine approach cannot be expected to give particularly good results. And much of the inefficiency legislators complain about is a result of short-term, erratic financing of programs by the legislative bodies themselves. Of course, the feast-or-famine, now-you-see-it-now-you-don't approach that makes everybody come as a suppliant for funds every session is gratifying to legislative egos and to executive-branch egos as well.

Legislators should be functioning as watchdogs over executive expenditures. But somewhat more method and consistency and consideration in the bird-dogging are most needed. For example, programs involving levels of price support might well specify that the price of the commodity in question will be supported at a level which will vary no more than some fixed percentage from last year's price. Give the people who are going to be affected half a chance to prejudge the process, to know roughly what the impact of the regulation is going to be.

Antidumping tariffs might be automatically imposed (and immediately) on a showing that imports are coming in at prices lower than those prevailing in the domestic market of the exporter. The law might specify that the exporter has to provide a document certifying the price for domestic sale in the exporting country. Understanding that prices and terms of sale are properly matters of public record is needed to facilitate this process. Once the information is in hand, the amount of the antidumping tariff is, or should be, automatically set as the amount of discount the importer received by comparison with the foreign domestic price. As matters stand, obtaining antidumping relief is a long-drawn-out, uncertain process, which takes much of the merit away from one of the few legitimate international trade restrictions.

Imperfect as the democratic process may be, it is the best we have, and it is the best we are likely to have. Improvement is an ongoing process. We do not, once and for all, devise an ideal world by a succession of national majority votes. We are not going to devise a definitive ideal world. Period! Arrow is correct, but it does not matter. Meanwhile, we had better concentrate on making the democratic process work better, as our self-correcting value judgments continually redefine "better," instead of concentrating on making it nonoperational.

Revolution and dictatorship: Historically the possibility of violent revolution has existed, and people have exercised this option frequently against autocratic power. And the revolution tool or the threat of its use has at times played a role in lessening the power of the bully, the autocrat, and the dictator.

In the 1970s, however, the underprivileged might well be a little bit coy about using violence in order to frustrate the working of our rather imperfect democracy. People in general, especially the underprivileged, had better take a long second look at their demagogues and inquire if they really want them as dictators. Whites should be a little more appreciative of the extremely high level of black diplomacy that has been expressed in the nonviolent movements of the Southern Christian Leadership Council and the National Association for the Advancement of Colored People.

The rebellious, in their insistence that they are being put upon and in their concern to destroy the system and the Establishment, should also be concerned that they do not destroy our last best hope—the freedom to orient one's own life much as one chooses. Certainly the world is not perfect, but the world of our parents is a darn sight better than the world of our grandparents.

John Dewey writes of democracy:

The political and governmental phase of democracy is a means, the best means so far found, for realizing ends that lie in the wide domain of human relationships and the development of human personality. It is, as we often say, though perhaps, without appreciating all that is involved in the saying, a way of life, social and individual. The keynote of democracy as a way of life may be expressed, it seems to me, as the necessity for the participation of every mature human being in formation of the values that regulate the living of men together: which is necessary from the standpoint of both the general social welfare and the full development of human beings as individuals.

Universal suffrage, recurring elections, responsibility of those who are in political power to the voters, and the other factors of democratic government are means that have been found expedient for realizing democracy as the truly human way of living. They are not a final end and a final value. They are to be judged on the basis of their contribution to end. It is a form of idolatry to erect means into the end which they serve. Democratic political forms are simply the best means that human wit has devised up to a special time in history. But they rest back upon the idea that no man or limited set of men is wise enough or good enough to rule others without their consent; the positive meaning of this statement is that all those who are affected by social institutions must have a share in producing and managing them. The two facts that each one is influenced in what he does and enjoys and in what he becomes by the institutions under which he lives, and that therefore he shall have, in a democracy, a voice in shaping them, are the passive and active sides of the same fact.[3]

Levels of Decision Making and Decentralization

The democratic process, such as it is, works on many different levels: school district, town, county, state, region, nation, world. And, in spite of the ardent states' righters, it just has to be true that, in case of conflicts among policies adopted by various governments at the lower levels, conflicts which the parties are not willing to resolve by themselves should be resolved by the next higher level of government. And a world authority just has to be the arbiter of disagreements among nation-states.

If we recognize the principle that the next higher level of government resolves conflicts, and if the spoiled child is not allowed to have its own way regardless of the interests of others, it may well turn out that relatively few problems actually have to be resolved at the level of the world authority. Much more actual decision making can be relegated to lower levels of government. Individuals will be able to participate in a more meaningful way in decision making. And national governments will be able to dispense with a lot of bureaucracy, the chief purpose of which was to protect "the national interest" against one's neighbors.

The Prohibition of Fighting
Other people suffer when society lets aggressive people or aggressive nations fight it out. It might not be too bad just to let them fight, if only they would not embroil others. But beyond a doubt the bellicose are going to manage to embroil others, as they will be interested in doing especially when they are losing. And the leaders are going to fix it so that most of the dirty work is done by the "common" people. Society just has to lay it on the line: no fighting, fellows, except in organized sports, where those who want to have a go at it may be permitted to do so under more or less controlled conditions.

Nations, *large and small*, should be eternally working to build up the prestige of the United Nations instead of tearing it down. Nationalism is probably the most vicious force loose in the world today. And the smaller nations would be especially well advised to appreciate that fact.

There are problems involved in establishing the institutional arrangements required to keep the sovereign nations and their belligerent leaders from starting wars. Nations insist on fighting and, when told to stop, their politicians instantaneously produce documentation of grievances, infinitely long and tear-jerking, describing rape and other atrocities, disregarded arbitral awards, flags spat upon, harassment at soccer games, and so on, grievances for which the only cure is obviously more fighting. The only way to handle this situation in the short run is for the school principal, without too much regard for the finer equities involved, to grab each kicking and screaming child and stand them in separate corners.

That is, the United Nations has to have a permanent and strong armed force of its own. And, in a setting where technology has been overworking itself to improve the killing power of military hardware, the United Nations peace-keeping force must also command the best technology. A procedure for financing this might well stipulate that each nation must give, say, 20 percent of its military budget to the United Nations. Such a procedure might both provide a reasonably strong UN force and stimulate arms reduction, as nations come to realize that their armed forces do not give them leverage to blackmail the rest of the world and are not the meaningful influence protecting them from aggression.

The United Nations desperately needs reform. It needs a police force strong enough to summarily prevent war. It also needs responsible decision-making machinery in control of that police force and its other activities. The Security Council with its veto power is a monstrosity. The General Assembly of some 150 nations with equal votes in a setting where four nations have half of the world population can scarcely be a responsible decision-making body. And the type of bargaining involved in selecting the secretary general is calculated to throw up an ineffective nonentity.

The Conflict of Policies

If certain dumbheads would get it through their thick craniums that in case of conflict the higher level of government has to have the final voice over the lower level, some agreement on policy patterns might make it possible for lower levels of government to perform much *expanded* roles and for the bureaucracies associated with the higher levels of government to become smaller, just as the international police force would decline in size as national armies decline in size. But meaningful and general decentralization demands centralized power when the chips are down.

For example, at present, at the level of the national governments in our nationalistic world, much of the bureaucracy is spending its time administering control systems involving tariffs, quotas, licenses, price controls, rent controls, gosh knows what all, controls that are standard operating procedures as each nation tries to use all the tools it can dream up to help solve some domestic problem (pseudo, real, or lobbyist-colored), without too much regard for the adverse effects that its particular measures may have on other countries.

For youths wanting to fight for great and noble causes, it may be of interest to know that there is a cause—world order—that is worth the candle. We need leadership that speaks for interdependence rather than for nationalism, for the human race rather than for national or state sovereignty. It bears saying several times: the world needs fewer declarations of independence and a few more declarations of interdependence.

NOTES

1. See, for example, Richard G. Lipsey and Peter O. Steiner, *Economics*, 5th ed. (New York: Harper & Row, 1978), chaps. 2, 3; Paul A. Samuelson, *Economics*, 10th ed. (New York: McGraw-Hill, 1976 [1948]).
2. Kenneth J. Arrow, *Social Choice and Individual Values* (New York: Wiley, 1951), p. 3.
3. John Dewey, *Intelligence in the Modern World: John Dewey's Philosophy* (New York: Modern Library, 1939), pp. 400–401.

ADDITIONAL READINGS

Boulding, Kenneth E. *Stable Peace*. Austin: University of Texas Press, 1979.
Dernburg, Thomas F., and Duncan M. McDougall. *Macroeconomics*. 3d ed. New York: McGraw-Hill, 1968 [1960]. This is a standard national income textbook which is going through many editions.
Hansen, Alvin H. *A Guide to Keynes*. New York: McGraw-Hill, 1953.
Klein, Lawrence R. *The Keynesian Revolution*. New York: Macmillan, 1948.
Nelson, Charles R. "The Prediction Performance of the FRB-MIT-PENN Model of the U.S. Economy." *American Economic Review* 62 (December 1972): 902–917.
Schelling, Thomas C. *The Strategy of Conflict*. Cambridge, Mass.: Harvard University Press, 1960.
United Nations. *National and International Measures for Full Employment*. New York: Lake Success, 1949.

7.
Dynamic Economic Process

THE CLASSICAL ECONOMISTS, Adam Smith, David Ricardo, and others, did concern themselves about ongoing economic process. It is true that Ricardo's dynamic process had it that the economy evolves into a stationary state, where the bulk of the population is not necessarily living very well. But, even so, the classical economists had a real concern for economics as ongoing process.

By contrast, the neoclassical economists of the late nineteenth and early twentieth centuries were principally concerned with static equilibrium, the epitome of which is the price (set by demand and supply) which will exactly clear the market during a given planning period.

Keynesian economics, which became influential in the 1930s, was developed in what has been called a comparative statics frame of reference. There was concern for the problem of adjustment but not for the process of long-run change or development itself. One begins a bit of analysis by visualizing the economy as being, for the moment, in some sort of equilibrium. In the basic case it is an equilibrium that involves considerable unemployment—an undesirable state of affairs—for Keynes was chiefly concerned with the business cycle and with depression unemployment. Then an autonomous disturbance (perhaps a block of new investment) is injected into the system. And, on the assumption that this disturbance has a certain clear-cut impact on the economy (via the marginal propensity to consume and the multiplier, both of which are generally assumed to be constants), the nature of the new equilibrium is determined. Such was Keynesian comparative statics—a description of "before and after" in a business-cycle context.

Analysis of economic, ongoing process is something yet again. There have, of course, been many efforts, since Ricardo, to conceptualize economics as ongoing process. The institutional theory of Thorstein Veblen and Clarence Ayres is one such effort. The various economic development and growth theories, such as that of Harrod and Domar, which have been much in vogue since World War II, are other examples.

The theories of production and capital accumulation have been recast in dynamic terms. John von Neumann, Joan Robinson, Paul Samuelson, Robert Solow, and various other persons have turned up growth paths, expansion paths, turnpikes and detours, golden ages, and golden rules, and dynamic equilibrium, labor-intensive and capital-intensive technological progress, embodied and disembodied technological progress, balanced and unbalanced growth, and so on. And the mathematical formulations which have gone with these economic models have been most impressive-looking as mathematics, even though the economics has generally been rather simplistic.

As has been indicated in preceding chapters, in economics much reliance has been placed on an assumption of constant relations. And generally in these growth models there develops a picture of a process in which, if all goes well, all the elements grow in a very orderly manner along a well-behaved expansion path. Rather typical is the requirement that, if the growth process is to stay out of trouble, all the ingredients have to develop in the same proportion and at constant rates. This has sometimes been called the golden age or balanced growth and is considered to be more or less the equivalent of equilibrium in static theory. If one ingredient insists on being individualistic and growing at a different rate (if the labor force does not grow at the same rate as the capital stock), all kinds of dire calamities may result, whether the razor's edge is too sharp or too dull—like Occam's.

One new development in this area, the pursuit of optimal growth paths, actually involves an effort to specify a welfare maximum (or something similar, the expression "bliss" being sometimes used) over time. How one can do that if one cannot specify a static maximum is a bit of a mystery, but . . .

The Closed-Circuit Flow Diagram and Say's Law

One way to get hold of the growth problem may be indicated by the relation between the closed-circuit description of the economic process which is generally presented in an early chapter of elementary economics texts (see figure 7–1) and the visualizing of economic process as a river with tributaries.[1]

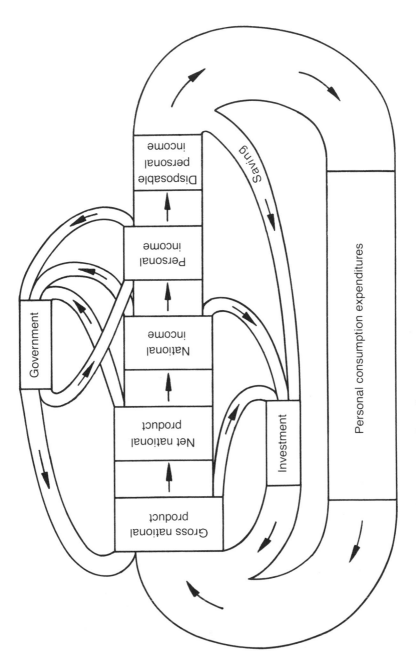

Figure 7-1. National income: circular flow diagram

The circular flow diagram seems to say that the return to the factors of production which create the gross national product is the purchasing power with which that same block of gross national product is taken off the market. If true, this would be an important natural equality, in fact, an expression of Say's law of markets.

Classical economics, after J. B. Say in the early nineteenth century, alleged an inherent equality between total demand and total supply as a sort of general equilibrium or macroeconomic manifestation of "demand equals supply" at equilibrium prices in the markets for the individual commodities. The purchasing power that took the goods off the market and provided the wherewithal to pay the factors of production was alleged to be identical to the purchasing power that was paid to the factors and was therefore the same thing as the purchasing power that the factors (playing the role of consumers) were using to take the goods off the market. Demand equaled supply because supply created and equaled the demand that took the supply off the market.

One type of difficulty with this argument involves a failure to distinguish between ex ante and ex post. There is a hen and egg problem. If the factors are paid first, they are clearly not being paid the same money that is the purchasing power with which they will later take the goods off the market. And, as far as the profit-taking entrepreneurs in particular are concerned, they are not going to be able to identify their profits until after the proceeds from the final sale yield proceeds that become their profits. There is a time element involved that Say's Law does not take into account.

In my innocence, I assume that I am saying little more than Keynes says in the passage in his *General Theory* refuting Say's Law:

> . . . the conclusion that the *costs* of output are always covered in the aggregate by the sale-proceeds resulting from demand, has great plausibility, because it is difficult to distinguish it from another, similar-looking proposition which is indubitable, namely that the income derived in the aggregate by all the elements in the community concerned in a productive activity necessarily has a value exactly equal to the *value* of the output.[2]

This is a way of saying that the equality between spending and receipts is an automatic equality. Whatever is spent is received by somebody. It is an equality that is not dependent on the proposition that a given block of income is expended on the purchase of goods whose costs of production were involved in creating that block of income. The latter type of closed circuit is one thing the economic process is not.

The Flow Diagram as a River

What all this means in terms of the flow diagram is that economic process is not appropriately described with a closed-circuit flow diagram. All money spent is ipso facto received by somebody. There is a genuine equality of sorts. But it is a far cry from the "supply creates its own demand" equality alleged by Say's Law. The meaningful equality between spending and receipt of spent funds is best represented by a cross section of a river which might look something like figure 7–2. One cross section is expenditure (= income or receipts) in 1961; the other is expenditure (= income or receipts) in 1962. Perhaps, needless to say, the river is flowing from left to right.

The left side of each vertical line represents spending; the right side of each vertical line represents the receipt of spent funds. The tributaries represent new spending power getting into the system or some spending power getting out.

If everything is taken into account, the equality between expenditure and receipts is continuous and automatic at any vertical cross section. For this automatic equality to exist, there is no necessity that income flow around a nonexistent circle and be spent on goods for whose production it represents payment. Instead, the given income may be spent on goods produced last year, or next, or whatever, or may not be spent at all.

The Implications of "Investment Equals Saving"

Another ostensibly automatic equality, which is much belabored in national income theory, is that between saving and investment. It is a bit difficult to find this equality in the national income accounts of most countries, including the United States. It is a bit hard to find, for example, in figure 7–2. But in figure 7–3 an effort is made to piece it together for the United States from United States and United Nations data.[3]

On the left side of each vertical line is an estimate of monetary saving, on the right side an estimate of monetary investment.

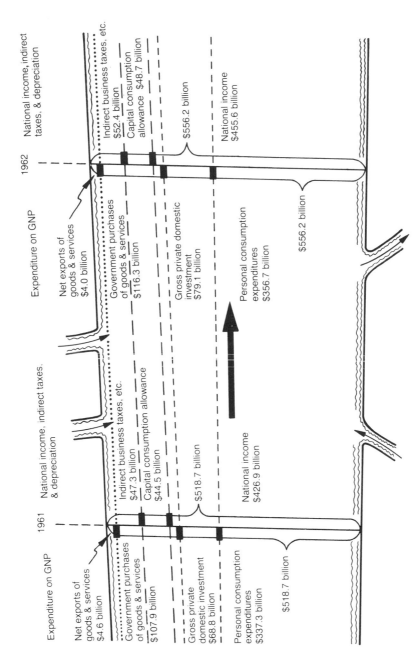

Figure 7-2. United States expenditure and income: flow diagram

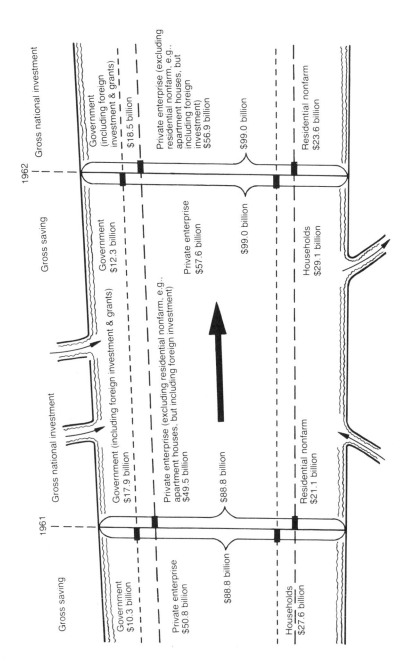

Figure 7-3. United States investment and saving: flow diagram

Again, the equality between investment and saving at any vertical slice is automatic. It corresponds with the precepts of both neo-classical and Keynesian economics, and it is almost entirely trivial in the sense that it tells us little about the nature of the forces that at one and the same time control the size of both saving and investment.

In fact, the identity itself is the result of classifying as saving a group of items that add up to equality with the group of items classified as investment. What is represented is monetary saving and monetary investment. And some of the monetary saving may well be just-created bank funds.

In a different sense, real saving must also equal real investment. In real terms, however, the saving that supports a given bit of real investment is the effort that goes into the creation of the capital (equipment). The effort which is saving is the same effort which creates investment. Involved is effort that might have been used to create consumer goods or might have been unexpended or never exerted.

Assuming a given bit of real capital creation is to be financed with money, the drawing out of the necessary equivalent monetary saving (failure to spend) which is envisaged in Keynesian analysis as equal to the amount of investment is a trivial logical exercise. The nature of the logic of the process is such that the savings are merely a residual drawn out regardless of the real content of the economic relations, regardless of the magnitudes of the propensities to consume and save, regardless of the length of the analysis period, and regardless of the stage in time when the process is cut off, if it is cut off. Also, the analysis blithely disregards the implications of the possibility that temporarily saved (and retired from duty) funds may be spent at a later date. Such funds may meanwhile be either under the mattress or deposited in a bank.

The Creation and Destruction of Usable Funds
Banks and other financial intermediaries may create and destroy usable funds or money. The manner in which they perform this in-stitutionalized behavior may have as by-product effect not only some inflation or deflation à la the quantity theory of money but also some real effects in increasing or decreasing real national income.

The goods produced in a given year may be taken off the market with current year income, with the income of earlier years, or with money (as distinct from income) created either this year or in earlier years. (For this purpose, visualize money as involving created money as yet unused.) Or the goods produced in a given year may be held as inventory, voluntarily or involuntarily, not taken off the market at all. However, at least some of the factors which produce the goods may be paid whether or not the goods are sold.

This approach alleges that held money which is ultimately used again is saving and destroyed money is not. Yet the operational distinction may not really be at all clear-cut.

A more important point is that a newly created dollar will have a mixture of inflationary and real expansionary effects. A destroyed (or saved until used) dollar will have a mixture of deflationary and real contractionary effects. And the relative importance of these effects will vary from case to case. Also, newly created dollars may be promptly killed off by the recipients and may consequently have little or no effect, either real or inflationary. This may have been the effect of much of the Reconstruction Finance Corporation's bailing out of bankrupt railroads in the early 1930s.

A crude example may help. New pesos created to help a speculator corner the frijole market in Guanatambo are going to have a different effect on production and inflation than new pesos put into building a plant to produce clothing of a type bought by people in the lower-income brackets.

Whether a given amount of demand deposits in banks is better visualized as money in circulation or as saving (even saving *retired from use*) is not knowable from the observable fact that banks have a certain amount of demand deposits. Statistical studies of how frequently the stock of money turns over and of how much total spending there is during a given time period are worth making. Estimating averages of these numbers is worth doing. Projecting trends is worth doing. And trying to forecast turning points is worth doing, although this is trickier business.

Far more important is the study of the block of new money or the block of spending in its actual setting. What is done with the money by different institutions, and why, and with what effects on production and luxury-goods consumption?

Investment in Real Property
Voluntary personal saving (or, perhaps better said, funds that might well become voluntary personal saving) may be vented in

directions other than investment. This circumstance has relevance for the oft heard statement that the predilection for land or property ownership in underdeveloped countries may absorb saving and frustrate capital formation. Traditional economic theory seems to say that this cannot be—because the land seller then has the money and has to do something with it.

But it is surely true that money in hand, which might be used to finance capital equipment accumulation, may be used to purchase land. Resources (and energy) that might, *at that time*, be mobilized to create real capital are, in fact, not mobilized. And this diversion of funds from more constructive enterprises may be repeated over time by the subsequent holders of these funds. An institutionalized preference for landownership may occasion such behavior.

Also, as part of this process, it may well be that the price of land will rise relative to other prices. Consequently, even more monetary "saving" will be drained off in bidding up the price of land.

In the frame of reference of the national income accounts of the United States, something called saving is vented in a manner which has no effect other than bidding up the price of real estate. That is, if I interpret the national income accounts correctly, an increase in the money value of real estate is handled as investment or as an increase in the capital stock of the nation.[4] For statistical evidence as to whether this particular phenomenon is going on, one might look to whether the price of land is rising relative to prices in general. However, the price of raw land is so mixed and so modified by the value of the improvements incorporated in it, the changing value of its location, and the exhaustion of its minerals that it may well not be possible to make a really satisfactory study of this sort.

Of course, if one does not define funds spent in bidding up the price of land as saving, no saving has been dissipated on land. But this is quibbling over semantics. The real question is in terms of whether the institutions of a society at a given time are or are not willing to mobilize a certain amount of otherwise unemployed effort and resources to produce real capital.

Conclusion
Let me hasten to claim some awareness of the fact that modern monetary theory is far more complex and takes far more into ac-

count than the preceding rather simple propositions recognize.

At all events, ongoing economic process is better visualized as a meandering river with tributaries and outlets, now deep now shallow, now swift now slow. At least it is better to visualize it so than as a closed circuit or as a stylized process where everything, or almost everything, must grow at the same rate.

Institutionalized Resistance to Change

Institutional theory views the process of change rather differently from neoclassical theory. The basic propositions involved were at the heart of the discussion in chapter 2. The institutional theory of economic progress is growth theory. Involved is dynamic economic process.

The consideration which is worth adding at this point to the picture presented in chapter 2 involves the conditions under which institutionalized resistance to change may break down. In a sense, this means that what is being looked for is the condition under which the "constants" of neoclassical theory and of the standard econometric models may cease to be constants. What happens in a time of crisis when the constant parameters no longer give the correct answers, if they ever did? What is involved at such times is far more important than the implications for policy that constant parameters can indicate during times when there are no real problems.

So, what of the conditions and circumstances under which institutional resistance to change may crumble and the institutions themselves may modify their attitudes?

The Concept of Threshold Resistance (The Timing of the Crumbling)

It is frequently true that institutions do not change perceptibly during a period of many years in spite of minor pressures. During this period those parameters, elasticities, and marginal propensities discussed in chapters 5 and 6 really are constants or, at least, are sufficiently so to justify econometric methodology; and the econometric model really may be a useful planning device. Then, one fine day, a somewhat stronger pressure (perhaps not a much stronger pressure) topples the house of cards and completely changes the nature of the behavior patterns of the institution. The Bastille falls, the Winter Palace is stormed, the Mongols breach the Great Wall, Madero finally challenges Díaz. A whole economic and social order (or something less) collapses—an order that only the day before had been thought to be firmly entrenched.[5] The behavior patterns are suddenly and drastically changed. Major new decisions need to be made. Yet the parameters, elasticities, and marginal propensities laboriously computed during the period of stability are now useless as guides in planning how to deal with the new situation.

The analysis of institutional change has some analogy with the role of the critical mass in nuclear physics and with sensitivity testing in statistics. "A test item will *respond* or *not respond* to a certain level of test stimulus (e.g., a shell will explode or not explode when subjected to a certain shock)."[6] This is the problem of measuring threshold resistance.

It would be nice if a formula could be developed to measure the amount of pressure it would take to break down the threshold resistance which a given economic institution presents to the assimilation of a given bit of new technical knowledge. Unfortunately, what is involved seems frequently to be more qualitative than quantitative. At a given time, most politicians have the same rules of thumb regarding what it takes to win elections. For example, advocacy of segregation was a standard rule of thumb in the South for many years. And anyone who suggests that a politician proceed counter to the current rule of thumb is considered politically naïve. Then some particularly striking contrariwise election occurs, and a lot of rules of thumb get changed.

There may be a useful analogy with the contraction of disease. Persons may live for many years as carriers of germs of a certain type without ever catching the disease in question. Then, one not-so-fine day, a slightly increased concentration of the germs may bring them down with the ailment. Or some outside event may activate the germs and change their role from endemic in the carriers to epidemic in other people. Foot-and-mouth disease may be endemic among cattle herds that have built up resistance and may become epidemic when fortuitous circumstances move the disease to a different setting, like Texas instead of Argentina.

A particular institution changes its ways drastically (or collapses) when technical change acquires sufficient force to compel the modification. The modification of behavior patterns then occurs in spite of institutional resistances, which are stronger the longer the institution has been set in its ways and the more isolated it has been from the forces of change. Francis Stuart Chapin has described a "societal reaction pattern" (in response to pressure or disturbance) that works something like this. In phase I, the group reacts against the change which seems to be called for by the pressure or disturbance. The group's reaction takes the form of an effort to enforce its mores on those trying to implement the change. In phase II, the significance of the inadequate adjustment is fairly generally felt. The group then reacts by expressing a willingness to experiment with some possible changes, by trying different expedients. During this period, the general feeling is one of chaos and unsatisfactory conditions. Then, in phase III, "the group integrates its trial and error efforts into a stable plan," and the result is one with which the group is reasonably well satisfied.[7]

In all this, the crucial stage is reached when the institution under pressure is still quite determined to defend its norms. Toward the end, collapse may be substantially speeded or delayed by whether the patient happens to go out on a cold, rainy night. Fate, and external forces, and human will can play an important role in influencing the timing of institutional change. But this does not mean that it is possible to quantify the resistance of institutional thresholds or to forecast the timing of major change by using statistical techniques. A consideration of overriding importance in these situations is that *this is not generally possible*.

An attempt to quantify threshold resistance is the wrong way to approach the problem. Using such an approach, one might try to develop methods for jolting undesirable institutions with shocks of increasing force until the desired change occurs, but that makes the process sound too orderly. It is probably not desirable to overwhelm an institution with far more force than necessary. Yet starting with shocks that are too mild may help build up the institution's resistance so that it takes, later, a much more disruptive shock than would have otherwise been necessary. The South was not hit hard enough in 1954, and it built up its resistance to desegregation. Perhaps President Eisenhower should have acted with more authority (an easy thing for someone else to say). But his personal presence in Little Rock might have prevented the occurrence of many similar incidents which followed.

David Landes tries to explain why French development lagged behind German from 1850 to 1914. In so doing, he points out that France had been ahead of Germany earlier for a long period, from perhaps 1780 to 1850, but was making progress slowly. This slow progress, he indicates, perhaps allowed French institutions to build up resistance to change. It permitted "the development within her body social of psychological and institutional antibodies to the virus of modernization."[8]

The "Usefulness" of Forecasting

I doubt that much can be, or should be, done along the line of forecasting the timing of the collapse of institutions. But maybe an inability to read the future and an inability to time catastrophe are not major problems. It would certainly be no favor to the family dog to tell it two weeks ahead of time that the family is going on a vacation and it is going to be boarded out at the vet's. Probably most of us would not care for the picture if we could see into the future: we would probably not care to anticipate either the gladness or the sorrow. And most of us, if we had a choice, would really not like to know ahead of time when we are going to become ill or when we are going to die.

> Heaven from all creatures hides the book of fate,
> All but the page prescribed their present state:
> . . . .
> Oh blindness to the future! kindly given,
> That each may fill the circle mark'd by Heaven.[9]

Forecasting is not, or rather should not be, the important job of economics. But the role of forecasting is even more dubious than this. As John Dewey has said: "The assumption is generally made that we must be able to predict before we can plan and control. Here again the reverse is the case. We can predict the occurrence of an eclipse precisely because we cannot control it."[10] If the fact of the forecast influences the likelihood of the event, forecasts tend to be either self-fulfilling or self-defeating. As John Jewkes has commented: "Peering into the future is a popular and agreeable pastime which, so long as it is not taken seriously, is comparatively innocuous."[11]

The chief duties of the economist should be working for the changes which society deems desirable and correcting undesirable situations. Much can be done along both of these lines without the ability to accurately quantify in forecasts.

We should not weep over our inability to forecast the future. Instead, we should relish the chance to use our judgment in an effort to shape the nature of that future. And what we desire of our policy tools is, modestly, that we know something about which way they are likely to work if we use them discreetly, not precisely by how much. Investment creates productive capacity and, very likely, jobs. Increased production generates higher income. More progressive taxes redistribute income and probably increase total spending. By how much? Do we really need to know? And, for better or worse, we must do the best we can without being entirely sure that these relations will always work in the indicated direction.

We probably do need to think more about the likely nature of the impact of new technology, to have scholarly outside assessments made. Is the new invention likely to be just a flash in the pan? Will it involve major institutional changes which can be identified, and can likely transitional difficulties be anticipated? Have we a tiger by the tail? Will the by-product, undesirable effects on the environment be hard to live with?

Implementing Change in a Limited Setting
Institutional change that permits the effective use of new technology will not necessarily destroy a whole social and economic order. In fact, it would probably be desirable if techniques could be developed for weakening institutions by just enough to permit the genuinely desired change. The chaos that goes with the destruction of whole social and economic orders is hardly desirable if it can be avoided. In fact, the construction of a better order may be a lot easier if we use much of the order that we already have as a base, rather than insisting on starting again from scratch.

It is worth looking at a few of the institutional change problems in this more modest and, perhaps, more important setting.

Change may be rough on people. Perhaps fashion renders obsolete the fur hat, or technology bypasses the horse and buggy. Jobs in the fur hat industry and in the smithies are threatened. At first the afflicted industry is likely to have a run at seeing whether higher tariffs will solve its problem. Next it may, reluctantly, try a little innovation. Detroit might actually manufacture a small car —but not before offering some pretty tough resistance, trying the Edsel first, and letting twenty-five years go by. Perhaps adapting to new technology will save the situation. It did not hurt the Singer Sewing Machine Company, after World War II, to start making sewing machines that would do some fancier stitching.

Maybe an industry is really dying instead of just being afflicted with the sniffles. Shifting workers, capital (where feasible), and entrepreneurs (this should not be too difficult if they are really living up to their name) is called for.

Although change may be hard on us, it may represent an interesting reorientation of life, depending on our personal reaction and on how much thoughtful help we get in making the transition—help from government, help from enterprise, and just plain help, not paternalistic bossy help but help involving meaningful understanding at the right time on the part of our fellows. It may be the lack of this sort of help, and the lack of a job guarantee, that sends the neurotic or the disappointed back to the farm, while the adaptable person makes a pleasant experience out of the changeover.

After institutional resistances break down, what happens next? The manner in which people have tried to analyze economic problems in the past may lead them to seek answers of the wrong type and to be frustrated when such answers are not readily forthcoming.

Human will and judgment in times of great institutional flux can play a powerful role in influencing the direction that the new pattern of behavior will take. In fact, it is at such times that individuals can exert a significant influence on the course of history. During the period that a static institutional order prevails, individuals, regardless of ability, can have little effect on the course of history. But energetic and aggressive individuals can have profound influence during a period of institutional commotion, influence perhaps out of all relation to the individuals' abilities or the real merit of their ideas. In Russia in 1917, Lenin seized a country which was in institutional turmoil, and he and a small number of associates effectively influenced the nature of the new order.

A similar situation existed in the United States in the New Deal days following 1933. Leadership at such times can accomplish more good in a year or two than could have been accomplished in fifty years of ordinary conditions. The circumstances that permit some change will likely permit a great deal, once institutional resistance is finally broken.

Gunnar Myrdal has observed that "often it is not more difficult, but easier, to cause a big change rapidly than a small change gradually."[12] What is involved is to seize the opportunity presented by a crisis or a state of flux. And society must just hope that the fates will put people of good judgment and compassion at the helm in such times. Most of the rest of the time, the effort to exercise diplomatic leadership is just an exercise in frustration.

For reasons that are not entirely clear, the new revolutionary leaders in Cuba, Algeria, Indonesia, Egypt, Iran, and Northern Ireland in recent years have not shown a knack for using their opportunities constructively. Rather, their chief efforts seem to have been directed toward denouncing foreigners, mounting foreign adventures, or fostering violence rather than toward making a constructive domestic effort. Fate is frequently unkind in terms of the character of the leaders thrown to the forefront in times of crisis. Or maybe, unfortunately, it takes such people to create and/or take advantage of a crisis.

The Role of Technology

Another point of contrast between institutional and neoclassical growth theory involves the conception of the influences that call forth new technology.

Statistical Evidence of the Importance of Technology

Neoclassical economic theory until the 1950s had almost completely disregarded the role of technology. However, common sense has urged for a long time, at least since the Industrial Revolution, the importance of technical progress. Finally, in the 1950s, some prestigious economists, working in the context of theory-of-production models, generated some statistical evidence indicating the very considerable importance of the accumulation of technical knowledge in fostering expanded production (by comparison with the importance of expanded labor supply and the accumulation of capital stock). This was pretty late in the day, but better late than never.[13]

At all events, Moses Abramovitz, using United States data on labor supply, capital stock, and output for the period from the 1870s to 1953, concluded that this research "tells us how net national product per capita would have grown had the productivity of resources remained constant at base period levels while only the supplies of resources per head increased. Such an index, based on the twenties, rises only some 14 percent between the seventies and the last decade. To account for the quadrupling of net national product per capita, the productivity of a representative unit of all resources must have increased some 250 percent. This seems to imply that almost the entire increase in net product per capita is associated with the rise in productivity." So, something different from increased labor stock and capital stock would seem to account for most growth.

Is this the real meaning of technical change, and is it fairly powerful evidence of the importance of technical progress in contrast to the importance of the traditional factors of production: labor, capital, and land? Perhaps so, despite the fact that some economists are not entirely happy with the nature of the Abramovitz test.

Various Methods of Incorporating Technical Progress in the Growth Model

After Abramovitz demonstrated the importance of technological progress in influencing production, economists rushed to get on the bandwagon and develop theories incorporating technical change in the growth process. In so doing, they used as a starting point the theoretical models with which they were familiar. Chiefly this meant modifying the Cobb-Douglas production function or the constant-elasticity-of-substitution production function so as to incorporate technical progress as though such progress occurred at a constant percentage growth rate.

The possible usefulness of such theories as the institutional, which has always assigned a major role to technology, seems usually to have been overlooked by economists brought up on general equilibrium theory, price theory, national income theory, and optimal growth theory.

Labor-Saving and Capital-Saving Technical Progress

Having somewhat more economic content than the equilibrium, constant-rate-of-growth models may be the models attempting to elucidate the implications of change in factor intensities (or capital-saving vs. labor-saving innovation) as part of the growth process.[14] Whether a new bit of technology is relatively capital- or labor-saving is important information. And an analysis that traces some of the implications of that distinction is worthwhile.

If the capital-labor ratio rises, there is an uncertain tendency for the rate of return to capital to fall relative to the wage rate. This is a valid, important point. But it does not take a particularly sophisticated model to make the point with all the precision that is appropriate to such a rough-and-ready relation.

The Causation of Technical Change
A particular technical change may be called forth by planning, as neoclassical growth theory alleges, because (1) it is qualitatively needed (it is functionally useful—such as a cure for the common cold), (2) it saves on the factor of production that is rising relatively in cost (cost saving), or (3) it is the next logical discovery (technologically appropriate), given the accumulation of technical knowledge up to the moment.

Functionally useful versus technologically appropriate developments: It is alleged by institutional theory that the more likely prevailing causal influence is the fact that a given discovery occurs when it is ripe in the context of the ongoing process of technological accumulation.

The nature of new technical discoveries is essentially dependent on the nature of previous discoveries. However, Landes, in his *Unbound Prometheus*, repeatedly indicates a belief that in the normal train of events technology provides the "needed" new techniques. But his actual examples frequently suggest a different story.[15]

In fact, Veblen alleges that the picture of "need calling forth invention" may have the story backward: "And here and now, as always and everywhere, invention is the mother of necessity."[16]

John Jewkes, also, seems very skeptical as to whether research projects directed toward discovering particular inventions, processes, or cures have a very good probability of accomplishing the desired results. He believes that research workers do not react favorably to having the direction of their effort controlled too closely by planners. Organized research projects directed toward particular, closely controlled ends are likely to be horrible boondoggles where the results are not very satisfactory. Jewkes quotes O. E. Buckley, then president of Bell Telephone Laboratories, to the effect that "one sure way to defeat the scientific spirit is to attempt to direct enquiry from above."

And Jewkes goes on:

> In seeking to provide a social framework conducive to innovation there are great virtues in eclecticism. The conditions under which inventions have arisen up to the present day are so diverse that safety would seem to lie in numbers and in variety of attack. . . . In so far as society can usefully interfere—and there is much truth in the belief that "the only thing men of power can do for men of genius is to leave

them alone"—its task would be to try to maintain a balance between the different sources of inventions, to strive to prevent any one dominating to the exclusion of others. . . .

The essential feature of innovation is that the path to it is not known beforehand. The less, therefore, an inventor is pre-committed in his speculations by training and tradition, the better the chance of his escaping from the grooves of accepted thought. The history of invention provides many instances of the advantages, if not of positive ignorance, at least of a mind not too fully packed with existing knowledge or the records of past failures.[17]

The description by R. J. Forbes of the evolution from fire and the fireplace to bricks and the kiln is an example of what has been a common pattern in which felt need for some particular development can hardly be identified as the crux of the explanation as to why some development has occurred: "Tending the fire required a suitable place in the middle of the hut or cave, usually a mud-plastered walled spot, the hearth. This was the birthplace of pottery, for prehistoric man soon discovered how hard the mud plaster became after being thoroughly heated. Also from the domestic hearth were developed our kilns, ovens, and industrial furnaces of a later period."[18]

In scientific research, one frequently, while trying to do something, discovers something else quite different and perhaps worthwhile. Bessemer discovered his steel process when looking for a cheaper way of making iron; Perkin discovered aniline mauve dye when trying to synthesize quinine.[19]

Also, sometimes the knowledge may already be in the cookbook, so that an expressed need for some particular new device may be met. The reservoir of unused knowledge may sometimes be adequate to meet this need, sometimes it may not. Robert Woodbury gives examples in the machine tool field of development where need seems to have called forth the appropriate tool.[20]

In the perfection of the steam engine, felt need may or may not have called forth the bored cylinder. Perhaps that development came along at the appropriate time in the natural order of things. Eugene Ferguson writes: "An accurately bored cylinder was of critical importance. Watt had since 1769 tried unsuccessfully to obtain a cylinder that would be steam-tight as the piston moved up and down inside it, and in the absence of such a cylinder, the development of his engine was at a standstill. Just such an iron cylinder, slightly over 18 inches in diameter, was finally cast and bored at John Wilkinson's iron works. . . . Wilkinson's contribution was to extend the supporting shaft all the way through the cylinder (which was cast hollow), encasing the shaft in bearings at both ends of the cylinder rather than at one end only."[21]

The preceding discussion has been addressed chiefly to the question of whether functionally useful discoveries can be called forth more or less as needed. The alleged answer was that, by and large, they cannot be. A particular discovery will generally occur when the sequence of knowledge accumulation makes that development natural, probably not before. Of course, appropriate innovations that are already in the cookbook can be used on call, sometimes when the profit motive dictates.

Cost-saving inventions versus technologically appropriate developments: A related question is whether, when labor costs are rising relative to capital costs, this influence tends to call forth inventions which will be labor-saving (or vice versa).

Charles Kennedy's induced bias in innovation, a closely related concept, concerns itself with the influences that may control whether the next innovation is likely to be capital- or labor-intensive.[22] As a qualification, it should be noted that the mere fact that labor unit costs are rising relative to capital unit costs does not necessarily imply that cost considerations automatically call for capital-using innovations. It might be that a certain labor-using innovation would reduce total costs more than some alternative capital-using innovation. In that case, the labor-using innovation would be the appropriate one on narrow cost considerations, even though labor unit costs may be rising relative to capital unit costs.

In the early days of the Industrial Revolution, there seems to have been no pronounced pattern in the sense of labor- or capital-saving discoveries being bunched according to which factor was falling in relative price, despite the fact that one might think that, if this concept is meaningful, there would have been such a pattern. Alan Milward writes of this situation:

> Many of the early innovations of the industrial revolution appear to have been labour-saving but by no means all of them. The speeding up of textile machinery was capital-saving: the steam engine required less capital than the water wheel for a given output of power and improvements in the steam engine concentrated on saving fuel. Some of the process developments of the late years of the nineteenth century,

requiring the use of hydro-electric power, were extremely capital intensive but in general, as the century wore on, more and more innovations saved on both factors though to different degrees in each case.

Railways . . . were capital intensive in themselves but the reduction in the time taken to transport goods allowed business men so to
reduce stocks that railways brought down the capital: output ratio of
the economy as a whole in spectacular fashion.[23]

In some cultures, the institutional order is such that labor-saving inventions are resisted (even when labor may be in fairly short
supply) because of workers' fear of possible unemployment. Such
behavior has been observed not only in western Europe and the
United States in recent times but also in ancient Rome. On the
other hand, in the China of a thousand years ago, where labor
seems to have been much more abundant by comparison with the
West, a more common attitude seems to have been to encourage
labor-saving innovation on the rather commonsense grounds that
it is better to work less.[24]

Conclusion

Growth is probably best visualized as a process in which the ingredients normally vary in rate of growth relative to each other. The
norm is change in the relative importance of the ingredients. And
we should be relieved that this is the situation, because variety and
change help make life interesting.

Technology plays a powerful, dynamic, innovating role in controlling the nature of change. It is not merely a passive factor in
response to the fact that society would like to have such and such
an invention and would also like it to be labor-saving, if you please,
because wage rates are rising.

NOTES

1. Such graphs appear in George Leland Bach, *Economics*, 3d ed. (Englewood Cliffs, N.J.: Prentice-Hall, 1960), p. 89, and Paul A. Samuelson, *Economics*, 10th ed. (New York: McGraw-Hill, 1976 [1948]), p. 42.
   Material in the following pages paraphrases text in my article, "Orthodox Economics and Institutionalized Behavior," in Carey C. Thompson, ed., *Institutional Adjustment: A Challenge to a Changing Economy*
   (Austin: University of Texas Press, 1967), pp. 41–67.

2. John Maynard Keynes, *The General Theory of Employment, Interest and Money* (New York: Harcourt, Brace, 1936), p. 20.
3. See *Survey of Current Business* 54 (July 1974); United Nations, *Yearbook of National Accounts Statistics, 1963* (New York, 1964).
4. See United States Department of Commerce, *National Income, 1954 Edition* (Washington, D.C.: Government Printing Office, 1954), p. 60.
5. This conception of institutional change has elements of similarity with the Stephen Jay Gould concept of biological evolution (à la Huxley) as a process of "punctuated equilibria"; see Gould's "This View of Life, Evolution's Erratic Pace," *Natural History* 96 (May 1977): 12–16.
6. Mary Gibbons Natrella, *Experimental Statistics* (Washington, D.C.: Government Printing Office [for the National Bureau of Standards], 1963), pp. 10–11.
7. Francis Stuart Chapin, *Cultural Change* (New York: Century, 1928), p. 228.
8. David S. Landes, *The Unbound Prometheus* (Cambridge, Eng.: Cambridge University Press, 1970 [1969]), p. 236.
9. Alexander Pope, "An Essay on Man," in *Great Poems of the English Language*, comp. Wallace Alvin Briggs (New York: Tudor Publishing Co., 1936), p. 266.
10. John Dewey, *Intelligence in the Modern World: John Dewey's Philosophy* (New York: Modern Library, 1939), pp. 952–953.
11. John Jewkes, David Sawers, and Richard Stillerman, *The Sources of Invention*, 2d ed. (New York: Norton, 1969), p. 170.
12. Gunnar Myrdal, *Asian Drama* (New York: Random House/Pantheon [for the Twentieth Century Fund], 1968), p. 115.
13. See Moses Abramovitz, "Resource and Output Trends in the United States since 1870," *Papers and Proceedings . . . , American Economic Association* (a supplement to the *American Economic Review*) 46 (May 1956): 5–23, especially pp. 10–11; Robert M. Solow, "Technical Change and the Aggregate Production Function," *Review of Economics and Statistics* 29 (August 1957): 312–320.
14. See J. R. Hicks, "An Inaugural Lecture," *Oxford Economic Papers* 5 (June 1953): 117–135; Charles Kennedy, "Induced Bias in Innovation and the Theory of Distribution," *Economic Journal* 74 (September 1964): 541–547.
15. Landes, *Unbound Prometheus*, pp. 87, 92, 317–320.
16. Thorstein Veblen, *The Instinct of Workmanship* (New York: Augustus M. Kelley, 1964 [1914]), p. 314.
17. Jewkes, Sawers, and Stillerman, *Sources of Invention*, pp. 75, 96, 111, 184.
18. In Melvin Kranzberg and Carroll W. Pursell, Jr., eds., *Technology in Western Civilization*, 2 vols. (New York: Oxford University Press, 1967), 1: 15.

19. See Alan S. Milward, *The Economic Development of Continental Europe 1780–1870* (London: George Allen & Unwin, 1973), p. 179.
20. In Kranzberg and Pursell, eds., *Technology in Western Civilization*, pp. 620–636.
21. In ibid., p. 271.
22. Kennedy, "Induced Bias in Innovation."
23. Milward, *Economic Development of Continental Europe*, pp. 172–173.
24. Joseph Needham, *The Grand Titration: Science and Society in East and West* (Toronto: University of Toronto Press, 1969), pp. 33–34.

ADDITIONAL READINGS

Allen, Francis R., et al. *Technology and Social Change*. New York: Appleton-Century-Crofts, 1957.

Ayres, C. E. *Science: The False Messiah*. Indianapolis: Bobbs-Merril, 1927.

Crombie, Alistair C. *History of Science*. Cambridge, Eng.: Heffer, 1962.

Ginzberg, Eli, et al. *Economic Impact of Large Public Programs: The NASA Experience*. Salt Lake City: Olympus, 1976.

Gurley, John G., and Edward S. Shaw. *Money in a Theory of Finance*. Washington, D.C.: Brookings, 1960.

Lave, Lester B. *Technological Change: Its Conception and Measurement*. Englewood Cliffs, N.J.: Prentice-Hall, 1966.

Mishan, Edward J. *Technology and Growth*. New York: Praeger, 1970.

Organization for Economic Cooperation and Development. *The Conditions for Success in Technological Innovation*. Paris: O.E.C.D., 1971.

Rostow, Walt W. *How It All Began*. New York: McGraw-Hill, 1975.

Schmookler, Jacob. *Invention and Economic Growth*. Cambridge, Mass.: Harvard University Press, 1966.

Strassmann, W. Paul. *Technological Change and Economic Development*. Ithaca: Cornell University Press, 1968.

United States, House of Representatives, Committee on Science and Astronautics. *Applied Science and Technological Progress*. Report prepared by National Academy of Sciences. Panel on Applied Science and Technological Progress, Harvey Brooks, chairman. Washington, D.C.: Government Printing Office, 1967.

8.

Marxian and Other "Radical" Theories

THE PRESENT economic orthodoxy does not seem to provide a unique solution to the value problem or to serve as a satisfactory policy guide. Does any one of the other more or less "general" economic theories enjoying some prestige provide satisfactory answers either to the basic value theory questions or to the questions of what the criteria for identifying appropriate economic policy may be? Such other theories include Marxian socialism, underconsumption, the single tax, and Catholic economic doctrine.

Marxian Socialism

Marx attacked classical economics in its own frame of reference. This involved working with most of the Ricardian assumptions and analytical tools. The procedure both strengthened and weakened his position. If he was to have significant scholarly impact in the midnineteenth century, this was probably good judgment. Besides that, in the world of scholarship and science, for institutionally controlled reasons, we usually work with the analytical tools and methods on which we were brought up and with which the people on whom we wish to make an impression are familiar. So, even Marx was bound into the institutional constraints imposed by the classical economics tradition—at least in large measure—but his use of this procedure meant that his theory incorporated many of the weaknesses of classical economics.

Thus, Marx assumed pure competition, Say's law of markets (demand equals supply), and the labor theory of value. At least, it seems that Marx adhered to Say's Law in connection with the development of his basic argument, although in his discussion of business cycles this may not have been the case.[1]

The Organization of Society

Marx divided society into a superstructure and a substructure. The superstructure included the noneconomic institutions, such as religion, ethics, the law, mores, and so on; the (economic) substructure, the economic base, included the modes of production. And the modes of production were divided into the forces of production and the (social) relations of production.

The forces of production were the material powers or means of production, the technological potential. There is a possible meaningful analogy here with technology as conceived in the institutional theory. The (social) relations of production may also have a meaningful analogy with the economic concepts of institutional theory. For Marx, the noneconomic institutions would not be found here, being in the superstructure instead.

To say that Marx's attitude on institutions substantially anticipated the position of institutional economics seems not to be a useful generalization. The matter is important enough to justify some discussion. One listing of the "institutions of capitalism" as identified by Marxists is (1) the labor market, (2) private property and the legal relations of ownership, (3) private ownership and control of the means of production, and (4) the economic man.[2]

This is a rather limited list. Two of the items involve the institution of property. In fact, the institution of private property seems—for Marxists—to overshadow, almost to the point of exclusion, all others. Ownership of property rights in capital, they say, provides the leverage that permits capitalists to exploit labor. The role of property is made basic in the context of the way Marxists have chosen to explain how exploitation occurs: the economic man (rational) capitalist uses the leverage of his property rights, operating through a labor market whose behavior norms the capitalists have created, to extract surplus value (profits) from the system. These are all the institutions the Marxists need as a basis for their theory. The economic man is motivated by the profit motive. Say's Law and pure competition operate to generate surplus value and the self-destruction of the capitalist system. This is pretty much the frame of reference of classical economics turned against classical economics, and it is an argument that was, for that very reason, telling in its time. But that was over a hundred years ago.

If, for example, property rights do not really provide capitalists and entrepreneurs with their basic leverage, the use the Marxists make of their concept of institutions (and of the institutions whose behavior norms they choose to emphasize) may be something less than crucial. Perhaps the real power base of capitalists, bankers, money changers, and entrepreneurs is gained from the way they utilize their strategic position in the money-changing process, and perhaps most of these people are not, at least until late in life, especially identifiable as property owners. And the person actually exercising the power derived from property ownership may well be the trustee who manages the estate rather than the widow who owns it, the ingroup in the corporation rather than the stockholder majority. In this setting, the class distinctions, of which Marxists make so much, seem ephemeral and shifting.

Conceptually, what Marx does with the forces and relations of production is in the analytical frame of reference of classical economics and is oriented around the profit motive and Say's law of markets. He and later Marxists do not seem to be working with a listing of institutions at all comprehensive in the sense that institutional economics conceives of institutions. Their conception of the role of institutions seems to belong to another world. The chief behavior norm, for them, is the profit motive. However, this emphasis does not seem to make much sense in a world where the dominant institution, the giant corporation, is run by managers rather than by the stockholder-owners who get (or fail to get) the generally extremely small dividends doled out by management.

Nevertheless, Marx did have much of the essence of the technology-institutions relation of institutional economics, early in his career at that. He wrote in 1849: "Thus the social relation within which individuals produce, the social relations of production, change, are transformed, with the change and development of the material means of production, the productive forces. With the invention of a new instrument of warfare, firearms, the whole internal organisation of the army necessarily changed."[3] It is too bad that he did not develop this insight more in later years and spend less time on the interminable development of the overrefined argument as to how surplus value falls into the clutches of the capitalists.

The Labor Theory of Value

The argument to which Marx devoted most of the time and energy of his mature years involved the description of the process by which the capitalists appropriate surplus value from the workers. This argument starts with the labor theory of value, stated in much the same form as Ricardo had stated it fifty years earlier. Marx apparently felt a compelling need to pin down and quantify (at least theoretically) the amount of exploitation of labor by capital. There was some point in this if the falling rate of profit generated by this process was to cause the collapse of the capitalist system. But there seems not to have been so much point if the falling rate of profit was a mirage and if the homogeneous, socially necessary unit of labor time (his starting point) was a fatally defective concept.

If Marx was to quantify the surplus value or the exploitation practiced by capitalists, he needed to start with a homogeneous unit of measurement. He wrote:

> The labour, however, that forms the substance of value, is homogeneous human labor, expenditure of one uniform labour power. Each of these units is the same as any other . . . , no more than is socially necessary. The labour-time socially necessary is that required to produce an article under the normal conditions of production, and with the average degree of skill and intensity prevalent at the time.[4]

He elaborated upon this in his *Critique of Political Economy*:

> To measure the exchange-value of commodities by the labour-time they contain, the different kinds of labour have to be reduced to uniform, homogeneous, simple labour, in short to labour of uniform quality, whose only difference, therefore, is quantity. . . .
>
> This reduction appears to be an abstraction, but it is an abstraction which is made every day in the social process of production. The conversion of all commodities into labour-time is no greater an abstraction, and is no less real, than the resolution of all organic bodies into air.[5]

My criticism of the homogeneous, socially necessary unit of labor time as a yardstick is basically the same as my criticism of the efforts in general equilibrium analysis to identify a unique maximum or even a unique solution, whether an optimum or not (see the appendix to chapter 4). Assume two qualities of labor, manual and skilled, producing two products. Depending on the relative demand patterns for the two products, manual and skilled labor will probably be combined in different proportions. The weather, or what-have-you, may cause demand patterns to change. This implies that their relative values will be appraised differently in the market depending on consumption preferences and that they cannot be synthesized into a homogeneous unit or a yardstick which is generally usable.

Accumulating Surplus

In Marxian theory, the prices or values at which goods have been assumed to be exchanged have been presumed to be controlled by the relative amounts of homogeneous, socially necessary labor time which it presumably took to produce them. And labor received a total wage corresponding to the amount of labor time it took to produce the goods necessary to provide minimum sustenance to labor (or was this some institutionally determined minimum acceptable standard of living?).

At all events, this formula for rewarding labor seemed to leave some surplus (if labor produced more than was necessary for its bare sustenance or for its institutionally determined minimum acceptable standard of living) for the individual in the strategic position that permitted appropriation of the surplus for personal uses. This strategically placed person was, according to the Marxists, the capitalist who owned the means of production. The capitalist then reinvested the gains in capital and the stock of capital grew and the ability of the economy to produce goods grew.

However, because wages were kept low, due to the fact that the workers were only getting barely enough to keep body and soul together (or . . .), mass purchasing power was not as robust as it might have been.

Given a belief in "demand equals supply," this situation, however, did not imply unsalable surpluses. Rather, it implied falling prices and falling profit rates as the capitalists desperately competed for the meager markets, hardly major problems in the 1970s. These conditions also led to the creation of a reserve army of the unemployed. This was a handy army for the capitalists to have around because it helped keep the wage rate where it should be, from the capitalists' point of view: at the subsistence level.

The Falling Rate of Profit and the Reserve Army of the Unemployed

So, in the society, there were at least two tendencies suggesting future trouble: falling profit rates and increasing unemployment. And these were presumed to lead inevitably to the collapse of the capitalist system. But Marx (or Engels) was somewhat ambiguous regarding just how this collapse was to come about. Was the revolution to involve a violent uprising, or was the system just going to fall apart because capitalists cannot live without profits? "The Communists openly declare that their ends can be attained only by the forcible overthrow of all existing social conditions. Workers of the world, unite, you have nothing to lose but your chains"—this sounds a bit like a clarion call for violent revolution. But these sentiments were expressed in the *Communist Manifesto* in 1848. The language and logic of the later *Das Kapital* were much more restrained. And, in the 1970s, there even seems to be a major block of young Marxist intellectuals who do not believe in revolution at all.

Parenthetically, if falling profits and massive unemployment were Marx's explanation of the forces that get the capitalist system into trouble, one may wonder why the Russians adopted a policy of cold war and repeated crises following World War II. Such policies kept the United States on the qui vive, stimulated Congress to heavy military expenditures, generally operated to keep the United States economy humming and productive, and kept the profit rate up and the unemployment rate down. But this is a digression.

Imperialism

As early as about 1900, Marxists were already disappointed because events were not moving, in the manner forecast by Marx, as rapidly as they would have liked. The cleavage between the workers and the capitalists was not unambiguously becoming more pronounced. If anything, instead of the economy polarizing into worker and capitalist groups, an unanticipated middle class was growing in relative importance. And there was perhaps some basis for saying that the standard of living of the mass of the population was rising. Profit rates were not obviously falling as a long-run trend; neither was unemployment rising. There were sporadic depressions, well described by Marx, but were they getting worse?

In any event, Lenin (and others) embellished Marxist theory with international imperialism as an explanation of the delay. That most of the essential ideas in Lenin's 1916 *Imperialism* had already been expressed in the bourgeois John Hobson's 1902 *Imperialism* might suggest that the ideas were not entirely dependent on Marxian logic. Be that as it may, Lenin argued that the capitalists in the capitalistic countries were desperately exporting both commodities because of the low returns from domestic sales and capital in the hopes of obtaining higher profits abroad. He also argued that the capitalists were using their power to extort raw materials from the backward countries at ruinously low prices and increasing their profits thereby.

That Marx believed that a pronounced feature of the capitalist system involved desperate efforts to export more in order to maintain profits may readily be documented in the *Communist Man-*

ifesto: "The need of a constantly expanding market for its products chases the bourgeoisie over the whole surface of the globe. It must nestle everywhere, settle everywhere, establish connections everywhere. . . . The cheap prices of its exports are the heavy artillery with which it batters down all Chinese walls."[6]

That capitalists export at cheap prices, however, is respectable Marxist doctrine only half the time and gut-reaction doctrine virtually none of the time. K. Izmailvo is probably speaking for more emotional Marxists when he says: "The capitalist monopolies sell their products in the underdeveloped countries at very high prices."[7]

For Lenin, the export of capital as distinct from the export of commodities became of dominant importance: "Export of capital as distinguished from export of commodities becomes of particularly great importance." It is clear that he believed that the export of capital was imperative, from the viewpoint of the capitalists, in order to hold up profit rates in the developed country, which would then have less of a glut of capital holding interest and profit rates down.

Lenin also wrote in *Imperialism*: "In these backward countries profits are usually high, for capital is scarce, the price of land is relatively low, wages are low, raw materials are cheap. The necessity for exporting capital [from the developed countries] arises from the fact that in a few countries capitalism has become 'over-ripe,' and, owing to the backward stage of agriculture and the impoverishment of the masses, capital lacks opportunities for 'profitable' investment."[8]

There are several difficulties with this argument. For one thing, it is simply not true that the price of land is relatively low, at least in the well-populated underdeveloped countries.

For another, Lenin's argument requires that profit rates or interest rates, on the average and in real terms, be higher in underdeveloped than in developed countries. It is by no means sure that this is the situation. Nominal interest rates are certainly generally high in underdeveloped countries. But, after allowance has been made for inflation, it is less than clear that the real interest rates are higher in the underdeveloped countries, especially after one averages profit and interest rates over all economic activity, including subsistence agriculture, and observes that the rates of return in some of these areas are abysmally low. The Lenin argument seems to require speaking in terms of national averages to justify, in a clear-cut way, the generalization that net movement of capital is in a given direction.

Also, in the way that Lenin presents the process of foreign investment as export of capital as distinct from export of goods, there seems to be an implication that capital migrates internationally by magic. In fact, for a transfer of capital to be meaningful in real terms, it seems it must be a counterpart of a net goods flow in the direction in which the capital is moving, and the distinction between goods flows and capital flows is artificial.

Lenin also argued that capitalists were busy exploiting underdeveloped countries by using power and leverage to extract raw materials and profits from them.

No doubt the capitalist countries have been interested in obtaining various raw materials from underdeveloped countries at prices as low as possible. Whether they have been any more anxious to buy them than the underdeveloped countries have been to sell them is much less certain. Of course, the underdeveloped countries have been interested in getting as high prices as possible. But there are at least two difficulties with imputing that all this implies successful and purposive exploitation by the developed countries and unfavorable prices or terms of trade for the underdeveloped countries. For one thing, it is not clear that the capitalist countries want to exploit in the sense of having net goods imports. Witness the developed-country efforts to use trade restrictions to hold down imports. Also, if exploitation is viewed as price or terms-of-trade exploitation, it is not clear that the developed countries have accomplished this or have even particularly tried to do so. Export dumping is such a common characteristic of the international trade behavior of capitalist countries that it is difficult to make a comprehensive case that there is a systematic effort at terms-of-trade exploitation. Also, such statistical evidence as we have with regard to the long-run movement of the terms of trade hardly seems to support the position that there has been secular worsening from the viewpoint of the underdeveloped countries.[9]

As to developed-country exploitation via profit taking to the benefit of the creditor country, for that to occur in real terms, the developed country would have to have a consistent import trade balance. And, as was alleged in the preceding paragraph, developed countries have fought that as though it was the fate worse than death. This observed, omnipresent capitalist-country reluctance to have an import trade balance does not keep Marxist or

Russian writers from arguing: "Today's imperialistic conquistadors no longer search for gold in Latin America. They prefer to 'create' it, squeezing huge profits from the exploitation of cheap Latin American labor and plundering their natural wealth."[10]

Since one of these behavior patterns seems to imply an effort to have export trade balances on the part of the capitalist countries (vis-à-vis the backward countries) and the others seem to imply net goods imports on the part of the capitalist countries, one may wonder whether Lenin was not having his cake and eating it too in terms of the alternative concepts of imperialism. The capitalists were presumed to be guilty of both foisting goods upon and taking goods away from the backward countries.

Another point of wonderment in connection with Marxian theory in general and imperialism in particular involves the Marxist endorsement of profit seeking as the basic explanation of motivation. The wonderment is that a theory, such as the Marxist, which ostensibly takes institutionalized behavior into account should actually concern itself so little with the factual study of how institutions behave. The assumption of the profit motive is ubiquitous in explaining the process by which capitalists accumulate surplus value. And it is essential to the result which alleges that exploitation can be measured in terms of a surplus value which is susceptible to quantitative measurement in a process where the capitalists are alleged to be trying to maximize the quantity of their profits. However, this picture disregards pretty clearly the phenomenon of the divorcement of ownership from control in the large, dominant corporations, a characteristic that seems well established.

Some Statistical Tests
The immiserization of the proletariat and the sharpening cleavage between the proletariat and the bourgeoisie seem to be phenomena that have not occurred in the manner Marx believed would be involved.

Unemployment is sporadically a serious problem, but it is not clear that it is a worse problem with each successive depression. There has been nothing comparable to the unemployment of the 1930s in a long time.

With regard to the declining profit rate, it is not possible to obtain the precise data needed for purposes of testing the proposition in terms of the definitions used by Marx. Yet miscellaneous bits of reasonably relevant data suggest that the burden of proof should be on the one who wishes to allege the existence of a secular downward trend. Figure 8–1, for example, hardly pictures a long-run trend downward in the yield on British government obligations. And figure 8–2 hardly demonstrates the existence of a secular trend downward in United States corporate profits.

Of course, the presence of high interest and profit rates may create a gut feeling that the "capitalists" are exploiting the "people." But those concerned about high corporate profits and high interest rates and unearned increments to *rentiers* should be at least aware of the manner in which they are deviating from the Marxist dogma on the declining rate of profits. Marxist dogma gets the capitalist system into trouble because the profit rate is falling, not because it is high or rising. Those who express concern about high profits may be expressing a very legitimate, but non-Marxist, concern about a real problem.

The Dialectic, the Revolution, and Communism/Paradise

Communism or Marxist socialism, like most religions, has a strong teleological aspect. Or does it? Many younger Marxist intellectuals now deny this. However, Marx's theory incorporated a version of the Hegelian dialectic which became a theory of history. The idea was that at any given time in a society a dominant group (the nobility, the bourgeoisie, the Establishment) exploits the rest of the population. This was the thesis of the dialectic argument. Then, with the passage of time, the exploited (slaves, serfs, workers, college students) would form a nucleus of opposition to the dominant group or elite, and this nucleus of opposition would become larger and stronger. This development corresponds to the antithesis in the dialectic. Eventually, the exploited group would become strong enough to seize power from and to eliminate the formerly dominant group. Thus, those who had previously been exploited would come to be the whole of society. This is the synthesis in the thesis-antithesis-synthesis sequence.

In the standard development of this argument, the new synthesis would become a new thesis over against which there would develop a new antithesis, and so on. For Marx this process was, for example, reflected in the argument that the medieval nobility (a thesis) was eventually opposed by a new class of bourgeois capitalists (an antithesis). The bourgeois capitalists eventually took power away from the nobility and became a synthesis, of sorts. But the bourgeois capitalists then became a thesis as worker opposition developed, the workers being the new antithesis.

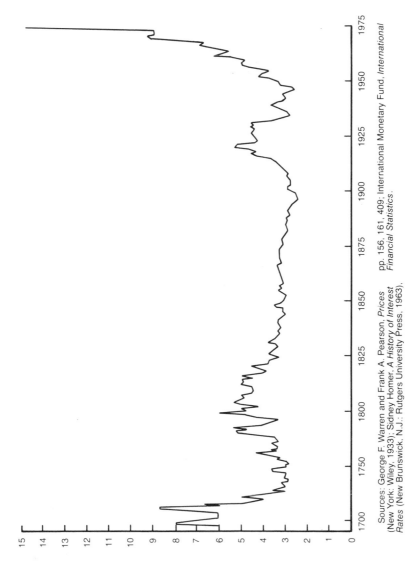

Sources: George F. Warren and Frank A. Pearson, *Prices* (New York: Wiley, 1933); Sidney Homer, *A History of Interest Rates* (New Brunswick, N.J.: Rutgers University Press, 1963), pp. 156, 161, 409; International Monetary Fund, *International Financial Statistics*.

Figure 8-1. Percentage yield on British consols

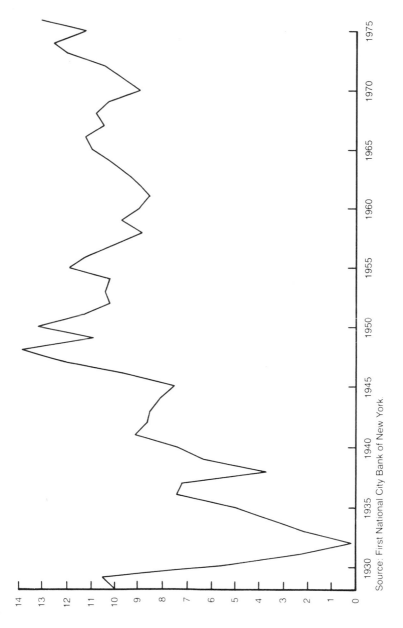

Source: First National City Bank of New York

Figure 8-2. Percentage return on net assets for a sample of leading United States corporations

According to this sequence, the workers would eventually come to dominate and would become the new synthesis. At this point Marxian socialism seems to allege that the historical evolutionary process comes to an end. There is no new thesis and antithesis. The workers (after the dictatorship of the proletariat) establish the ideal society: communism (with a small c).

So, there is considerable parallel between the communism of Marxian socialism, the heaven of various religions, and so on, and this is a point of difference between classical Marxian socialism and institutional-instrumental theory. The latter theory does not have this conception that the ideal society can, now or ever, be described definitively or, even, that we are evolving into an ideal society in any meaningful sense. Rather, institutional theory conceives that people's ideas of what is desirable will change as time passes and circumstances change. At any given time, on the basis of prevailing knowledge, we have ideas as to whether one or another behavior is more or less desirable, but we are not committed to retaining these views under later, changed circumstances. The institutional theory does not conceive that the ideal society is something attainable, with which we will be content to live for all eternity once we have it.

Another difficulty with the dialectic argument and its implication of the polarization of positions is that positions have not polarized. There are many lines of cleavage in present society between different antagonistic groups, not just one between capitalists and laborers, and there is no indication that the number is decreasing or that the polarization between capital and labor is becoming more clear-cut. One example of a different line of cleavage is the confrontation between producers and consumers, which may be more important than that between capitalists and laborers. Another is the confrontation between OPEC and much of the rest of the world.

Other lines of cleavage include those between people at different income levels. Also, in many professions, such as the academic and the military, salary-level cleavage difficulties are compounded by the existence of ranks, which are the basis for very strongly felt invidious comparisons. There are cleavages between men and women, between students and teachers, between parents and their offspring, among the races, among the religions, among the social classes.

Some of these cleavages are between aspects of behavior, with one individual being on one side of the argument in one setting and on the other side in another. The cleavage between producers and consumers is of this type, with (almost) everybody playing both roles.

Another implication of the dialectic seems even more objectionable ethically and factually. The dialectic argument points to bilateral confrontation and violent revolution in which the antithesis destroys the previous thesis, the proletariat destroys the bourgeoisie—or at least the Russian nobility. This confrontation seems to be a situation devoutly hoped for and worked for on the part of Marxists in general and latter-day, gut-reaction Marxists in particular but, perhaps, not on the part of the new generation of Marxist intellectuals. This seems clearly true whether or not the last words in *Das Kapital* are: "Long live *violent* revolution." And almost the last words in the *Communist Manifesto* certainly are: "The Communists . . . openly declare that their ends can be attained only by the forcible overthrow of all existing social conditions."

Kenneth Boulding has written of this aspect of dialectic process:

> A dialectical philosophy, however, whether nationalistic, racist, or Marxist, which stresses victory rather than problem solving, beating down the enemy rather than cooperating with him (and which therefore tends to justify and excuse the immoral behavior which dialectical processes always produce), is likely to intensify the dialectical processes themselves to the point where they will become damaging to all parties, and unfriendly to human welfare and development.[11]

Underconsumption

In the late nineteenth century, John Hobson argued that an economy may get into trouble as a result of the inability of the mass of the population to buy all goods that the productive process is placing on the market. Sheer lack of adequate effective demand by the needy was frequently the trouble, according to Hobson. He wrote in 1902:

> If a tendency to distribute income or consuming power according to needs were operative, it is evident that consumption would rise with every rise of producing power, for human needs are illimitable,

and there could be no excess of saving. But it is quite otherwise in a state of economic society where distribution has no fixed relation to needs, but is determined by other conditions which assign to some people a consuming power vastly in excess of needs or possible uses, while others are destitute of consuming power enough to satisfy even the full demands of physical efficiency.[12]

By this time, Hobson had been saying the same thing for many years, and where had it gotten him? Such a position represented a denial of the truth of Say's Law. Orthodox economists in the late nineteenth century generally regarded Say's Law as sacrosanct; anybody who did not appreciate the inner logic of the "supply creates its own demand" argument was a booby.

Pretty obviously, however, especially during depressions, all the available goods are frequently not bought. Marx had pointed this out in his pioneering work on the business cycle, although he held pretty much to a Say's Law assumption in the core of his analysis describing the processes leading to the undermining of the capitalist system.

Despite a century and a half and more of argument on the issue, there still remains a good deal of uncertainty as to the sense, if any, in which demand need equal supply. If poverty is due to the fact that the economic system does not provide the poor with purchasing power adequate for taking all the actually produced goods off the market, and if surpluses tend to hang over the market in an ominous manner, we have a pretty powerful argument against the capitalist system. But it is not exclusively a Marxist argument; it is not even essentially a Marxist argument. It sounds like basic common sense: poverty in the midst of plenty is not a reasonable condition.

Exactly what Say's Law is stating is that inadequate purchasing power for purposes of taking all the produced goods off the market cannot exist as a simple logical proposition because supply creates its own demand. The return paid to the factors of production has to equal purchasing power adequate to take all the goods off the market—and to pay off all the factors who produced them—because these two quantities are the same thing. This argument was considered in chapter 7, but it seems worth considering again.

What is paid for goods becomes the return to the factors, but those receipts may be supplemented by a little bank borrowing. On the other hand, it is not true that the return to the factors automatically creates purchasing power which will in fact be used to take the goods they produce off the market. If the relations are in terms of money, inequality between receipts and spending is obviously possible as money is created or withheld by individuals or by the banking system. If the relations are in real terms, it is obviously possible to produce something that nobody will swap anything for and that even the producer does not want.

In any event, Hobson does not now seem to be quite the discredited peddler of faulty logic that he was generally thought to be in his lifetime. And inequality in income distribution creates the conditions where income received is likely not to be used in a process that comes out even in taking all the produced goods off the market.

A good deal of inequity in income levels and levels of buying power can result from the manipulations which are possible because some people are closer to the processes by which money is created and destroyed than are others. The nature of the institutional arrangements controlling the manner in which money is created and destroyed can affect both total production and income, the possibilities of unsold stocks of goods, and income distribution.

Also, inequality in income distribution may exist as a result of the fact that some people are more adept at profitably exploiting some prevailing set of institutional arrangements. Other people would be more adept in another setting. Competition, pure or impure, pays off for one type of shrewdness. Another institutional setting would reward physical strength better.

We may detect what we consider to be patently objectionable results of the interaction of institutionalized influences without working out the labor theory of value/theory of surplus value relations of Marxist theory.

The Single Tax

It is also possible for a non-Marxist to believe that major unearned income is a by-product of landownership. For example, the economist Henry George (an American, where Hobson was an Englishman), whose views were colored by the conditions of the gold-rush days in California, came to believe that much of the wealth that dominated the United States in the late nineteenth century was a by-product of landownership and the rise in the value of land. The single tax which George proposed was to be, depending on the perspective, a tax on unearned increment in the value of land or a taxing away of economic rent. Just as much of Marx's argument used the logical tools of Ricardo and other early classical economists, so did Henry George's single tax argument use the logic of the classical economics explanation of a phenomenon: this time the source and nature of land rent. Pure land rent, it was argued, was a happy by-product of the fact that one happened to own land which was more productive than the marginal land which it just barely paid to cultivate.

George wrote: "The rent of land is determined by the excess of its produce over that which the same application can secure from the least productive land in use. . . . The reason why, in spite of the increase of productive power, wages constantly tend to a minimum which will give but a bare living, is that, with increase in productive power, rent tends to even greater increase, thus producing a constant tendency to the forcing down of wages." The true remedy is: "We must make land common property." But, to accomplish the desired result, "it is not necessary to confiscate land; it is only necessary to confiscate rent." And sufficient revenue will be raised to permit us "to abolish all taxation save that upon land values." "The elder Mirabeau, we are told, ranked the proposition of Quesnay, to substitute one single tax on rent (the *impôt unique*) for all other taxes, as 'a discovery equal in utility to the invention of writing or the substitution of the use of money for barter.' And so we have proposed: the single tax on rent from land." [13]

So, Henry George found a source of unearned wealth but failed to convince governments to enact his single tax on land rent— perhaps in part because of the political power of landowners, an institutional phenomenon, perhaps in part because of the difficulty of quantifying rent with reasonable precision. The popularity of Proposition 13 indicates this difficulty.

Marxists also make much of the allegation that it is the ownership of land and of the means of production (capital) by capitalists that gives capitalists their leverage to appropriate the surplus value unto themselves. But Marxists try to prove a good deal more than did Henry George with regard to the implications of ownership (and their emphasis is on the ownership of capital rather than of land). George's simpler theory may have a more clear-cut element of truth than does the more complicated Marxist theory.

Catholic Economic Doctrine

Historically, many reformers have denounced the economic position of the Catholic church as being reactionary and tending to protect the vested interests of the wealthy. The strong opposition of the church to communism, and to Marxian socialism, and to the Soviet regime has been well known. Also, the church advocacy of a well-ordered society savors a bit of dictatorship. (However, one would not expect some reformers to object to the "well-ordered" society, per se. There is nothing many of them would rather have than the power to "well-order" a society to their own taste.)

There is another side to the church record. In recent years, many ecclesiastics have been in the vanguard in working for improved social and economic conditions.[14]

The church has always approached economic problems from a moral viewpoint. Church precepts describe the economy as it should be, not necessarily as it is. The individual who enjoys more than a proportionate share of the good things of the earth *should* give of the excess as charity. It is meritorious to give away much or all of one's wealth, but the church has not considered that the individual is obligated to give away all of the excess or even all of the excess over a proportionate share. Tithing has been a rather common standard but has been a bench mark, not a requirement.

The church opposed usury during the Middle Ages, but it has long since come to the position that it is legitimate to charge a small interest to cover the cost of making loans. The church opposes high interest charges, however.

The church still subscribes to the concept of the just price, somewhat as it did in the Middle Ages. To sell goods at any price other than the just price was formerly thought to be both criminal and immoral. The concept now runs somewhat to the effect that a just price would be a price set between a buyer and a seller after free bargaining where prevailing conditions guaranteed that each has equal bargaining power. Perhaps this would not be too far from the price pure competition would set, if there were such a thing.

Particularly as a precept in the papal encyclical *Rerum novarum* of Leo XIII in 1891, the church came to sponsor labor unions. Its unions, however, did not actively foster strikes, picketing, and so on. Rather, they emphasized the desirability of getting along, and they sponsored systems of mutual insurance and mutual assistance. Pope Leo XIII wrote: "It is capital error . . . to believe that the classes are natural enemies of each other."[15]

Less well known than the church opposition to communism is its opposition to the "capitalist spirit." Joaquín Azpiazu, a Jesuit writer in Spain, wrote several decades ago:

> Neither capital nor capitalism—understood in the manner of Diehl as a system, in its two aspects of productive capitalism and rent-earning capitalism—is condemned in any way, nor is it illegal in its fundamental essentials; but the anti-Christian capitalist spirit and the results of that spirit, self-serving and uncontrolled ambitious capitalism, appear condemned at the very heart of the fundamental Christian doctrine.[16]

And Azpiazu quotes Pius XI:

> First, there comes to view that in our times it is not only that [capitalists] accumulate wealth but also that they acquire enormous power and a despotic economic predominance in the hands of a very few. Many times they are not even themselves the owners, but only the custodians and administrators who manage the capital as they choose. These potentates are extraordinarily powerful when, as absolute master of the money, they control the credit and distribute it at their pleasure.[17]

An interesting difference between the Catholic and the Marxist positions emerges. In the Marxist argument, capitalists get leverage for purposes of exploitation as a result of ownership of land. In the church position, capitalists get leverage as a result of being in a key position in the money-changing process; they need not own anything to profit from this position. (In a socialist society, exploiters [bureaucrats] might get leverage from their position as bureaucrats.)

At all events, and in spite of opposition from many ecclesiastics, the modern Catholic church has much support to offer the idealist reformer.

Conclusion

Actually, there has been a lot of opposition to oppression on the part of earlier generations. Finding things wrong with the system and penning fiery denunciations is nothing new. It would seem to have been and to be an appropriate activity in many times and places, including the present.

The real problem is how to move effectively to overcome institutional resistance to the implementation of desirable changes and how to do this without destroying the very considerable progress that has been made through the ages. Joan Robinson quotes a challenge by a Chinese scholar to the first Han emperor: "You conquered this country in a chariot—can you rule it from a chariot?"[18] The same challenge might well have been made in the post–World War II period to many reformers, from Perón to Castro to Nasser.

The great challenge to idealistic rebels is the knowledge that the real problem is not the staging of a successful revolution. That has been done many times. The real challenge is the constructive work of building a better society. A better society surely can be built more effectively and quickly if we begin on the foundations of what we have rather than insist on starting fresh. This is true in spite of the frustrating effectiveness of institutional resistance to change.

To return, however, to Marxism and its present vogue with idealistic reformers, perhaps the most important criticism of Marxism involves its predilection for polarizing conflict and class struggle in the apparent hope that justice will triumph after the great showdown and that thereafter we will automatically have an ideal society. We seem to like to visualize our troubles as involving conflict between clear-cut good and clear-cut evil; we like to assume that it will be helpful, in resolving our difficulties, if this cleavage becomes sharper and finally culminates in a holocaust where good destroys evil. This seems pretty clearly to be the view of the emotional Marxist, whether or not it is the commonly held doctrine of the new generation of Marxist intellectuals.

Much of the appeal of Marxism seems to be due to the fact that it lends itself to painting a picture of this sort. Yet, surely, this is its great, even its vicious, weakness. There is nothing humanistic, or tolerant, or democratic, or even civilized about such a forecast for the world, even though many of those painting such a picture are of the finest.

NOTES

1. See Howard J. Sherman, *Radical Political Economy* (New York: Basic Books, 1972), p. 387. Baran and Sweezy seem to adhere to the more traditional Say's Law view of Marxian theory; see Paul A. Baran and Paul M. Sweezy, *Monopoly Capital* (New York: Monthly Review Press, 1966), p. 108.
2. Richard Edwards, Michael Reich, and Thomas E. Weisskopf, *The Capitalist System—A Radical Analysis of American Society* (Englewood Cliffs, N.J.: Prentice-Hall, 1972), p. 89.
3. Karl Marx and Frederick Engels, "Wage Labour and Capital," *Selected Works* (Moscow: Progress Publishers, 1968), p. 81.
4. Karl Marx, *Capital*, trans. Samuel Moore and Edward Aveling (Chicago: Encyclopaedia Britannica, 1952 [1867]), p. 15, and pt. 3, chap. 7, sec. 2.
5. See Karl Marx, *Contribution to the Critique of Political Economy*, trans. S. W. Ryazanskaya (Moscow: Progress Publishers, 1970 [1859]), pp. 30–31, 38.
6. Karl Marx and Friedrich Engels, *Manifesto of the Communist Party* (New York: International Publishers, 1948 [1848]), pp. 12, 13.
7. K. Izmailvo, *Voprosy ekonomiki* (September 1954); *Mezhdunarodnaya torgovlya* (Moscow: Vneshtorgizdat, 1954), p. 359; see also Academia de Ciencias de la U.R.S.S., *Manual de economía política*, 2d ed. (Mexico City: Editorial Grijalbo, 1957), p. 239.
8. V. I. Lenin, *Imperialism: The Highest Stage of Capitalism*, rev. trans. (New York: International Publishers, 1933 [1916]), pp. 81, 58.
9. See Wendell Gordon, *International Trade: Goods, People, and Ideas* (New York: Knopf, 1958), pp. 64–70.
10. V. Vol'skii, *Latinskaya Amerika, neft' y nezavisimost'* (Moscow: Izdatel'stvo "Mysl'," 1964), p. 3.
11. Kenneth E. Boulding, *A Primer on Social Dynamics* (New York: Free Press, 1970), pp. vi–viii.
12. John A. Hobson, *Imperialism: A Study*, 3d ed. (London: George Allen & Unwin, 1938 [1902]), p. 83.
13. Henry George, *Progress and Poverty* (New York: Appleton, 1879), pp. 168, 282, 328, 405; 406, 433.
14. Much of the doctrine which follows is from the encyclicals: *Rerum novarum* (1891) and *Quadragesimo anno* (1931).
15. Pope Leo XIII, *Rerum novarum* (Rio de Janeiro: Edição "Organização Simões," 1950 [1891]), p. 29.
16. Joaquín Azpiazu, *Moral profesional económica* (Madrid: Ediciones FAX, 1940/1943), pp. 85–86.
17. Ibid., p. 88.
18. Joan Robinson, *Freedom and Necessity* (New York: Vintage Books [Random House], 1971), p. 52.

ADDITIONAL READINGS

Balinky, Alexander. *Marx's Economics*. Lexington, Mass.: D. C. Heath, 1970.

Berndt, E. R., and L. R. Christensen. "Testing for the Existence of a Consistent Aggregate Index of Labor Inputs." *American Economic Review* 64 (June 1974):391–404.

Bernstein, Richard. *Praxis and Action*. Philadelphia: University of Pennsylvania Press, 1971.

Burns, Emile, ed. *Handbook of Marxism*. London: Gollancz, 1935.

Cleaver, Harry. *Reading "Capital" Politically*. Austin: University of Texas Press, 1979.

De Sanctis, Frei Antonio, ed. *Encíclicas e documentos sociais de "Rerum novarum" a Octogesima adveniens*. São Paulo: Ediciones LTr, 1972.

Foyaca, Manuel, ed. *As enciclicas sociais*. Rio de Janeiro: Agir, 1967.

Marcuse, Herbert. *Soviet Marxism*. New York: Columbia University Press, 1958.

Ollman, Bertell. *Alienation*. Cambridge, Eng.: Cambridge University Press, 1971.

Owen, Roger, and B. Sutcliffe. *Studies in the Theory of Imperialism*. London: Longmans, 1972.

Robinson, Joan. *An Essay on Marxian Economics*. London: Macmillan, 1942.

Schumpeter, Joseph A. *Imperialism and Social Classes*. New York: Augustus M. Kelley, 1951 [1919].

Winks, Robin W., ed. *British Imperialism*. New York: Holt, Rinehart & Winston, 1963.

Winslow, E. M. *Pattern of Imperialism*. New York: Columbia University Press, 1948.

PART II
Research Methods

9.
Research Methods

The Research Methodology of Institutional Economics

Institutional economics consists of (1) a theory of economic progress, (2) a value theory, (3) a research methodology, and (4) empirical applications. Case studies and research in the frame of reference of institutional economics may take many forms. In fact, an
important consideration is that such studies not be forced into a
stylized mold. Despite this need for flexibility, which derives from
the nature of the institutional value theory itself, it is desirable to
try, in some degree, to indicate the nature of worthwhile studies in
the area of institutional economics.

There would seem to be three chief types of such studies: (1)
the study of the behavior pattern of an institution, (2), the study of
the working out of the institutional response to the appearance of a
new technology, and (3) the rationalization and formulation of a
policy proposal.

The Study of Institutional Behavior

The Problem
There are difficulties in identifying institutionalized behavior
norms. One can do justice (or half justice) to an institution's behavior only after living with the institution for a long time and observing its behavior under many circumstances. Yet those who have
lived with an institution long enough to have this sort of insight
should feel a degree of loyalty to the institution that would prevent
their being objectively caustic about much of what the institution
does. They should feel such a loyalty or they should not have remained with the organization. If they know enough about the institution to write about it, they will not—except in one case. But

denouements by insiders (or, more likely, former insiders who have had a falling-out with the institution) are more likely to reflect special pleadings or spleen than accurate reporting. Of course, one way that the scholar, working from the outside, may try to get at the truth is to obtain special pleadings from various of the parties involved and then to engage in judicious questioning and weighing (this was the method of the Ervin Committee of the United States Senate in studying the workings of the White House in 1973). In rare circumstances, conditions may make it feasible for the investigator to pursue an inquiry in such a reasonable manner; in most circumstances, this is not feasible. Meaningful study of cartel practices was made possible by the disclosures of the early years of World War II. Walton Hamilton's *Price and Price Policies* and George Stocking and Myron Watkins' *Cartels in Action* are models of what can be done under such special circumstances. Most of the time, however, it is simply impossible for the outsider-scholar to find out what is going on in the way of cartel-type practices in business.

Competent, muckraking reporting in the tradition of Ida Tarbell, Lincoln Steffens, and, more recently, Anthony Sampson in some degree fills the gap, and maybe professional economists should do more of this sort of thing.

Be the difficulties as they may, the study of the behavior patterns of institutions should be the meat and drink of economics (and of sociology and the other social sciences). Understanding the behavior patterns of institutions may be more helpful in the formulation of public policy for dealing with the nation's problems than can be the most assiduously constructed econometric model. Intelligent understanding of oil industry behavior norms and environmentalist behavior characteristics may well be the best basis for dealing with the energy problems of the 1970s, better than any amount of econometric model building which tries to forecast how much more wildcatting will occur if the industry's profit rate is allowed to rise 1 percent or if the price of gasoline or crude rises by some other percent.

An example of a behavior pattern that is, by now, pretty well documented concerns agriculture. During periods of falling and low agricultural prices, speakers for the industry, with a mighty voice, demand government assistance. In periods of rising and high prices, they are generally paragons of free private enterprise who want only one thing from the government: that it get out of the farmer's hair. Farming is not the only branch of the economy where this is true, although certain of the characteristics of agriculture seem to give this aspect of farmer and rancher behavior a high level of visibility.

Economists could well make more use of the insights of anthropology, sociology, psychology, and political science as they try to understand the behavior of economic institutions better. Analysis based on an oversimplified assumption that "the effort to maximize" profits or individual income can explain or motivate behavior may lead to wrong answers—even though "the effort to gain higher profits" is actually an important and highly institutionalized influence in the economy, one among many. There still remains the question as to just what the profit-seeking phenomenon is, how the profit-seeking influence works itself out, and how it interacts with other influences in the hands of "uneconomic man," who is the creature of his genes and, even more so, of his cultural and physical environment.[1]

How can we conduct research on the behavior norms of institutions, especially when we approach the problem without prior knowledge of the workings of the institution? As a preliminary, we can read as much as is available about the institution. Working, at least for a time, in the company or agency or industry, if feasible, will be helpful. Sample questionnaires may be used. However, the difficulties involved in preparing the questions, selecting the sample, extracting the responses, and evaluating them may well be considerable. Such activity is an art or a profession, or both, involving a knack of a very high order. And the questionnaire procedure should not be used unless we are prepared to take the difficulties seriously.

Interviewing members of the institution is an obvious, but not necessarily easy, procedure. Introductions to the "right" people may not come easily, and such people may or may not respond to a direct request for an interview. We can request permission from high-level officials to look at the books or to interview the personnel, although the chances are extremely good that an economist will be denied permission to look at accounts or records which are at all sensitive. An economist working for a congressional committee, or for a prestigious research organization such as Brookings or the National Bureau of Economic Research, may have better luck—or worse. It may well take a subpoena before the congressional committee can get access. The recipient of a substantial research grant may use the fact of the grant as leverage. But, after all is said and done, some people are just naturally better at this sort of bird-dogging than others.

It is a mystery to me how Wassily Leontief obtained access to corporate accounts in the early days of his work with input-output matrices. Perhaps the corporate realization that Leontief was not muckraking may have helped. But, when economists give adequate assurances to the corporation that they will not rake muck, they may also pretty well have gutted the usefulness of their research.

In any case, what is one looking for: indications of standardized behavior, indications that the institution will respond in some particular way in a given situation? The loan officer of a bank spontaneously reacts negatively when asked to make a loan to someone from a certain part of town. During a certain period, society's favorite cliché is "separate but equal"—the more separate and the less equal the better. Or we may find a setting where the members really choose to believe that "there is no such thing as a free lunch" and act accordingly. Some such behavior regularities may be of a type that can be picked up by regression analysis, but many are not—or are identified as well or better by direct observation.

At all events, the research worker uses ingenuity to identify standardized or customary behavior patterns and, perhaps, their consequences. Executives raise prices because others have raised prices (and they feel they are suckers if they do not), even though in the back of their minds they may not relish the resulting general pattern of rising prices. We can observe these mental processes in the boardroom or in conversation with the executives. They may even pound the table. Yet once such a process, with its built-in interactions, has commenced, it has an institutionalized character of its own: "onward and upward."

An Academic Department
I have had some experience with the workings of an economics department in an American university. My viewpoint is likely biased in various respects. Nevertheless, a description of some aspects of the behavior of such an institution may help clarify the nature of some of the issues involved. Let me address myself particularly to the manner in which the program of the undergraduate economics

major is handled by such an institution. I allege that the behavior pattern which I am about to describe has prevailed in economics departments since the early 1930s—and probably was typical even before that. It is not unique to any particular university or decade.

In general, the program of an undergraduate major is designed to prepare the student to be a graduate major rather than a good citizen who is reasonably knowledgeable of desirable economic policies. It does not matter that most students are not going on to graduate school and that most of what is important in economics is independent of calculus and matrix algebra, constant coefficients and multiequation models. The highly esoteric price theory and national income theory courses frequently required as a prerequisite to other advanced courses involve levels of mathematical and geometric sophistication which are by no means necessary to make the worthwhile points. Such courses do provide useful methodology, however, if one is going on to graduate theory courses. As a result, the undergraduate major with a real social science concern for society and an abhorrence for artificial mathematical models avoids economics like the plague.

A passage from Kenneth Boulding deserves quotation:

> It is a sad commentary on the American scene in economics that the only really indigenous American school of economists, the institutionalists, represented for instance by John R. Commons at Wisconsin, left only a handful of descendants. I would not be surprised if the majority of graduate students studying economics in American universities do not even know the names of the great American empiricists and institutionalists of the past. It is fashionable indeed to decry the history of thought as a luxury in these days of econometrics, to proclaim that it is of no greater significance than, shall we say, the history of mathematics. This attitude it seems to me is disastrous, for it limits the graduate student to the fashions of the present and easily leads him into a tight little intellectual box from which there is no escape. The successes of economics should not blind us to the fact that its subject matter is a system far more complex than the systems which are studied by the natural scientists, for instance, and we must recognize that our most elegant models can be no more than the crudest of first approximations of the complex reality of the systems which they purport to represent. If we educate out of our students that almost bodily sense of what the real world is like even though we may see it through a glass darkly, a trait which was so characteristic of the great economists of the past, something of supreme value will be lost. Our graduate schools may easily be producing a good deal of the

"trained incapacity" which Veblen saw being produced in his day, and this is a negative commodity unfortunately with a very high price.[2]

One of the stranger aspects of this process is the role of the younger faculty members in insisting on increasing the requirements involving the more abstruse theory at both the undergraduate and the graduate levels. The more interesting aspect of this operation is not the ability of the young to wield power in such decision making but, at least in economics, their insistence on making the degree program standardized, esoteric, highly mathematical and theoretical (just like it was back at that high-grade graduate school they came from), and largely sterile. Why should the young act this way? Young faculty members are frequently very liberal in their attitudes on social behavior and public issues and in their eagerness to unhorse the full professors. It is the old who are supposed to be conservative.

I believe I even detect a tendency for the junior members of other social science faculties, such as political science and sociology, to advocate the strait-jacketing of degree programs, the demanding of "more specific" course requirements, and the requiring of more standardized theory. Some political scientists even seem to think they can build a theoretical model identifying "the national interest."

The attitude of the young in insisting on the requirement of some pretty sterile theory in degree programs may be explained somewhat as follows. Young Ph.D.s have a major stake in the theory and methodology to which they were exposed as they struggled for their Ph.D. We have a vested interest in what we know—and we *know* dogmatically so young. So, young Ph.D.s seem to react by believing everybody else should undergo an initiation just as painful and involving the same hazing. Also, for their own self-respect, they have an interest in proving that all the stuff they know is not useless. So, we may have a situation where to some degree it is stodgy oldsters who, these days, are the chief defenders of a liberal curriculum—a curriculum that will permit the student a respectable range of experimentation in searching out problem areas that really seem important and in developing methods of study appropriate to the problem. A less complimentary explanation of the oldsters' behavior is that they do not understand the new, sophisticated methodology and call down a plague on anything new.

Probably a core of knowledge on which to test the apprentice has to be isolated, and it has to be a core on which there is general agreement among the experts in the field. They have to agree that a problem is important and legitimate, and they also have to agree on the analytical method and the solution if the question is to be a legitimate one, say, on a nationwide, professional qualification examination. Otherwise, it will not be possible to grade the questions in a comprehensive (not course) examination covering a field or even possible to make up the examination. (This means that there is difficulty in including challenging questions on new developments.)

The result is that tests controlling professional accreditation are oriented to a lowest common denominator of the standardized, theoretical, difficult material in a field. Applicants who have mastered the traditional core of knowledge will be more likely to get accredited than will imaginative experimenters. In fact, the latter may well have already dropped out of the program because they could not stomach some of the required courses. This should not be a problem with the undergraduate economics degree, which should not be a professional degree anyway.

(Let me hasten to add that this situation is frequently used by students who "can't get organized" and who "disliked every course they ever took" to justify their chronic inability to get anything done. Nonconformity is not necessarily evidence of genius any more than it is evidence of stupidity.)

Economists should concern themselves with problem solving, and they frequently do. In so doing, as creatures of their own institutional background, they are likely to insist on using familiar tools. This is only natural: we cannot solve problems with unfamiliar tools. In this age, economists frequently assume constant propensities and elasticities and pure competition, and they often use price theory, national income theory, linear programming, and multiequation econometric models. Some of them rise above these models to use a little common sense when the model obviously gives wrong answers, some do not. Some never come to grips with a real problem in their whole professional careers. Others deal with real problems in utterly unreal ways. And frequently it is difficult to tell whether the model is really giving a wrong answer or not. Some, like Everett Hagen, become sufficiently disillusioned with the usefulness of the economic models to attempt to reformulate their approach in terms of a special aspect of the institutional theory, such as the importance of the role of outcast minorities in performing the entrepreneurial function. Some, like Vilfredo Pareto, completely shift over to sociology but take their analytical methods with them, and economics' gain is sociology's loss. Frequently, however, the pedestrian economists go on applying price theory and national income theory and production theory in unimaginative ways to problems those tools cannot solve. This is the nub of what has been wrong with much of the advice on economic development which has been given to underdeveloped countries in the post–World War II period and with much of the advice on policy which the Council of Economic Advisers has given the president in recent decades.

Leonard Goodwin and Joseph Tu comment: "What stands in the way of carrying out research that meets traditional standards of quality while bearing upon significant public issues? . . . The professional training one receives tends to shape what one perceives to be interesting and useful research topics. Topics may be ignored because they do not come within the angle of vision of traditionally trained social scientists rather than because the topics are fundamentally useless or uninteresting."[3]

The Study of the Technology-Institutions Interrelation

The Problem

A full case study in the field of institutional theory might involve (1) identification of a major technological change, (2) discussion of the reaction of those controlling the prevailing institutional arrangements as they become aware of the possible implications of the new technological development (this is the initial reaction to the technological imperatives), (3) discussion of the process by which the new technology may have been allowed to become operational or of the influences that may have frustrated its use, and (4) identification of the institutional changes that occur as a result of the introduction of the new technology. If the introduction of the new technology aborts in step 3, there is no step 4.

The information needed for conducting such studies is hard to come by. The identification of technological change and the appreciation of its significance in the context of the general sweep of the history of technology are not tasks for which economists are particularly well qualified. Nevertheless, major technological changes have such an impact that at least a particularly important discovery may be fairly readily identified: the internal-combustion engine or the vacuum tube, for example. And, with a particular technology in mind, economists should be able to learn enough about it from the scientific and technological literature and from history of science material so that they will not "accidentally" reveal themselves as ignoramuses when they study its economic significance.

The catalog, in table 9–1, of some of the major inventions of recent decades may help give some feel for the starting point in this process. And most of us, after a little meditation, can identify ways in which various of these inventions have modified institutions, affected our lives, and influenced economic attitudes. This list of inventions, as well as an allegation as to the country where the basic research occurred, has been prepared by Arthur Ross.

Understanding the technology as technology calls for a real effort on the part of economists. They should not assume away the uniqueness of each invention by such devices as the concept of induced technical change of Charles Kennedy, Paul Samuelson, Robert Solow, and Jan Tinbergen. Especially, the device frequently used in neoclassical growth models, which involves simply assuming that technology accumulates at a constant percentage growth rate, does not get hold of much of what matters in reality.

Next, ascertaining and understanding the reaction of the prevailing institutions as their members become aware of the possible implications of the new technological development involve the range of problems already discussed in connection with the basic institutional behavior problem.

Discussion of the process by which the new technology is allowed to become operational (if institutional rigidities do not frustrate its use) goes beyond the static issue as to what the behavior norms of an institution are at a given time. Involved is the sensitive and important question of technology-institutions interaction. Adaptation (innovation) requires permissiveness on the part of the institution; it will result in modification of the behavior norms of the institution (the next step), and all this will influence further technical progress and further modification of the behavior norms of other institutions. The discussion of the influences proper that effect the innovation, again, involves penetration by the investigator of the inner workings of the institution. However, in this case, the difficulties involved in getting the facts and identifying the influences may be ameliorated by the fact that, after the event, the successful innovator may like to talk. This is a starting point, even though some double checking is probably in order. At least one has

Table 9-1. Selected Inventions and Technology Imported into the United States

Austria
Oxygen steel making

Belgium
Prestressed concrete
Solvay process

Czechoslovakia
Soft contact lenses

France
Polyacrylamides
Radial tires
Rayon-cellophane

Germany
Atomic fission
Continuous casting of steel
Cryogenic air distillation
Electrodialysis
Inertial guidance
Liquid and solid propellant rocketry
Methacrylate resins
Microporous filter membranes
Nitrogen fixation
Polyacrylonitrile (Orlon)
Polybutadiene rubbers
Polystyrene
Polyurethanes
Rocket technology
Synthetic rubber polymers
Wacker process for acetic anhydride
Wacker process for acetylaldehyde
Wankel engine

Hungary
Gas-filled lamp bulbs
Holography

Japan
Contact lenses
Polyvinyl alcohol textiles
Tantalum electrodes for chlorine cells
Tunnel diode amplifier

Netherlands
Electron microscope

Sweden
Dynamite

Switzerland
DDT

United Kingdom
Dacron (Terylene)
Float glass process
Graphite fibers
Ion exchange resins
Radar
Vertical take-off aircraft (VTOL)

U.S.S.R.
Automated bridging
Ion exchange membranes

France–Israel–Italy
Marine surface-to-surface missiles

Germany–France–United Kingdom
Mobile, low-altitude air defense
  systems

Germany–Italy–United Kingdom
Polyethylene
Polypropylene

Germany–Netherlands–Switzerland
Nylon 6

Germany–United Kingdom
Jet-powered aircraft

Source: Arthur Ross, "International Investment: A Two-Way Street," *Columbia Journal of World Business* 8 (Spring 1973): 11.

an allegation to check. This is not always the case in connection with the identification of the static behavior norms of an institution, especially when one of those norms is on the border line of legality.

Identification of the institutional changes and the new institutions that come into being as a result of the new technology is likely to involve a mixture of some pretty obvious developments with others where the cause and effect relation, although important, may not be quite so obvious. It may also involve situations where those concerned have a real interest in suppressing awareness of the connection. The effects of new technology on the ecology are an example of the latter influence. On the other hand, the Wilderness Society and the Sierra Club would be institutions with certain behavior norms called into being by the influence of technical change on the ecology.

Such a case study of the inception and implications of a bit of technical innovation can make a coherent and worthwhile research project. But, of course, any one such innovation is only an incident in the ongoing sweep of all such happenings as they accumulate to make history.

In spite of the difficulties, the effort to develop a satisfactory methodology for institutional economics (and for economics in general) needs to be made. No one of the studies in the chapters which follow will be an entirely satisfactory example of the genre, but the studies will at least illustrate something of what is involved in the effort to understand economic process.

The When and Where of the Industrial Revolution
The Industrial Revolution itself may be looked upon as such a case study. The major technological advances that were prime movers in connection with the Industrial Revolution, which occurred in northwestern Europe in the mid eighteenth to mid nineteenth centuries, were, in the background, gunpowder and printing, perhaps brought by the Mongols from China, arabic numerals and the concept of zero, paper brought from China via the Arabs, spectacles, the casting of iron, the astrolabe and the magnetic compass, the mechanical clock, and Viking ships with keels and the sternpost rudder capable of sailing the open ocean. Major advances in the foreground were Newton's physics, Darby's coke, Watt's steam engine, and the major inventions in spinning and weaving of

the eighteenth century, beginning with John Kay's flying shuttle in 1733.[4]

These inventions were not all made in northern England and southern Scotland, but they were put together into the Industrial Revolution there. Why there, instead of somewhere else? Why then, instead of some other time? An attempt to answer requires backtracking in history to explain why English institutions were less resistant to change than were the institutions of other areas which were at least as technically advanced as England in, say, the fifteenth century.

The older civilizations which were the prime repositories of the technological knowledge of the world in the fifteenth century— Italy, Byzantium, Arab Spain, China, Egypt—were operating under the dead hand of powerful ancient institutionalized constraints: the Catholic church in Italy, the icons in Byzantium (until the 1450s), the Koran around half the Mediterranean, the system of writing in China, the stirrings of the Inquisition in Spain.

England, as a frontier region which had been part of the Roman Empire (and had had fairly free access to the technology of the civilized ancient world), had not evolved into a highly stylized culture, set in its ways, by the fifteenth century. "A frontier is a great breeder of ingenuity."[5] And the Protestant Reformation of the sixteenth century, even more, freed northwestern Europe in general and England in particular from the institutionalized behavior patterns, fortified by the Inquisition, that were stymieing development in southern Europe.

England (thanks to one of the provisions of the Magna Charta) was also, by the later Middle Ages, one of the largest areas in the world that was substantially free of trade barriers. And in the fifteen hundreds the English Merchants of the Staple had succeeded in wresting control of England's trade from the German merchants of the Hanseatic League. England was also taking positive measures to attract technical knowledge by overtly hiring foreign artisans. Spain and France were rejecting skilled labor; England was attracting it—as public policy. And English international trade barriers featured an export tariff on raw wool—to encourage woolen textile manufacture in England rather than to try to encourage domestic woolen textile manufacture with an import tariff on woolen textiles. Then, too, during the period from 1500 to 1750, the enclosure movement freed a substantial labor supply for work in the factories to be. (Or did it? Apparently there is disagreement among economic historians on this point.)

At all events, by the eighteenth century English industry was receptive to the implementation of new technology in the textile industry. It was not hidebound in its practices. One may add that the humidity of Manchester (a raw-material resource) helped: it helps to have raw materials and natural conditions peculiarly appropriate to the use of the current bit of new technological development. Readily available coal and iron ore were also important. Ireland is probably just as humid as the region around Manchester, but Scotland and England had had more institutional shake-up than had Ireland, and they had coal, and they were more amenable to the assimilation of the new textile industry technology. Ireland was freezing its institutional order in a defense of Catholicism.

The institutions that evolved to permit the effective use of the technology of the Industrial Revolution were (1) the corporate form of business organization, allowing limited liability on the part of the owners and consequently the tapping of the "savings" of large numbers of people, (2) the factory system, a not unmixed blessing,[6] (3) commercial banking and the power to create money against fractional reserves, and (4) the conceptions of free competition and laissez faire (keep the government out of business) as the appropriate machinery for managing and running the economy. The (5) profit motive itself may be visualized as an institutionalized arrangement that acquired its present role and meaning in influencing the behavior of people as a by-product of the pressures and needs created by the technological developments of the Industrial Revolution. The most important new phenomenon of all, however, was probably (6) the industrial city, with its transportation problems, its ghettos, and its filth.

Institutional arrangements that were forced into retirement included the guild system and the putting-out system. Cottage industry and the rural farmer-artisan lost importance. By-employments became less available to country dwellers. And the nature of family life changed drastically as the worker—often a child—instead of being employed at home or nearby, customarily left home for the whole day to work in the factory. Family and home life were substantially modified. The factory, an institution quite apart from the home, became a major part of life. Its smoke and its great fires and its grime and din produced a very different sort of worker—

different from the farmer and the artisan. And the twelve, four-
teen, and sixteen hours a day passed in its sordid confines under-
lined the impact of the change.

The rise of the industrialists in England between 1750 and
1850 was strenuously resisted by the land-based nobility. One manifestation of this contest between the entrenched interests of the
landlords (the nobility) and the rising industrial class was the
struggle over the repeal of the corn laws, tariffs protecting British-
grown grain from the competition of imported grain. The industrialists wanted cheap imported grain to feed their workers so they
could pay them less (as Ricardo assured them would be possible if
they could get the tariffs on grain repealed). The landlords resisted
the loss of their tariff protection with tenacity and perseverance.
However, in the 1840s they lost the battle, and the industrialists,
who were adapting to and using the new technology, came to dominate England.

"So capitalism emerged from the working of the handicraft
system, through the increased scale and efficiency of technology."[7]
This development occurred in spite of the opposition of the nobility, resistance which, however, was not remotely comparable to
the resistance offered by the church and the Inquisition in southern Europe.

The Rationalization and Formulation of a Policy Proposal

Its Relation to Value Theory

Individuals generate ideas as to what is desirable policy as a
by-product of the influences described in the theory of economic
progress and the value theory of institutional economics. A recom-
mendation that the depletion allowance in connection with oil production be discontinued would be an example of a policy proposal,
and various self-correcting value judgments would provide the
basis for making the proposal.

The Justification of the Details

Circumstances alter cases. An initial proposal by an academic
and/or an idealist may well argue general ideas, whereas the text
of a bill before a legislative body needs to involve far greater precision in wording and far greater thoughtfulness with regard to the
operational workableness of the proposal, especially in terms of

the behavior norms of the institutions being set up. The job guarantee proposal presented in chapter 17 is an example of an initial proposal in connection with which a good deal of the detail has been worked out. At the same time, much reworking would need to be done before the proposal would be in a form suitable for congressional action.

The Philosophical Basis

Case studies may be especially oriented to policy proposals. Individuals, in the context of their prevailing values, observe a problem and make a proposal for dealing with it.

It should be noted that, unlike many other economic theories, institutional theory does not, in general, provide the analytical framework for making a definitive judgment as to the desirability of a particular policy. National income theory may provide a basis for saying, in certain circumstances, that government expenditures should be increased. Price theory may provide a basis for saying that monopoly is undesirable. An individual who is an institutionalist in economic outlook may endorse the findings of price theory or national income theory in these regards.

The role of institutionalism is to provide a frame of reference for understanding what is going on. It does not provide the logic for proving the validity of solutions. But it does provide a frame of reference that encourages us to think in terms of change and improvement, and it does indicate the nature of the ongoing processes.

Consequently, the policy proposals made later in this book are not to be thought of as having their validity proven by some logical interrelations hidden away in the logician's black box of institutional model building. There is no such black box, no logical model capable of grinding out unique and definitive solutions.

On the basis of our currently held values, we make judgments about policy proposals. We endorse policies publicly and perhaps get supporters. We and others test our proposals in the technology arena. Do they work to our satisfaction or to society's satisfaction? We back and fill in a process of self-correcting value judgments, as does society, as we reappraise our position in light of results and in the context of our perhaps changing values. And society, influenced by all this, is the ongoing arbiter of the process, working through the institutions which make it up and which are themselves being changed in the process.

Evaluation

Institutionalism alleges that it is useful for economists to assemble data on the manner in which economic institutions behave and on the manner in which technology and institutions interact, as well as on the substance of policy issues. The whys and wherefores of actual behavior do matter.

NOTES

1. Wilbert E. Moore, *Order and Change* (New York: Wiley, 1967), pp. 118-133.
2. Kenneth E. Boulding, *Economics as a Science* (New York: McGraw-Hill, 1970), p. 156.
3. Leonard Goodwin and Joseph Tu, "The Social Psychological Basis for Public Acceptance of the Social Security System," *American Psychologist* 30 (September 1975): 875.
4. See C. E. Ayres, *The Theory of Economic Progress* (Chapel Hill: University of North Carolina Press, 1944), chap. 7; see also A. E. Musson, ed., *Science, Technology, and Economic Growth in the Eighteenth Century* (London: Methuen, 1972), especially p. 40; and Joseph Needham, *The Grand Titration: Science and Society in East and West* (Toronto: University of Toronto Press, 1969).
5. C. E. Ayres, *The Industrial Economy* (Boston: Houghton Mifflin, 1952), p. 74.
6. As Charles Dickens, in *Martin Chuzzlewit*, says: "Bethink yourselves . . . that there are scores of thousands breathing now, and breathing thick with painful toil, who . . . have never lived at all, nor had a chance of life. Go ye . . . teachers of content and honest pride, into the mine, the mill, the forge, the squalid depths of deepest ignorance, and uttermost abyss of man's neglect, and say can any hopeful plant spring up in air so foul that it extinguishes the soul's bright torch as fast as it is kindled." See also John Stuart Mill: "It is questionable if all the mechanical inventions yet made have lightened the day's toil of any human being." In *Principles of Political Economy*, 6th ed., new impression (London: Longmans, Green, 1904 [1848], p. 455.
7. Thorstein Veblen, *The Instinct of Workmanship* (New York: Augustus M. Kelley, 1964 [1914]), p. 282.

ADDITIONAL READINGS

Allen, Francis R. *Social-Cultural Dynamics*. New York: Macmillan, 1971.
Ayres, C. E. *Divine Right of Capital*. Boston: Houghton Mifflin, 1946.

Barnes, Harry Elmer. *An Economic History of the Western World*. New York: Harcourt, Brace, 1935.

Barzun, Jacques, and Henry F. Graff. *The Modern Researcher*. New York: Harcourt, Brace, & World, 1957.

Chapin, Francis Stuart. *Cultural Change*. New York: Century, 1928.

Goode, William J., and Paul K. Hatt. *Methods in Social Research*. New York: McGraw-Hill, 1952.

Hamilton, Walton H. *Price and Price Policies*. New York: McGraw-Hill, 1938.

A Manual of Style. 12th ed. Chicago: University of Chicago Press, 1969 [1906].

Polanyi, Karl. *The Great Transformation*. Boston: Beacon, 1957 [1944].

Rostow, Walt W. *How It All Began*. New York: McGraw-Hill, 1975.

Stocking, George W., and Myron Watkins. *Cartels in Action*. New York: Twentieth Century Fund, 1946.

Toynbee, Arnold. *Lectures on the Industrial Revolution of the Eighteenth Century in England*. 2d ed. London: Rivingtons, 1887 [1884].

Turabian, Kate L. *A Manual for Writers of Term Papers, Theses, and Dissertations*. 3d ed., rev. Chicago: University of Chicago Press, 1967 [1955].

United States, Government Printing Office. *Style Manual*. Rev. ed. Washington, D.C.: Government Printing Office, 1959.

PART III
Case Studies and Policy

10.
The Institution of Property

ALTHOUGH it has been customary to cite the Marxist appreciation of the importance of institutions ("relations of production," in the Marxist jargon) and the role they play in influencing the economy, in such a listing typically the only institution actually cited will be that of property. It is, according to the Marxists, the institution of private property rights with respect to capital that gives the capitalists the leverage to extract surplus value from the workers, who are left with only subsistence or the "customary minimum" as a reward for their efforts as they sell the only thing they have to offer—perishable labor time.

Certainly this institution, property rights, has played an important role in society. It is not necessary to claim that it is either the only or even the primary institution before granting it much importance.

What is not true is that property rights are unique. It is not true that the expression "ownership of property" is enough to clearly define the behavior norms of the institution or of the people involved: the property owners. Property in the sense of land, subsoil, and other things has existed since the beginning of time, and humans and other animals capable of asserting themselves in this context have staked claims on property with varying degrees of success. Certainly property exists and norms describing control over it exist even in socialist societies. On another extreme, dogs or snakes or rats may implement a proprietary claim to a bit of area, even though a person wishing to evict them may wave a copy of a title deed.

Types of Property Claims

Communism

A group of people (a tribe, or a clan, or an extended family) may occupy an area of land and defend it with more or less success against trespassers. The use of the land may be controlled by the group as a whole by some decision-making process that is more or less democratic, more or less spontaneous consensus, or more or less autocratic. The members may have varying degrees of independence or autonomy in consenting regarding what their individual roles in the use of the property may be.

Probably typically in communities that have approximated the communistic form of organization, small personal objects have been recognized as the property of individuals. Pasture, woodland, village commons, and perhaps a source of water may be used freely by all. The agricultural land may be assigned in some sort of usufruct tenure to individuals. (They may keep the plot during such time as they continue to farm it effectively, or it may revert to the community on the death of the possessor. In such arrangements, the possessor typically cannot "sell" the plot. But, possibly, she or he may be able to "rent" it out.) The agricultural land may also be farmed in common, with chores assigned or agreed upon, in various possible arrangements, including more or less equal shares or shares distributed on the basis of need.

Feudal Tenure

In a system of feudal tenure, some autocrat, king or whatnot, is conceived as owning all the land of the country. Perhaps the mythology is that the sovereign was endowed with the property rights by some divinity (or by long tradition). The monarch then parcels out the right to use of the land to nobles, who in turn parcel out plots to serfs. In exchange, the nobles owe services and taxes and royalty fifths, eighths, or tenths to the king. And the serfs owe shares and services, and maybe their lives as well, to the lords.

In such a system, typically, neither lords nor serfs can convey to third parties their interest in the land. The land may revert (if duties are not performed) from serf to lord and from lord to sovereign, and the sovereign or the lord could then dole out the land and its corresponding rights and duties to somebody else.

The Freehold (Fee Simple)

Then there is the sort of property right that is generally thought of as being *the* system of private property, especially in the United States—as though the Lord on high had ordained a certain set of rules or norms describing the eternal nature of property rights.

One of the major steps in the transition from the system of feudal tenure to the freehold (or fee simple) system of tenure was taken at the time of the Restoration in England in 1660. John Commons has described this development:

> Finally, the parliament of 1660, controlled by the landlords, proceeded to abolish the military tenures, altogether without compensation to the King, but they substituted in lieu thereof, a perpetual hereditary excise on the drink of the people. . . .
>
> Indeed the royalist tenants of the Restoration, by this act of Parliament, truly created modern landed property, for, by commuting the sovereign's arbitrary rentals into pecuniary taxes they resolved themselves from tenants into owners, and gave to themselves that "sole and despotic dominion" over external things which constitutes both sovereignty and property.
>
> Thus the right of private property in land emerged from the struggle of 450 years between the sovereign as landlord and his vassals as tenants, over the rental value of land. The collective bargaining over rents, begun with Magna Carta in 1215 and ending with the Restoration and a limited monarchy in 1660, transferred dominion from the will of the sovereign to the will of the tenant, by the simple device of making fixed and certain, in terms of money, instead of arbitrary in terms of commodities and services, the rents owed by the tenant to the monarch. Private property emerged from the rent bargain carried on collectively in terms of money between the supreme landlord, the King, and his tenants. The duty to pay definite taxes in cash, determined collectively by monarch and the representatives of the taxpayers, was substituted for the indefinite duty to pay rent in commodities and services, determined individually by the chief landlord. As long as the King could arbitrarily fix rents, whether in services or money, he was truly the owner as well as the sovereign. When the rents were fixed collectively in cash, he became only the sovereign and his tenants became the owners.[1]

In the case of the freehold title, the property owners have complete authority over the property—more or less. They can use and abuse it as they see fit, prohibit trespass, and profit from the sale of its products. However, these powers are subject, in some degree, to the right of society to interpose to abate a nuisance. Perhaps the burning of garbage in such a way that the smoke passes into a neighbor's living room would be the basis for some abatement of nuisance procedures.

Property owners take as their own accretions in land values, including those that may be due to the activities and general progress of the community—for example, the proximity of a new highway may well raise land values.

In the United States, and fairly generally in common-law countries (but with exceptions), the surface owners usually own the subsoil, meaning that the minerals in the ground under their property are theirs to sell. In the civil-law (Code Napoleon) countries, and this would include southern Europe and much of Africa and Latin America, the surface owners usually do not own the subsoil. Ownership of minerals is reserved by the state, which may mine the minerals itself or give the right to exploit them to private interests other than the surface owners in the form of concessions.

Actually, society generally reserves certain rights with respect to property. And the power of the property owners is not as exclusive as the foregoing might suggest. There is the already mentioned power of intervening to abate a nuisance. This is an exercise of the state's police power.

Typically, the government can tax the land and set the tax rates. And the existence of the taxing power raises the question of tax rates becoming so high as to be confiscatory. Such taxing policy by the government might occasion, and generally does, considerable indignation on the part of property owners (as well as the possibility of international complications if foreigners are involved), but, basically, one has to say that a government has the power to impose confiscatory taxes if it chooses. However, it may deny itself this power by virtue of the manner in which it words its constitution. Also, a government that confiscates property may pay for its temerity shortly thereafter if the dispossessed property owners succeed in defeating the government in the next election or overthrowing it by revolution.

Governments typically avail themselves of the right of eminent domain, expropriating private property for public purposes, contingent on the payment of a more or less reasonable compensation, the amount of which is fixed by the state. Land needed for transportation right-of-way or for public buildings is frequently taken away from private-property owners in this way. Also, abandoned land typically reverts to the state.

Still and all, allowing for the rights reserved to society, property owners typically visualize the property as being theirs, to do with as they choose.

What is the source of such a right or such a claim on property? The above brief history of the evolution of property rights in England does not dispose of the basic question. A present owner may have acquired property by purchase or inheritance but, way back in the beginning, what was the source of the ownership claim of the original owner? The answer is neither simple nor unambiguous, nor is there just one answer. On the contrary, there are many possible explanations or theories as to the basis for the institution of private property. Some of the theories are the occupation theory, the natural rights theory, the labor theory, the social welfare theory, the social expediency theory, and the institutional theory.

Something of the nature of the philosophical problem is revealed by this poem by Carl Sandburg, which runs in part:

"Get off this estate."
"What for?"
"Because it's mine."
"Where did you get it?"
"From my father."
"And where did he get it?"
"From his father."
"And where did he get it?"
"He fought for it."
"Well, I'll fight you for it."[2]

Theories as to the Basis for Freehold
Conceiving that the essence of the freehold is more or less complete control by the owner of the property, we ask what is the philosophical basis for such control. What is the logic of the legitimation of the owner's rights?

The occupation theory: This theory alleges, rather simply, that whoever occupies the property first is thereby the owner and is endowed with freehold-type rights with respect to the land. The theory does not explain why freehold-type rights are exactly what they are but, in general, neither do the other theories.

Another difficulty with the occupation theory involves the problem of justifying how much area one individual can reasonably occupy. The concept of effective occupancy is most imprecise.

The area that one individual can actually stand on at any given time, or even lie on, or farm, is rather limited.

The natural rights theory: It is not entirely clear that the natural rights theory is essentially different from the occupation theory—except in terms of the stage in the process where the explanation starts. The natural rights theory involves observing that in fact at a given time people (owners) are exerting freehold-type powers over property and then goes on to say that every situation which exists naturally is right and should (must) prevail. "Whatever is, is right." This then is the simplest form of natural-law concept.

The labor theory: The labor theory with relation to property rights should not be confused with the Marxist (or Ricardian) labor theory of value. The labor theory as to the origin of freehold property rights may be attributed to John Locke:

> . . . it is very clear that God, as King David says (Psalm 115.16), "has given the earth to the children of men," given it to mankind in common. But, this being supposed, it seems to some a very great difficulty how any one should ever come to have property in anything. . . .
>
> Though the earth and all inferior creatures be common to all men, yet every man has a "property" in his own "person." This nobody has any right to but himself. The "labour" of his body and the "work" of his hands, we may say, are properly his. Whatsoever, then, he removes out of the state that Nature hath provided and left it in, he hath mixed his labour with it, and joined to it something that is his own, and thereby makes it his property. It being by him removed from the common state Nature placed it in, it hath by this labour something annexed to it that excludes the common right of other men. For this "labour" being the unquestionable property of the labourer, no man but he can have a right to what that is once joined to, at least where there is enough, and as good left in common for others. . . .
>
> Though the water running in the fountain be every one's, yet who can doubt but that in the pitcher is his only who drew it out?
>
> But the chief matter of property being now not the fruits of the earth and the beasts that subsist on it, but the earth itself, as that which takes in and carries with it all the rest, I think it is plain that property in that too is acquired as the former. As much land as a man tills, plants, improves, cultivates, and can use the product of, so much is his property.[3]

So, in this Lockean theory, it is the fact that individuals have worked land which vests them with freehold-type property rights. This theory is also very similar to the occupation theory. But, perhaps, one can say that it goes a little further. There may well be a meaningful difference between occupation (by force or by physical presence) and effective working of the land. Also, Locke says there must remain idle land for others to appropriate.

Nevertheless, this labor theory leaves some of the same questions as does the occupation theory. It does not explain the details of the rights that go with the freehold system of tenure, and it does not effectively explain the criteria for determining how much land one individual can appropriate in this way.

The social welfare theory: This theory alleges that some such system as freehold tenure is necessary for the general welfare, but it leaves unanswered the question as to just how particular people got their claims on property in the first place. And some statements specifically allege that such a system is the appropriate one for maximizing the general welfare. How one might demonstrate this maximization solution mathematically is not clear, but then the solution of sophisticated maximization problems has acquired vogue only since World War II. In the seventeenth and eighteenth centuries, when much of the theorizing about property rights was going on, the allegation about the maximization effect was little more than pure assertion—or appeal to intuitive reasonableness.

The social expediency theory: It has been said that this is the only theory that can justify the institution of freehold property rights in its present form. The theory defends property rights on the ground that they are the best device that society has yet been able to develop as a means of relating the individual to property (wealth) in a manner calculated to contribute effectively to an increase in that wealth.

It should be noted that a theory stated in this form cannot be used to defend the inviolability or sacrosanct nature of the institution of property in its present form.

The institutional theory: In fact, the expediency theory has considerable affinity with the institutional theory. The chief difference, perhaps, is that the expediency theory appears to play the role of justification, whereas the institutional theory claims merely to play the role of explanation.

In the institutional explanation, the system of freehold property rights evolved out of the feudal tenure system as a by-product of the pressures of evolving technology. The process of change was conditioned by the rest of the institutional setting of those times and was guided by people making value judgments in the context of the then prevailing influences.

So, the freehold system of land tenure should be looked on as a stage in an evolving process in which what was immediately involved was modification of feudal arrangements under the pressures of the commercial and industrial revolutions.

One cannot explain the rationale of a system which has sprung full-blown from a state of nature. There it is—what more can one say? One attempts in practice also only the much more modest task of explaining how a prevailing system evolved from the conditions which preceded it. And one should probably presume the existence of influences that will almost certainly result in further changes.

In particular, the system of feudal tenure, in which the lords' rights were dependent on the caprice of kings and the serfs' rights were dependent on the caprice of lords, was not conducive to the accumulation of capital equipment and the development of manufacturing in the towns. The willingness, on the part of the new capitalist class, to engage in the accumulation necessary for the developing manufacturing system required property rights titles that seemed to give protection against arbitrary loss at the whim of kings and nobles and their men-at-arms.

We might be interested in studying in much greater detail the intricacies of the evolution of feudal tenure into freehold property holding. Or we might be interested in trying to identify the influences which led from various ancient systems of property rights to the feudal tenure system. Or we might be interested in determining whether even earlier more or less communistic systems existed which evolved for one reason or another into the various systems of Egypt, Mesopotamia, Greece, and Rome. Or we may observe how the more or less communistic systems of pre-Spanish Mexico and Peru were completely jolted by the sudden imposition of the legal norms with respect to property rights of Spain and the Catholic church.

The freehold system of property rights is not to be explained as an exercise in rational decision making as a result of which the system may be either justified or accounted for. It is, rather, to be understood—as much as possible—in historical perspective.

Comments about Property Rights

Some miscellaneous comments about property rights, especially freehold property rights, may help clear the air a bit with regard to the nature of the institution we are actually living with at the moment.

Property owners are dependent both upon society and its police power to protect their property rights and upon the law to adjudicate disputes (of which there are many).

Rights may be (or have been) held in many different kinds of property, tangible and intangible: land, people, buildings, more or less movable objects, especially clothing, food, household equipment, and jewelry (tangible personal property), stocks and bonds (intangible personal property), contract rights, rights in patents and copyrights, vested interests (in a certain scenic view, in the "quality" of the neighborhood, in a given property tax rate—matters can get pretty sticky here), and all sorts of conditional equities dependent on a fantastic range of possibilities and on human imagination.

It may be remembered that the United States Declaration of Independence spoke of "life, liberty, and the pursuit of happiness," not "life, liberty, and property."

Property rights are among the most vulnerable of rights. They involve a procedure for freezing out much of the human race from the enjoyment or the use of much of the natural endowment of the earth. Given the fragility of the rights involved, it may behoove property owners to be reasonably circumspect in pressing their claims to the last possible iota of special privilege. It may also well behoove them not to be too obstreperous in avoiding taxes—Proposition 13 in California and other tax avoidance measures of a similar sort during the late 1970s probably enjoyed their success more because of discontent with bureaucrats and taxes in general than because of any commonly held feeling that property owners are among the more meritorious recipients of tax relief.

NOTES

1. John R. Commons, *The Legal Foundations of Capitalism* (Madison: University of Wisconsin Press, 1968 [1924]), pp. 219–221.
2. Carl Sandburg, *The People, Yes* (New York: Harcourt, Brace, 1936), p. 75.
3. John Locke, "An Essay Concerning the True Original Extent and End of Civil Government," chap. 5, "Of Property," in *Great Books of the Western World*, vol. 35: *Locke, Berkeley, Hume* (Chicago: Encyclopaedia Britannica, 1952 [1690]), pp. 30–31.

ADDITIONAL READINGS

Dixon, Russell. *Economic Institutions and Cultural Change*. New York: McGraw-Hill, 1941.

Krueger, Robert O. "Corporate Property and Corporate Responsibility." Ph.D. dissertation, University of Texas at Austin, 1967.

Lafargue, Paul. *The Evolution of Property from Savagery to Civilization*. Chicago: Kerr, ca. 1905.

Leipziger, Danny M. *Seabed Mineral Resources and the Economic Interests of Developing Countries*. Cambridge, Mass.: Ballinger, 1976.

Mill, John Stuart. *Socialism*. New York: Humboldt, 1891.

Proudhon, Pierre Joseph. *What Is Property?* New York: Fertig, 1966 [ca. 1890].

11.
The Limited-Liability Corporation

THE LIMITED-LIABILITY corporation is probably the crucial institution of capitalism. It evolved as a by-product of the technical changes that created the Industrial Revolution—it, or something much like it, was necessary to implement the system that the new technologies made possible. Some such institution was necessary if capital was to be mobilized, if the enterprise was to have reasonable assurance of longevity, if the total operation was to be big enough to use the new machines effectively.

Single proprietorships and partnerships, with their limited assurance of longevity, their limited access to capital funds, and their unlimited legal liability (applicable to the individual owners taken separately), could not effectively mobilize the large sums needed, build the large plants, assemble the work force, assure supplies of raw materials, and develop the markets that were appropriate to efficient use of heavy equipment.

Adolf Berle and Gardiner Means point out that "in both Europe and America the development of the modern corporation appears to have received its impetus from the industrial revolution." Speaking of the first half of the nineteenth century, they say: "The corporation as the principal means of providing necessary large capital acquired increasing economic importance and more definite and liberal legal recognition." It was 1811 in New York when the individual American states "began to substitute general incorporation laws for the process of negotiating with the state legislature for a charter." Berle and Means go on to say: "The history of the nineteenth century in American corporation law is in fact that of a slow abdication by the state of control over corporations."[1]

Definition

This institution, the corporation, which has emerged to service modern productive technology has been defined as being "artificial, intangible and existing only in the contemplation of law."[2] And John Commons has written:

> The meaning of a corporation, like the meaning of property and liberty, has been changing during decades and centuries, and when a corporation appears in court it takes on a variety of shapes derived from different parts of its history. It is not a citizen within the meaning of the Federal Constitution but is a "person" within the meaning of the Fourteenth Amendment. At one time it appears to be an *association* of persons, at another time a *person*; at one time it is an independent existence separate from its members, at another a dummy concealing the acts of its stockholders. At one time it is a fiction existing only in contemplation of law and limited strictly to the powers granted in the act that created it; at another it is a set of transactions giving rise to obligations not authorized expressly by the charter but read into it by operation of law. To Hedges it might appear to be a Leviathan controlling twenty thousand jobs, but when he gets into court it is only Coppage, a person like himself. With this elastic ability to change its shape and slip out of your hands when you think you have it, the definition of a corporation is truly intangible.[3]

At any rate, as far as the law is concerned, the corporation is handled as though it were an individual, as though it had a legal personality separate from that of anyone associated with it. As such, it can sue and be sued, contract and buy and sell, own property, and hire workers. And in its ability to live on and on, perhaps for ninety-nine years, perhaps forever (depending on the law of the state in which it is incorporated), it has a characteristic which many individual human beings would sell their souls to possess.

The corporation is legally owned by its stockholders (a form of slavery, if you will), theoretically controlled by them. However, as far as the debts of the corporation are concerned, the involvement of the individual stockholder generally extends only to those funds personally invested in the corporation's stock. That is all the stockholder can lose, no matter how large the unpaid debts of the corporation may be. In this connection, the corporate stockholder-owner is much more privileged than the single proprietor or partner, who may be required to regurgitate virtually all private wealth to meet claims against the business enterprise. The money-raising capabilities of the corporation are much beholden to this difference be-

Table 11-1. Types of Business Enterprises, 1975

Type	Number	Business Receipts (in billions of dollars)	Net Profits (Income) (in billions of dollars)
Single proprietorships	10,882,000	339	45
(of which farms)	3,367,000	69	6
Partnerships	1,073,000	146	8
Corporations	2,024,000	3,199	143
(of which farms)	56,000	27	1
Total	13,979,000	3,684	196

Source: Statistical Abstract of the United States, 1978 (Washington, D.C.: Government Printing Office, 1978), p. 561.

tween the potential liability of stockholders and that of free private entrepreneurs and partners. This is the redoubtable "limited liability" characteristic of the corporation.

Types of Business Enterprise

There exists an almost infinite variety of possible types of business enterprise. Perhaps the single proprietorship, the partnership, and the corporation will suffice as a listing of the chief basic types. In the United States in 1975, the numbers were as indicated in table 11–1.

Table 11–2 summarizes and compares the basic characteristics of these types of business enterprise.

The single proprietor typically really runs the single proprietorship and is responsible for it. In a legal sense, she or he is the enterprise and gets what profits there are. If the enterprise requires little capital this arrangement may work very well or as well as the capabilities of the proprietor (plus a little luck) permit. There are vast numbers of single proprietorships, perhaps ten million, but their combined capital is small, they often do not survive their first year, and they do not have the dominant influence on the economy possessed by the corporations. However, their proprietors have a lot of votes and their interests are ostentatiously, if not effectively, served by politicians.

Partnerships also have no legal personality separate from that

Table 11-2. Characteristics of Types of Business Enterprises

Characteristic	Single Proprietorship	Partnership	Corporation
Legal personality	No separate personality	No separate personality	Possesses own legal personality
Source of funds	Personal funds and personal borrowing capacity	Personal funds and personal borrowing capacity	Securities (stocks and bonds) and other borrowing capacity
Nature of liability	Unlimited on the proprietor	Unlimited on each partner separately	Stockholder liability limited to investment
Duration	Death of proprietor or sooner	Death of any partner or sooner	Unlimited or indefinite or as provided in charter

of the individual partners. To the extent that there are more partners in a given partnership than proprietors in a single proprietorship, the partners have more money-raising ability, generally speaking, than does the single proprietor. Even so, that ability is limited to a few personal fortunes and the borrowing capacity of a relatively small number of individuals. In the case of a lawsuit against the partnership, each partner separately is completely liable for the whole of a judgment against the group—this means that partnerships should be established only among those with considerable confidence in each other. Also, the range of activities where partnerships are common is quite limited: the law, some associations of physicians, real-estate agents, and a few other areas. The partnership comes to an end automatically on the death of any partner, but, especially in the legal profession, it may almost as quickly be revived minus the deceased member.

By contrast, the corporation has a group of characteristics that permit it to assemble the great quantities of capital demanded by the new discoveries of the Industrial Revolution. The corporation has its own separate legal personality. It can obtain funds via issues of stocks and bonds in arrangements that do not require that any single stockholder or bondholder advance a major sum. The stockholders are favorably disposed to such arrangements because of the possibility of sharing in the profits combined with the circumstance that, if worse comes to worst, all they can lose is the sum they have invested in the securities; their other assets are safe. Also, the probable greater longevity of the enterprise makes it possible to undertake activities involving longer gestation periods than the single proprietorship or the partnership can reasonably expect.

The Structure of a Corporation

The structure of a typical corporation may be schematized as in figure 11–1.

Theoretically, the stockholders are the owners, and they legally control the activities of the corporation. In practice, this control is largely a myth: the phenomenon of the divorcement of ownership from control is elaborated on later in this chapter. Actually, given the way things are typically done, the annual stockholders meeting is the only occasion when it would be organizationally feasible for the stockholders to assert themselves—and on that occasion it is not practically feasible.

The board of directors is elected by the stockholders at their annual meeting. At least nominally this is the situation. In fact, the stockholders pretty much rubber-stamp the election of the board and/or the administrative officers. In the typical situation, those people are a self-perpetuating ingroup, although there certainly may be power struggles among the members of the ingroup. At all events, the board of directors, in the name of the stockholders, nominally controls the corporation in the interests of the stockholders between meetings of the stockholders. And the board selects, supervises, and controls the administrative officers, at least formally. However, interaction between the board and the administrative officers is complex and personal, and one needs to study a particular corporation to determine how in fact the division of functions is handled. There is not much doubt as to the subordinate position of the run-of-the-mill employees, except that an effective labor union may give them a voice in some matters and a favorable wage and salary position. The bondholders are outside the formal ownership-employee structure; theirs is a debtor-creditor relation with the corporation.

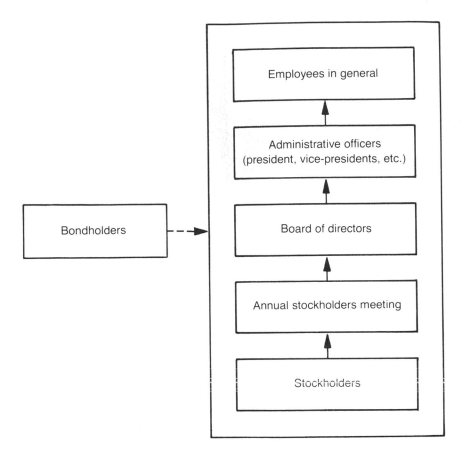

Figure 11-1. The structure of a corporation

Raising Funds

The actual money-raising instruments used by corporations are, characteristically, stocks, bonds, and bank borrowing. Stocks represent an ownership claim; bonds and bank borrowing represent debt. Fantastic ingenuity has gone into designing stock and bond issues with slightly different characteristics and slightly different investor appeals: common and preferred stocks, par and no-par stocks, voting and nonvoting stocks (it is not exactly true that all stockholders, because they are "owners," can necessarily vote on corporate matters), debentures, and mortgage bonds with all kinds of maturity periods (ten years or forty), and all kinds of interest rates, and all kinds of ratings as to quality from AAA to pretty poor.

New security issues are generally handled for corporations by investment banking houses. In the old days J. P. Morgan was the most famous. Currently important firms include Merrill Lynch, Morgan Stanley, Salomon Brothers, First Boston, Goldman Sachs, and Dean Witter Reynolds. They generally act as a group, or syndicate (including many or most of the important investment banking houses), in the marketing of each and every major new issue of securities.

Promotion

On the occasion of the initial establishment of a corporation, a small group (or a single individual) may be the promoters (the entrepreneurs). They may themselves provide the front money needed for the initial promotion (perhaps several hundred thousand dollars) and may thus really be risk takers, at least to a modest degree, or they may obtain such funds from obliging bankers or from friends and relatives, and the identity of the true risk taker may thus become a bit blurred. When the corporation is finally established, it is likely to repay the promoters for their services in midwifing (or mothering) by turning over to them blocs of stocks (very likely voting stock, if some of the stock is voting and some is nonvoting). In later periods, much of the actual earnings of corporate executives will be not their salaries proper but fringe benefits in the form of expense accounts, stock options, generous retirement plans, and so on.

The Stock Market

Why should some 10 percent of all the footage of all the newspapers of the country for the past hundred years have been devoted to stock market security price quotations? (But, then, why should some 20 percent have been devoted to sports?)

Since the technology of the Industrial Revolution called forth the limited-liability corporation and the corollary issuances of stocks and bonds, it was not unnatural that a secondhand market for those stocks and bonds should develop. One institution called forth another.

The miracle is the status which this secondhand market has acquired. Savoir-faire about the stock market in the United States in the last half of the twentieth century establishes one's credentials as a true sophisticate, perhaps, even, a beauty contest judge:

> Or, to change the metaphor slightly, professional investment may be likened to those newspaper competitions in which the competitors have to pick out the six prettiest faces from a hundred photographs, the prize being awarded to the competitor whose choice most nearly corresponds to the average preferences of the competitors as a whole; so that each competitor has to pick, not those faces which he himself finds prettiest, but those which he thinks likeliest to catch the fancy of the other competitors, all of whom are looking at the problem from the same point of view. It is not a case of choosing those which, to the best of one's judgment, are really the prettiest, nor even those which average opinion genuinely thinks the prettiest. We have reached the third degree where we devote our intelligences to anticipating what average opinion expects the average opinion to be. And there are some, I believe, who practise the fourth, fifth and higher degrees. . . .
>
> Even outside the field of finance, Americans are apt to be unduly interested in discovering what average opinion believes average opinion to be; and this national weakness finds its nemesis in the stock market. . . .
>
> When the capital development of a country becomes a by-product of the activities of a casino, the job is likely to be ill-done. . . .
>
> In the absence of security markets, there is no object in frequently attempting to revalue an investment to which we are committed. But the Stock Exchange revalues many investments every day and the revaluations give a frequent opportunity to the individual (though not to the community as a whole) to revise his commitments. It is as though a farmer, having tapped his barometer after breakfast, could decide to remove his capital from the farming business between 10 and 11 in the morning and reconsider whether he should return to it later in the week.[4]

Keynes suggested that one possible policy for dealing with the situation would be a stiff government transfer tax on security transactions.

At any rate, the stock exchanges and the dealings on them are a complicated jungle of rules and behavior patterns sufficient to challenge the imagination. And the stock market is an example of an institution whose characteristics have been made pretty much what they are in response to the role of another institution, the corporation.

One of the resulting relationships is that amounts equivalent to the market value of all the stock on the New York Stock Exchange are turned over on the exchange roughly every five years. For example, in 1973 the market value of stock sales on the New York Stock Exchange was $146 billion, and the market value of all the quoted stock on that exchange was $721 billion.[5] (But, then, Americans turn over their real estate at a pretty rapid rate also.) This extreme fluidity means that capital values are being reappraised at a great rate, in large part because the exchanges are organized to facilitate such reappraisals and to encourage turnover. The greater the volume of sales, the more money made by the brokers, and they are prone to encourage their clients to reappraise their portfolios (meaning buy and sell a lot of stock) frequently.[6] Thus, to the extent that people are conditioned to view the stock markets as a barometer of the economy, and to the extent that the market machinery encourages turnover and consequently price fluctuations, the market as such is a destabilizing influence on the economy.

Policies that would tend to discourage turnover would seem desirable. For one, earnings on stock speculation might be treated as regular income for income tax purposes if the sale occurs within, say, two years of the purchase (the present figure is six months). Another possibility is a much higher tax on the value of securities traded, as suggested by Keynes.

The Divorcement of Ownership from Control

All in all, the corporate form was a tremendous conception, generating further behavior patterns and permitting all sorts of ramifications. Much of this permissiveness is a by-product of the relationship known as the divorcement of ownership from control, a rather natural development given the other characteristics of the corporation and the fact that nobody was watching.

The stockholders, again (at least some of them), have voting rights in setting corporate policy. But, especially when there are hundreds of thousands of stockholders, it is not really possible for them to exercise supervision and control on a day-to-day basis. In fact, typically, stockholders meetings occur only once a year. At those meetings the few stockholders who actually appear are given a snow job by management and, except for a few chronic malcontents who occasionally protest futilely, the meeting is little more than a formality.

However, the formality includes one important vote: the election, or reelection, of the board of directors. It is not feasible, as a matter of organization, for the stockholders to run the company on a continuing basis. But the ten or twelve directors whom they elect can meet more often and may exercise more or less meaningful control over the hired employees, beginning with the chief executive officer and/or the president. The board could function as an institution through which the majority of the stockholder-equity interest (a stake in terms of money value of investment in stock, not a representation in terms of a head count of stockholders) might control the operations of the company.

The workings of the proxy system, however, pretty much assure that this does not happen. When corporate management sends stockholders the notices of their annual meeting, accompanied by a statement strongly encouraging their attendance, it also sends a request for a proxy. "If you cannot attend, please sign the form designating so-and-so as your proxy at the stockholders meeting." In fact, then, at the stockholders meeting there may well be (especially in the case of the larger companies) stockholders owning no more than 5 or 10 percent of the stock outstanding. But there will also be proxyholders, originally selected by management (in fact, they are likely to be two or three individuals from top management), with the right to vote most of the stock outstanding—except for the stock of those who fail to return their proxies and whose ownership interest is consequently not represented one way or the other at the meeting. Thus management, by means of the proxy procedure, and more or less as a result of a default by the stockholders, is in a position to control the election of a board of directors which will be committed to ingroup management and its policies.

This customary procedure does not preclude the possibility of stockholder revolts, but such incidents are rare. When they occur, they are more likely to involve powerful outside interests trying to take over rather than stockholders genuinely mobilizing to influence policy. If the outsiders manage to organize enough votes to take over, they rather than the majority of the stockholders will be effectively controlling the ongoing activities of the enterprise.

So, in general and with sporadic exceptions, one may speak of corporate management as being self-perpetuating. And the insiders in management select their own successors. This is not an effectively working democracy—it is not even a democracy in the sense of a dollar of investment representing one effective vote. It is certainly not a democracy in the sense of one individual stockholder having as much voting power as another. Unhappy as we may be with some of the manifestations of political democracy and its perversions of the voting process, the workings of the democratic political process have to be given at least a C+ by comparison with the D− (or F) that the voting process in the corporation earns, if the criterion is effective representation of stockholder interest.

An attempt to describe more precisely the extent of divorcement of ownership from control in the case of corporate enterprise is important as one tries to get a little better conception of what is really going on and whose interests are really being served.

Thorstein Veblen commented on this phenomenon in his 1923 *Absentee Ownership* with great insight but in fairly general terms. Adolf Berle and Gardiner Means, in their 1933 *The Modern Corporation and Private Property*, went a good deal further in the effort to quantify the degree of divorcement of ownership from control in the case of the two hundred largest corporations in the United States. Their original findings were as follows:[7]

> Let us examine the type of control exercised over the 42 railroads, the 52 public utilities, and the 106 industrials which compose the list of 200 largest companies at the beginning of 1930, remembering that their combined wealth amounted to nearly half of that of nonbanking corporate wealth. Of these companies ultimate control appeared to be:

	By Number	By Wealth
Management control	44%	58%
Legal device	21%	22%
Minority control	23%	14%
Majority ownership	5%	2%
Private ownership	6%	4%
In hands of receiver	1%	Negligible
	100%	100%

Since 1933, other studies have attempted to describe the divorcement of ownership from control, but it is difficult statistically to get hold of the concept with precision. The Berle and Means numbers probably remain roughly accurate and give about as good a feel for the phenomenon as statistics can give.

Motivation

Much of economic analysis is predicated on the assumption that owners of businesses control the operation of their enterprises in an effort to maximize profits. The prevalence of the divorcement of ownership from control raises serious questions for economists (orthodox and Marxist alike) as to the validity of this basic working assumption.

How should the profit maximization assumption be rephrased? One possibility would be to assume that management visualizes itself as a trustee for the stockholders and is indoctrinated with the concept that it is its function to try to maximize profits to the greater benefit of the stockholders. (This tendency might be strengthened to the extent that individuals in corporate management are likely to own some stock.)

Even so, those in management have a more immediate and obvious interest in higher salaries for themselves, larger expense accounts, stock bonuses, better retirement programs, and similar perquisites which, as far as corporate bookkeeping is concerned, are costs and, as costs, tend to reduce profits. So, there is a not unimportant contradiction built into the attitude of management toward the desirability of maximizing corporate profits.

Over and beyond these immediate pecuniary considerations, individuals in top management may have other interests. They may relish empire building. This would mean a tendency toward plowing profits back into expansion instead of distributing them to stockholders, who would then be making the decisions as to the use of these profits instead of management making such decisions. But the decision as to which of these possibilities will exist is made not by the stockholders but by management. How likely is it that the decisions would be the same in either case? Not very, particularly if management feels disrespect for or even repugnance toward so-called carping, ineffectual stockholders, especially small stockholders of the type who comes regularly to the annual meetings, eats the free box lunch that may or may not be provided, and then creates a disturbance during the business meeting by complaining about management.

Management's attitude toward laissez faire is mixed. Management is interested in being let alone, insofar as its autonomy in decision making is concerned, by both government *and* owners. But this independence is not a two-way street. When in difficulty, management is more than willing to demand assistance from the government in the form of rapid write-offs of new capital expenditures for income tax purposes, protective tariffs, and subsidies. The free competitive market and its alleged merits can be quickly forgotten, as can the owners' right to make decisions on the disposition of profits—in times of difficulty, management is almost completely free to reduce dividends to stockholders, even to zero.

Appreciating the interplay of these influences and attitudes is probably more important for understanding how capitalism works than is comprehending how a purely competitive market would work if the profit motive ruled.

Corporate Accounts (Double-Entry Bookkeeping)

Double-entry bookkeeping is an example of a technology or a technique for keeping track of what is going on in the corporation at the same time that its procedures are replete with institutionalized behavior norms. The basic double-entry accounts in terms of credits and debits oversee, on an ongoing basis, the activities of the firm. Providing that each transaction has two faces and is entered twice was a tremendously powerful technological innovation because of its usefulness in checking for accuracy. At every instant, the sum of all the credits must exactly equal the sum of all the debits or something is wrong.

All the transactions during a time period, such as a year, are summarized in a profit and loss or income statement. The static situation at the end of the time period is summarized in the balance sheet. And such and other information is summarized, ostensibly for the benefit of the stockholders, in the annual report.

However, it is probably not too unfair to say that annual reports are designed not so much to give information as to impress. They are costly documents on slick paper, evidencing a lot of fine photography. They are an example of the fine art of the care and feeding of stockholders, which has as its basic purpose keeping them contented and quiet.

Concentration

There is a basis for believing that a very large, probably undesirably large, proportion of the country's production is concentrated in too few firms. Also, there are grounds for believing that the degree of concentration is getting more pronounced. In any event, if the concentration is undesirably large, it is not a major issue to determine whether it is slightly more so or slightly less.

As far as the situation in manufacturing is concerned, William Leonard reports the following comparative percentage shares of value added in manufacturing as being accounted for by the largest manufacturing companies:

	1947	1958	1972
Largest 50 companies	17	23	25
Largest 100 companies	23	30	33
Largest 200 companies	30	38	43

He adds: "But these data on value-added seriously understate the real hold on manufacturing of the top 200 companies. The Census Bureau fails to include among its top 50 firms many of the largest companies . . . including at least 10 leading oil companies which because of tax advantages allocate much of their operations to mining and are classified by Census as mining enterprises."[8]

Holding Companies

The holding company is the most important intercompany structural arrangement. One company may own some or all of the stock of another company. One "artificial, invisible, and existing only in contemplation of law" enterprise may own another. Slavery has not been entirely abolished, at least among artificial persons. In fact, with considerably less than 100 percent stock ownership, one corporation may establish the basis for controlling another.

A perhaps desirable policy might prohibit one corporation from owning stock in another. It was probably a bad mistake, in the nineteenth century, to sanction the practice of stock ownership by one corporation in another. By what conceivable rule of reason can one bit of property own another bit of property? Corporations or, rather, the humans who control them would wail to heaven if the practice were stopped. But it should be, and some effective procedure such as one providing that a corporation sell off perhaps 5 percent per year of its ownership of stock in other corporations (and abstain from buying stock in other corporations)—should not be too great a hardship. Certainly corporations should be estopped from new acquisitions of each other's stock. What kind of massive, out-of-control game has been going on? Who does own, who does control, large industry? Those who pursue logical possibilities to their limit may like to speculate on the implications of the quite possible situation where most large corporations might be owned virtually in their entirety by each other—not by individual stockholders in any significant degree.

Disqualifying Corporate Officers

Perhaps one fairly simple measure might make corporate executives more cooperative and understanding in observing the antitrust laws: a provision disqualifying corporate officers from continuing in their positions if the firm is found to be in violation of antitrust laws as a result of their activities. If it cannot be determined which officers are responsible for the violation (if they are protecting each other), it might not be too unfair to order the severance of perhaps one-third of the board of directors, chosen by lot, or three people out of top management, chosen the same way. Such a sanction might turn out to be surprisingly effective, more so than the possibility of fines and short jail sentences that are almost never assessed. (Similar procedures might well be used in government bureaus and military units when the existence of institutional impropriety has been established.)

Learning more about the whys and wherefores of the behavior of industries and developing concepts for controlling their group behavior are important. The study of the regulation of that behavior in the public interest is, or ought to be, a fertile, challenging, difficult field of work for economists. So, economists generally avoid this area of specialization like the plague.

Summary

Five notable characteristics of corporations are legal personality, longevity, limited liability, money-raising ability, and the divorcement of ownership from control. Central measures for control might eliminate, or at least limit, the possibilities for corporations to own stock in each other and provide for the removal of corporate officers involved with violations of the antitrust laws.

NOTES

1. Adolf A. Berle, Jr., and Gardiner C. Means, "Corporation," in *Encyclopaedia of the Social Sciences*, ed. Edwin R. A. Seligman (New York: Macmillan, 1935), 4: 414–423.

2. Dartmouth College v. Woodward, 4 Wheat. 518, 636 (1819); also see H. H. Liebhafsky, *American Government and Business* (New York: Wiley, 1971), pp. 157–158.
3. John R. Commons, *The Legal Foundations of Capitalism* (Madison: University of Wisconsin Press, 1968 [1924]), pp. 291–292.
4. John Maynard Keynes, *The General Theory of Employment, Interest and Money* (New York: Harcourt, Brace, 1936), pp. 156, 159, 151.
5. See *Statistical Abstract of the United States, 1974* (Washington, D.C.: Government Printing Office, 1974), p. 466.
6. See Adolf A. Berle, Jr., and Victoria J. Pederson, *Liquid Claims and National Wealth* (New York: Macmillan, 1934).
7. Adolf A. Berle, Jr., and Gardiner C. Means, *The Modern Corporation and Private Property* (New York: Macmillan, 1933), p. 94.
8. William N. Leonard, "Mergers, Industrial Concentration and Antitrust Policy." Paper read at the Association for Evolutionary Economics meeting, Dallas, Texas, December 1975.

ADDITIONAL READINGS

Bogen, Jules I., ed. *Financial Handbook*. 3d ed. New York: Ronald Press, 1952 [1925].

Dewing, Arthur Stone. *Corporation Finance*. Rev. ed. New York: Ronald Press, 1935 [1922].

Gordon, Robert Aaron. *Business Leadership in the Large Corporation*. Berkeley and Los Angeles: University of California Press, 1945.

Livingston, J. A. *The American Stockholder*. New York: Collier Books, 1958.

Nader, Ralph, Mark Green, and Joel Seligman. *Taming the Giant Corporation*. New York: Norton, 1976.

Veblen, Thorstein. *Absentee Ownership*. New York: B. W. Huebsch, 1923.

Welsch, Glenn A., Charles T. Zlatkovich, and John Arch White. *Intermediate Accounting*. 3d ed. Homewood, Ill.: Irwin, 1972 [1963].

Whyte, William H., Jr. *The Organization Man*. New York: Simon & Schuster, 1956.

12.
Government and Business

Regulation or the Market

Historically, economics has customarily approached the study of production and consumption via the market. Much ratiocination goes into explaining how the competitive market can generate maximum welfare. Sophisticated mathematics is used to demonstrate how Adam Smith's invisible hand is really supposed to work to generate the desirable maximum welfare result. However, orthodox economics also grants that this meritorious system may be distorted by monopolistic practices, and some attention is given to preventing or neutralizing such pernicious practices. This is the antitrust approach, which is important but will be passed over here. Some believers in pure competition, who do not take the distortions of monopoly very seriously, claim that the market does work "in general and well enough." Others believe that effective antitrust policy is extremely important if the benefits of the competitive market are to be obtained.

In any event, there has been a rash of articles, texts, books of readings, books ostensibly advising on policy, indicating how all problems can be solved by deregulation and letting the market work.[1] This movement has had massive public appeal in the 1970s. Large numbers of students have acquired an automatic reaction when considering any problem: deregulate and let the market work, or enforce competition and let the market work, or grant accelerated depreciation and let the market work, or maintain the depletion allowance and let the market work. (The incongruity of the presence of the regulatory aspect in the last two proposals seems to disturb ostensible advocates of the free market solution very little.)

That pure competition is completely incapable of assuring

equilibrium, a unique solution, a welfare maximum, or even reasonable stability over time represents a consideration that strong advocates of the market solution brush aside. That pure competition, even assuming it was attainable, can give no assurance of a unique maximum was discussed in the appendix to chapter 4.

More generally, it is hopelessly clear to me (but not to some people) that, if we had pure competition, innumerable situations would arise which the public would not be willing to tolerate. Some degree of regulation would be demanded—for example, in connection with the effort to solve the energy problem (one hears speakers for the oil industry saying both "Give us deregulation" and "Give us an energy czar"). So, why not think about the problem in these terms? What regulations are appropriate? Under what circumstances? Even Adam Smith recognized the need for police and the arrest of thieves, a position with which any property owner (regardless of the degree of commitment to competition or Proposition 13) would agree heartily.

The question is not whether to have regulation. It is what type of regulation is suitable and when and where. Any argument in the abstract about the appropriateness of a system with no regulation in contrast to a situation where some amount of regulation exists is a sterile waste of time.

There is the problem of the natural monopoly, or the naturally large company, or the decreasing-cost industry. There are problems connected with the essentialness of a product or service. There are quality-of-product (product contamination) questions that the market does not adequately police. There are questions of health and sanitation, questions related to ecology and pollution of the environment, police and fire, dope and public morality. All these issues get mixed up in varying ways with questions involving the ability of the competitive market to come to grips with them. These questions raise different issues and may call for different solutions in each different industry and situation; and the appropriateness of various policies for different industries may change with the passage of time as attitudes, institutions, the social setting, technology, and even human biology change.[2]

There has been a temptation to subsume all these problems under one rubric, the public-utility umbrella, and discuss two alternatives: (1) the regulation of privately owned public utilities or (2) public enterprise. The essence of the problem of regulation of privately owned public utilities has seemed to be the rate-setting problem—how to set a rate or price that permits a fair return on a fair value of the investment, while protecting the public interest in not being gouged by monopoly prices. Concentration on these issues, however, may lead to disregard of more important matters, such as what should determine whether passenger trains should disappear.

Socialism (Public Enterprise) or Capitalism

The possibility exists that a new institutional form may represent a response to a previously created unsatisfactory institutional form—rather than being a direct response to technological change, it may be an indirect response. Thus the socialist movement, in the forms it took in the mid nineteenth century, was probably more directly a response to the institutionalized evils involved in the manner in which the corporation was implementing the factory system than it was a response to the technological imperatives of the factory system. Perhaps one of the chief weaknesses of socialism results from this origin. The proponents of the various forms of public enterprise have not thought primarily in terms of policies that could properly screen and assimilate new technology.

One of the burning questions of yesteryear involved the relative merits of capitalism and socialism. Can socialism, that is to say, the government, run a business as well as or better than free private enterprise? Such dichotomies have never been as clear-cut as the disputants have frequently implied. Nevertheless, there may exist significant differences in the degree of private or governmental participation, and it is conceivable that an economy might operate at one of the extremes, all-private or all-government.

At least since the Industrial Revolution, the inequities and the business-cycle fluctuations that seem to result from the free private enterprise, pure competition, laissez-faire approach have led compassionate people to seek alternatives in the various forms of socialism. The present generation of radicals, unable to find a really worthwhile new approach, seems to be reverting to an advocacy of socialism, particularly Marxian, just as former generations did, just as the generation of 1848 did.

But, in truth, the extremes of neither socialism nor pure competition can really assure the "proper" working of an economy. We are just going to have to struggle along with mixtures of socialistic and free private enterprise ingredients—using one alternative as a kind of watchdog for the other. Maybe that is not so bad. When private enterprise botches up a job, we can turn to government, and vice versa. "A plague on both your houses" as far as the socialism versus free private enterprise argument is concerned.

As for the eternal argument as to whether things are botched up more when private enterprise (big or little) does it or when the government does it (or when the government and private enterprise, especially the Defense Department and private enterprise, get together and do it), there is continually going to be new evidence indicating that, whatever the balance has been, it was not quite right. We must try to establish control devices (of a not too onerous or inhibiting nature) that tend to encourage improvement in the performance of both private business and government. And shifting the balance from time to time will put pressure on whichever type of management is doing the shoddier job at the moment.

Maybe we are now in a better position to state fairly dogmatically that there are three possibilities for organizing business: laissez faire (or private enterprise operating without any government regulation), regulation of private enterprise, and public enterprise. Society is eternally operating and the various industries are eternally operating under the aegis of various mixtures of these institutionalized possibilities. Changing technology and biological evolution impact on the institutional order. As individuals (and groups) respond to these changing situations, rethink their values and their opinions as to how well one or another of these institutions is doing its job, they change the institutional behavior norms. They may even acquire the leverage someday (but they will certainly take a deep breath before doing it) to require that all automobile bumpers must be the same height.

Or, for some particular industry, we might want to have capital creation and production without paying the profit-rate bribe that industry is demanding at the moment—or the accelerated depreciation.

More or Less Public Enterprise

If a government, itself, owned or operated much or all of the productive enterprise of a country, we might call that government socialistic (or, less aptly, communistic). The Soviet government comes pretty close, but not completely, to meeting this description of socialism (much agriculture in the Soviet Union is organized in cooperatives, but there also exists a not inconsiderable amount of small-scale private retailing). There is a much higher proportion of public enterprise in the United Kingdom than in the United States, but there is perhaps more in the United States than we sometimes realize when we speak of this country as being characterized by free private enterprise, capitalistic competition. For example, quite a few U.S. municipalities provide water, gas, electricity, and garbage collection as public enterprises. And the federal government is up to its ears in the post office and whatnot. Meanwhile, in the United States, the attitude that government ownership is anathema is more or less institutionalized. There is a whole lot of public enterprise in the United States, there ought to be a lot, and there will continue to be a lot. The problem is how to run it better, not whether or not it should exist.[3]

Some More or Less Regulated Industries

It should be useful to develop a perspective on the importance of that part of the economy which is regulated relative to that part of the economy where market influences dominate. The following examples will indicate that the regulated areas are major sectors of the total economy, sectors that affect our daily lives continually. Also, despite our general predilection for the "free market," as these sectors are identified individually we will probably become aware of a spontaneous feeling that some regulation is appropriate for that particular sector and that these sectors add up to a major fraction of the economy. This does not mean that we will automatically be jubilant about the way the regulatory agency handles the situation. Continual reappraisal of the regulators and their practices is an essential part of the picture.

The local gas company, if it is private, probably has a virtual monopoly, except for certain options. The consumer may be able to opt for electricity instead of natural gas—but frequently that is not much of a choice, especially if the electricity is generated with gas. The local gas company in its turn is likely to be dependent on one or two possible suppliers: pipeline companies capable of delivering gas to the city. All in all, these complicated interrelations and the paucity of alternatives for years on end surely mean that governmental supervision and regulation are appropriate parts of the picture, perhaps with regard to the substance of the original contract with the pipeline company and also with regard to the rates

236 Case Studies and Policy

to be charged the ultimate consumers. And study and restudy as to appropriate policy are called for. Miraculous answers that will solve the problems for all time (or for decades) probably simply do not exist.

Ditto, more or less, for the local electric company. And ditto, more or less, for the water supply, except that the municipality is more likely to supply water through a public enterprise than gas or electricity.

The Tennessee Valley Authority is an example of a useful, major, governmentally handled power and valley development project. Knowledge acquired about costs and distribution problems has been useful as a yardstick in establishing regulatory practices in connection with private electric power companies. (However, this does not mean that there is utopia in the Tennessee valley.)

The American Telephone and Telegraph Company and its Bell System are fond of pointing out that there really are a lot of independent telephone companies in the United States. But that does not create competition in the industry or the possibility that rates and quality of service can be effectively controlled by market forces. The small independent telephone companies must rely on connections with the A.T.&T. system if they are to provide long-distance service to their customers at all, and the federal government regulates interstate rates to deal with the problem of possible monopoly pricing at that level. Thus, in states, such as Texas, that do not have effective regulation of intrastate long-distance rates, long-distance calls between intrastate points two or three hundred miles apart are likely to cost more than many interstate calls involving far greater distances.

Frequently, local telephone rates are regulated by city councils. This involves a continual hassle in which the city council may lack the expertness and leverage to regulate the rates effectively. Also, it seems that the Bell System pretty skillfully plays one city off against another as it pushes rates up, gets rate increases from the more accommodating city councils, and uses that happenstance to pressure more resistant councils. Better procedures are generally needed for setting local rates, but what sane person would leave these matters to the complete discretion of the Bell System?

That the oil industry really understands that regulation is appropriate is indicated by the tendency of private industry leaders to discount industry shortcomings by pointing to the lack of a national energy policy. Talking about the situation as though there is a choice between regulation and pure competition is simply a red herring, a ploy, in a setting where the real issues are otherwise.

Then there is garbage, a not unimportant commodity. Garbage is generally collected by the municipalities, sometimes ostensibly gratis. Also, there generally exist commercial, private garbage-collection services which large generators of garbage may be required to use. Possibly garbage collection could be handled, more or less workably, by free private enterprise. But would the public really relish this? In any event, the problem of where to dump the stuff after it has been collected would remain—and social pressure is definitely going to influence that decision. Most municipalities are in almost continual dispute with adjacent (or potentially adjacent) landowners as to the appropriateness of using one or another location for a dump. Nobody wants to live near it, but the stuff has to go somewhere (or does it?). It is hard to see that this aspect of the problem can be reasonably handled without the use of the eminent domain powers of government. However, no doubt there are still some die-hard free private enterprise advocates, Chicago's Professor Coase, for example, who think that the free market can work all this out down to and including allowance for the danger of contaminating underground water.

The railroads are in a mess. They have been since the early days when the private railroad builders, unfortunately, made most of their profits from the land grants which the government gave them to encourage the building of the systems, rather than getting squared away to make their money from more or less honest railroading. The railroad rate structure was an unbelievable mess before the Interstate Commerce Commission was set up in 1887. Freight rates on short hauls between points served by only one railroad were frequently fantastically higher than rates between more widely separated points (on the same line) served by competing railroads. Regulation was certainly needed. Whether the particular regulation that has resulted has been all that the heart could desire is another matter: some say that with the passage of time the railroads have come to control the ICC, rather than the other way around. Certainly the railroad situation in the United States as concerns both freight and passenger traffic is most unsatisfactory, but surely better regulation (and perhaps less regulation), not absence of regulation, is called for.

The problem is being struggled with, and the struggle will be ongoing. Hindsight being better than foresight, one can now say that it would probably have been better if the railroads had stuck with that abundant fuel, coal, instead of shifting over to diesel, but that is only one issue. With regard to the passenger service, competition from intercity buses, airplanes, and the private automobile has been destructive. But need it have been? In any event, it hardly seems that the free competitive market could have used its standard rules to work out appropriate costs and fares given the fact that the railroads have to maintain their roadbeds and the buses (and trucks) use roadbeds provided by the state. There is no way around the proposition that regulation is appropriate.

As for the airlines, the need for pooling terminal facilities concentrates a good deal of the cost and necessitates public handling of that aspect of the service. There seems some difference of opinion among knowledgeable people, however, as to whether it would be reasonably workable to let competition and the market then determine which airlines would give how much service and to what towns at what fares. One may be excused for guessing that, if this were tried for a little while, we would quickly be back with intercompany agreements on services and prices and, subsequently, a lot more regulation. For one thing, it seems likely that the quality and quantity of the service to smaller communities would be reduced drastically as all the airlines tried to serve the profitable trunk lines. And government subsidy of the local routes would certainly be an important measure of regulation.

Urban public transportation in the past forty years has declined severely in quantity and quality as the private automobile and urban sprawl have proliferated. It might seem that the energy crises of 1973 and 1979 would contribute to a revival of urban public transportation. But little that is effective has been done. The phenomenon of urban sprawl itself makes it extremely difficult to serve the outlying suburbs with adequate public transportation. There is no way a major improvement in urban transportation can occur without substantial population concentration and a reversal of the tendency to urban sprawl. High-rise apartments along arterial streets (with greenbelts behind the apartments) would probably be a good idea as the core concept in the urban planning of the future.

As for the streets themselves, except for a very few toll roads, any suggestion that private enterprise might provide for them (somehow charging for the use) seems scarcely imaginable.

As for taxis, would anyone seriously suggest that the meters not be regulated? Perhaps so, for in quite a few cities of the world one hurriedly negotiates with the driver before starting a trip. It can be done. But the weary traveler, arriving late at night and unfamiliar with the city, is not going to be much of an economic man in the bargaining process.

In the area of communication, there have been the publicly operated pony express and postal service and the privately operated Western Union, United Parcel Service, and assorted cable services. Surely no one would want such vital services completely in private hands and completely unregulated. Too much is at stake, although it may be helpful, when the post office is having troubles, to have the United Parcel Service as an alternative.

Anybody who can visualize how Adam Smith's invisible hand might regulate television, in particular which promoters would get which channels, deserves some credit for ability to conjure up fantasy. There are the additional complicated questions of the appropriateness and availability of programs for small children (and adults as well) and the availability of worthwhile cultural and educational programs, which are a little more likely to be shown if a regulatory agency is prodding. All of which does not deny the possibility that British public television is pretty stodgy.

An expensive and problematical enterprise like atomic energy virtually required public funding to move at all. How much help it may be with the energy situation remains uncertain, even with the help of public funding. Pretty clearly, the use of nuclear power needs to be regulated in many ways, including careful supervision for safety and radioactive-refuse disposal.

Probably almost everyone would agree that many of the aspects of hospital and ambulance services ought to be subject to careful regulation—including the fees charged, especially when ambulances make long runs into the country or answer emergency calls. Hospitals, although certain phases of their operations may be usefully guided by not so competitive market forces, can stand a lot of regulation. Also, given the high cost of various types of special equipment, some sort of planned division of responsibility for different services among different hospitals seems important in an effort to provide inexpensive service at the same time that highly specialized equipment may be made reasonably available.

Then there is agriculture. If ever there was a regulated industry it has been agriculture in the United States for the past fifty years, and if ever there was a group of producers that asked to be regulated it was the freedom-loving farmers. In the early 1970s, because agricultural prices had been relatively high, there was, temporarily, considerable clamor from the farmers for discontinuance of the various agricultural support programs. However, one can be sure that, as soon as agricultural prices fall relatively, farmers will be back pleading for and getting regulation, and that hardier breed —the Texas rancher—will be doing the same thing. Let us hope that next time the regulatory tools will be better than they have been. The old parity price approach can certainly be dispensed with to advantage.

Lumbering largely occurs on public lands, as does offshore oil drilling, and much of the potential oil shale development will be on public lands. Any way you look at it, the government will be handling leasing and influencing who gets leases.

Fishing on the high seas requires the occasional support of the navy, or the State Department may pay the fine for some fishing boat out of San Diego which has been arrested by Ecuador for fishing within two hundred miles of the coast of that country. In that sort of context, one might expect that the government has some legitimate interest in regulating where United States fishermen can fish.

Auto insurance rates are pretty generally regulated, and there seems to be agreement that they need to be. Probably all drivers ought to be required to have liability insurance.

The reader may be interested in glancing back over the items just reviewed and speculating on the desirability of complete deregulation. Surely the appropriateness of some judicious regulation in most of these areas stands to reason. These are hardly minor and peripheral segments of the total economy. And old-age pensions and socialized medicine are not even mentioned. One might well wonder: where are the industries that do not need a little regulating? Surely not pharmaceutics?

Public-Utility Regulation
Gas, water, and electricity are standard examples of industries which might be identified as public utilities, natural monopolies characterized by decreasing costs, providers of especially crucial services to the public. However, the clarity of the classification leaves much to be desired.

In economics, discussion in this area used to be pretty much limited to the rate-setting problem.[4] An attempt might be made to judge what a fair profit rate might be, for example, 8 percent. An estimate of the capital value of the enterprise might be attempted. There would then be discussion of the relative merits of historical cost and reproduction or replacement cost as methods for determining the capital value. Historical cost involves an effort to take into account the expenditures actually made over the history of the enterprise, suitable allowance being made for depreciation. Replacement cost involves attempting to estimate what it would cost to duplicate the facilities at the present time. Which method the company preferred would depend on whether inflation or deflation was going on. If the times were inflationary, the company would prefer the replacement-cost method of valuation because that would put a higher value on its plant and equipment, and 8 percent of a larger number is better (as profits) than 8 percent of a smaller number. Historical cost would be preferred by the company in deflationary times. Having made these estimates, it was then necessary to estimate how much of the product or service the consumers would use at various possible rates, deduct estimated operating costs, and determine what rate would generate the identified amount of profits.

Almost complete disillusionment with the possibility of making these calculations in a reasonable way has led to some cynicism with regard to regulation in general and to something of a movement toward letting the market do the job.[5] No doubt dissatisfaction with unregulated price-gouging will cause the pendulum to swing back.

Price, Wage, and Rent Regulation

It is desirable that business in general be viable and reasonably profitable and that there be substantial availability of high-quality goods. These considerations are not in question here. What is in question is the role of governmental measures in directly affecting and/or regulating the prices, wages, and property rentals paid and received.

Price Control as Producer Protection

Producers want higher prices and consumers want lower prices. Producers should have protection against violent price fluctuations, at least if it is reasonably feasible to provide such protection. Producers are hardly, however, entitled to protection against continuing low prices, if those prices are a result of the fact that times have changed, people do not want their product anymore, or they have not kept up with the new technology. Yet raw-commodity prices do fluctuate violently, especially in relation to manufactured-goods prices. On the assumption that this is so and that producers, especially farmers, are entitled to protection against such fluctuations, the following policy is suggested.

In the past in the United States, effort along this line has involved trying to provide farmers with prices that maintained a given relation between the prices of the things they buy and the things they sell (parity farm price supports). Such a system attempts to maintain the prices of qualitatively very different goods in some sort of fixed relation to each other. But, if demand and supply and competition mean anything as economic yardsticks, the machinery for effecting appropriate adjustments in the quantities produced of different commodities requires flexibility in such price relations. The rise of productivity in one industry should be a force tending to lower that industry's prices relative to other prices. An economy which behaves in a manner calculated to prevent the occurrence of such "natural" adjustments is not doing itself any great long-run favors.

The problem is to find a procedure which will mitigate the violence of short-run price fluctuations without preventing the natural long-run adjustments among prices. A procedure that might do this job is as follows.

The working principle would be that the price paid the original producer of a given commodity should be allowed to fall no more than some percentage, say 5 percent, by comparison with the year before (not by comparison with other commodities). Meanwhile, all buying and selling actually continue to occur on the open market at open-market prices. There is no formal price control. However, if a particular sale by an original producer occurs at a price that is more than 5 percent below the price of the year before, the seller would be entitled to certify to the appropriate government agency the quantity of the goods sold at the lower price. The amount of subsidy paid would be the difference between what the total value of the sale would have been if it had occurred at a price 5 percent lower than the price of a year before (perhaps this is computed to be $130,000 for that quantity of goods) and the total value of the sale at the price prevailing on the day of the sale (perhaps this is $115,000). This comparison would call for a subsidy of $15,000. In computing the value involved in the actual sale, the publicly quoted price on the day of the sale would be used, not the actual sale price. This procedure should help avoid the possibility of collusion between buyers and sellers such as might involve understated prices and, perhaps, kickbacks from the seller to the buyer.

Price and Rent Control as Consumer Protection

Producers have been known to price-gouge consumers. Give some of them a little monopolistic leverage, and they will do what they can with it. The natural reaction of consumers is to howl rather ineffectively. If the situation gets bad enough, and if there is a war going on, the government may set or try to set maximum prices by any one of many possible methods, each of which works slightly worse than the one before. Maximum prices are especially likely to be set on such necessities as basic food items and movie admissions—and rent. In fact, fairly commonly in the developed countries and quite generally in the underdeveloped countries, there is a complex, massive, almost beyond comprehension proliferation of poorly enforced, poorly coordinated regulations trying to set maximum prices. The chief result of all this is to convey the message loud and clear to the landowners that they will do better to produce coffee for the international market rather than beans for the domestic market. In the private construction industry, they get the message that building housing for low-income families is not a worthwhile racket.

So, in a setting where there are surpluses of the internationally marketed staples, there are, in the underdeveloped countries, likely to be shortages of basic food items. In a setting where the construction industry is proliferating luxury apartment houses, millions of people may be living in shacks and mud huts. And the soldiers returning to the United States after World War II could not find housing at any price, while a lot of people rattling around in rent-controlled housing were enjoying much more space than they really needed.[6]

Meaningful protection for consumers is just not found in the regulations trying to set maximum prices (the current euphemism being "incomes policy"), despite the immediate appeal of such measures during periods when prices are rising rapidly. Help for consumers comes from abolition of tariffs and international trade controls. It is not a by-product of tariffs and suchlike restrictions. It is found in the job guarantee which assures consumers a respectable income, in the enforcement of laws against restraint of trade, in countervailing power. It is found in goods availability, not in goods scarcity. And it may be found by other means that economists should be trying to discover.

The overriding solution is that there be expanding production of goods and housing plus a system that sees to it that these expanded quantities get on the market, instead of being held off by collusive agreements and production limitations. This is the chief argument for the price-support schemes discussed in the preceding section by comparison with the modus operandi of the typical raw-commodity control scheme of recent years, which has been oriented to base-year quotas, parity prices, and keeping goods off the market. And heaven protect us from generalized price setting and the bureaucracy which would come with it.

Trade Taxes and Subsidies
Because they distort the meaningfulness of price and wage comparisons, excise taxes and other interferences with goods as they move through the channels of trade are generally undesirable, unless there is a social decision that the discouragement or encouragement of some type of consumption is advisable. If the government wants to influence production, the job is more likely to be effectively done by interference at the production stage, perhaps by a production subsidy. If it wants to aid consumption, let it do so by interference at the consumption stage, like the job guarantee, which provides people with freely disposable purchasing power.

Behavior Norms of Regulatory Agencies

Regulation implies regulatory agencies. But there is a hitch: nobody seems happy with the behavior of the regulatory agencies. Their efforts to make the concept of "fair return on fair value" meaningful have been ridiculed. It is charged that the regulated generally come to control the regulators and that the courts too frequently interfere with the determinations of the regulatory bodies. The results then seem arbitrary, chaotic, changeable, and a return to reliance on the market seems preferable. However, the problems that call for regulation and that *cannot* be resolved by the market remain.

The trouble with the regulatory agencies has to be recognized for what it is. The agencies are trying to do a job which society wants done. The problems, what needs regulating and how, vary from industry to industry. Each industry is unique; each regulatory agency has unique problems; but to deal with this situation there remains society's perennial and ongoing method: self-correcting value judgments. As ongoing process we judge and rejudge the performance of regulation and change our procedures for selecting the regulators, the norms they apply, and the controls over the process.[7]

There is work for the League of Women Voters and the American Association of University Women and Ralph Nader and Common Cause and a lot of other public-spirited citizens bird-dogging these processes. The average citizen should hope that such groups grow in influence relative to the growth of special interests.

It should be emphasized that regulations and rules had best be as clear as possible, and as consistent as possible, and as simple as possible, and as nonexistent as possible, and the criteria used in establishing them should be set forth as understandably as possible. The obfuscation and mysticism traditionally practiced by the board of governors of the Federal Reserve System are not good models. Whim and spontaneous instinct (or "trust me") do not provide a good working base. Where possible, the rules should permit the public to know ahead of time what will actually be done policywise in certain eventualities. An example of this sort of regulatory procedure is indicated earlier in this chapter, where it is alleged that sellers might well be guaranteed prices no lower than 95 percent of the prices they received the year before.

Regulation, Economists, and the Public

Sure, the fewer the rules the better, the simpler the rules the better, and the absence of rules where possible even better. And let not so pure competition do the job during periods when it manages reasonably well. The economists' job should be a leadership role in connection with the hows, and whats, and whens of regulation. Economists—many with some legal training working with lawyers with some training in economics, others with some engineering training working with engineers with some training in economics—[8]should be actively working with all levels of government (municipal, county, state, federal, assorted authorities with assorted geographical coverages and jurisdictions) to try to make regulation in the public interest as reasonable and light-handed as possible.

All levels of government, especially local and state levels, need to place much more emphasis on the hiring of professionally competent economists, knowledgeable in the problems of the particular industries with whose regulation they are concerned. Too many municipalities are using well-meaning committees of amateurs to suggest policy on regulation and then depending on those amateurs to stand up to the Bell System lawyers, and the gas company executives, and the professional lobbyists of the American Petroleum Institute on matters of technical detail, which is where the industry representatives are expert at discrediting their well-meaning opposition.

Initial suggestions as to regulation procedures need to be made by professional people knowledgeable in the industry and employed by the agency doing the regulating. Also, the channels for receiving suggestions and advice from the concerned public should be open.

Then, as H. H. Liebhafsky especially emphasizes, preliminary decisions on regulations should be made by hearing examiners employed by the regulatory agencies at the end of adversary-type proceedings at which all sides have an opportunity to be heard. The agency then reviews the findings of the hearing examiner and perhaps endorses them, perhaps not. Disgruntled parties may then appeal to the courts, with two provisos: (1) in general, the agency decision will be enforced pending final determination by the courts, and (2) the role of the courts should be to assure that procedural due process has been observed—not to second-guess the economic analysis or the value judgment of the agency.

There is, or should be, a lot of work for economists here, even if their econometric models merely play the role of evidence which may be controverted by other evidence or arguments. In fact, probably the chief knowledge that economists should bring to the fray should be much understanding of the history of the industry and its technology, labor relations, marketing methods, capital formation problems, and so on; experience with the types of regulation used in that industry or similar industries elsewhere; and considerable feeling for the whole problem of regulation—feeling which, by and large, economists imbued with econometric models presently lack. Their models have possibilities for being a useful part of this process, but only a part.

At all events, this sort of participation in the regulatory process should be the principal activity of economists, but their principal analytical perspective should be the self-correcting value judgment concept of institutional economics and instrumental value theory.

There is, then, no automatic arithmetic solution for the best profit rate or price. There is merely ongoing consideration and reconsideration of all this information. The battles will be fought over and over in different contexts, and new industries with new problems will come and old industries with old problems will go.

The problems of a given industry should be considered in light of the problems of the economy as a whole, but no one should operate under the illusion that these relations have a unique, best form. Rather, there will be common concerns and the possibility of conflicting interests and the continuing necessity to restructure this or that industry's place in the economy. The industry and its regulators will have certain interests. The larger economy may have contrary interests. And there is and will continue to be a higher decision-making process for society as a whole, which can override the industry and which will also be making its self-correcting value judgments in a context of institutions and evolving technology, the weather and available resources.

Recapitulation

Understanding the implications of regulation and the reasonable control of the regulatory process is an important social skill which economists should learn to work with—industry by industry, problem by problem. Also, always, they should reconsider decisions made in such a limited setting in the context of the general welfare but with some appreciation of the nature of the general welfare as a manifestation of an ongoing process of self-correcting value judgments—not as an exercise in logical positivism.

Society will use regulation more effectively if it understands that regulation is the normal and appropriate state of affairs but that it may be botched up. However, the solution for a botch up is not an appeal to unattainable pure competition. Conceivably, more reliance on not so pure competition may be helpful. Or what is called for may be a change in the norms involved in the regulation or a change in the identity of the regulators. Insofar as it chooses to utilize the control devices available to it, society naturally regulates the operation of society. Individuals are neither above society nor in a position to assert their independence of it: there is certainly no presumption that things would be better if everybody had total freedom. However, in a setting where society it-self is understood to be the arbiter or regulator, as little regulation and as simple regulation as possible is desirable. Thus a high de-gree of individual freedom of action is surely a meaningful value.

Advocates of the use of the market to determine which airlines will serve which routes at what rates do not generally recommend "catch as catch can" to decide which airplane is going to use the runway next. Nor do advocates of the market as a device for con-trolling which bus routes will go where also advocate the abolition of traffic signals. As for the railroads, it seems pretty clear that they have been fouled up both by private enterprise and by regulation and that some rethinking of their role is in order in a setting where it is realized that simplistic clichés about the market or regulation or government enterprise hardly help much.

These carefree comments and policy proposals hardly resolve all the issues in the troubled areas of business-government-con-sumer relations. Junk mail has not been dealt with, for one thing. We are stuck with the necessity for large corporations and large-scale production in many industries and with fantastically high innovation costs in many areas, such as the development of the communications satellite. We need a mixture of private and gov-ernment enterprise to protect us from each other. There is going to be abuse whether the projects are privately or publicly developed, and keeping the abuse to a minimum will be a continuing chore. In the public sector, the salary arrangements to some degree keep officials under control. In private industry, where upper-level man-agement can come close to writing its own salary-bonus-pension ticket, there are more problems, haters of government bureaucrats to the contrary notwithstanding. Also, the relation between corpo-rate decision making and the will of stockholder-owners, who have no effective voice in that decision-making process, poses some un-resolved questions.

It will probably be better to concentrate on establishing effec-tive controls piecemeal rather than chucking the whole sorry mess. Our sorry system might look pretty good compared to the mess we would have if we tried to start over from scratch. There does not seem to be much indication that the proponents of the "chuck the whole sorry mess" approach have much conception of what would be involved in building an entirely new order.

In concluding this chapter, an obvious but often forgotten rela-tion between producers and consumers should be indicated.

The Relative Strength of Pressure Groups

In the private enterprise economy in many sectors, there exist a limited number of producers or sellers. This is true in automobile production, petroleum, or steel, or barbering (in a given residential area), or grocery shopping (in terms of the number of stores reasonably available to a family). The number of producers is generally sufficiently limited so that it is feasible for them, if they so choose, to cooperate in setting production and pricing policies. They certainly have continuing occasion to discuss industry problems and to acquire a common feeling for those problems. The instruments of such cooperation are frequently the great, effective trade associations—the National Association of Manufacturers, the American Petroleum Institute, the Iron and Steel Institute—as well as similar organizations at the local level.

On the consumer side, such interchange and cooperation are not generally feasible. All the buyers of automobiles cannot organize to tell Ford or General Motors what they will pay for cars, on pain of there not being any cars bought, nor can buyers of gasoline organize to tell the oil companies what they will pay for gasoline. Prices—"administered prices"—are typically set by producers or sellers. Sellers can and do confront buyers with prices on a take it or leave it basis, and buyers take them or leave them. The circumstances of price changes are also pretty much up to the sellers, although the sellers are of course influenced by the state of the market.

The difficulty is organizational. It is not practicable as a matter of organization, generally, for buyers as a group to say how much they will pay for things. There are too many of them and they are too widely dispersed. Also, their interest in the price of any particular commodity is too small a proportion of their total interest in purchases for it to be worth their while to spend large amounts of time trying to set a commonly agreed-on price with which they could confront the producers of, say, vitamin pills on a take it or leave it basis.

On the other hand, it is quite feasible and natural for the producers in one industry to organize either overtly or tacitly and reach an understanding about or acquire a feeling for what it is best for them to do, what price it is best for them to charge. There are generally few of them in most industries, and they are naturally thrown together because of similar activities and interests at the Rotary luncheon or the country club. The institutionalized pressures for conformity and cooperation become strong. This does not debar the possibility of occasional price wars, and bitter inter-company struggles, and a bit of judicious nonprice competition, but the chief lesson learned from such forays into the area of major conflict is that cooperation is the desirable standard pattern of behavior. All producers have a stake in a more orderly and profitable industry, and competition is likely to make the industry less profitable. (Of course, each has an interest in a larger share of such profits and gains as there are.)

So, the economy is more effectively organized to raise prices and costs in the interest of higher profits and wages than it is organized to promote lower prices and greater goods availability. Things happen this way in spite of the fact that the population as a whole has just as much interest, in its role of consumer, in getting more goods at lower prices as it has, in its role of producer, in charging higher prices and getting higher wages and profits. To say that there is a conspiracy by a little group of producers (the Establishment) to exploit consumers (the great exploited masses) misrepresents the problem. We are all producers and we are all consumers, but we are all more effectively organized to push our interests as producers than as consumers. As Pogo once said: "We have met the enemy and they are us."

Note the difference between the nature of this cleavage of interests and the cleavage emphasized by the Marxists. Marxists emphasize the cleavage between capitalist and worker interests. But, in the situation looked at here, it is the relation between *producer* and *consumer* interests which is relevant. The capitalists and the workers have a common interest in raising prices and costs (meaning, among other things, expense accounts and wages). And, in recent years, because of effective organization, both capitalists and workers have been remarkably successful in these activities—to the detriment of the interest of both capitalists and workers, viewed as consumers, in more goods at lower prices. This relation would seem to explain, in large part, the inflation of recent years.

The implications of the relative strengths of these pressure groups make it sound as though people are rather schizophrenic in their attitude toward villainy.

Even though it is difficult to quantify exactly the relative strengths of producer and consumer pressures, significant rough but reasonably accurate judgments can be made. It is possible, for example, to count registered lobbyists and tell, in a general way, whether they are representing producer or consumer interests. One may also have some pretty good impressions as to which lobbyists are better heeled. And one may conclude from this comparison whether legislative bodies are hearing producer or consumer interests more effectively expressed. On the basis of such counts, there are many more and more powerful pressure groups in Washington, and in state capitals as well, obviously representing producer interests against consumer interests (see table 12–1).

Of course the figures in table 12–1 are very approximate. They represent the result of some sort of institutionalized compromise between Congress and the lobbyists as to who will report what and who will report anything and who may be late with reports.[9] It is certainly a healthy influence to have reports of this kind, but nobody should be under any illusion that they present an accurate total picture. For one thing, figures that cover only one-quarter of one year cannot begin to catch the sweep of activities of those lobbies which may be dormant for long periods of time until there is some proposed legislation that touches home.

In many cases, the classification of particular lobbyists in the table was fairly arbitrary. And many who would properly belong in one category or another ended up under "Other reporting lobbyists" as a result of the ignorance of the compiler.

The great labor union lobbies almost certainly represent producer interest more effectively than consumer interest, although it may be that they come to the defense of the consumer occasionally. Nevertheless, all in all, their prime concern is higher wages, and that is an influence on the cost side. Also, this is generally the role of the professional associations of lawyers, doctors, teachers, and realtors and of the skilled hard hats.

Regarding the interest of such powerful lobbies as the National Association of Manufacturers, the United States Chamber of Commerce, the American Farm Bureau Federation, the Independent Petroleum Association of America, the Iron and Steel Institute, and hundreds of other trade associations, there can be no doubt: their prime concern is with their role as producers. Also, each of these organizations, when foreign trade questions arise, will want to keep out competing imports and be helped in the promotion of its exports.

The figure of $147,000 for organizations with a genuine interest in the general welfare is almost entirely due to Common Cause. Before the recent advent of Common Cause, that figure was negligible.

Table 12-1. Washington Lobbyists: Numbers and Expenditures, Fourth Quarter, 1971

Classification	Number	Expenditures
Reporting lobbyists representing producer interest		
Manufacturers	185	$ 131,000
Farmers and ranchers	55	97,000
Other producers (e.g., mining, petroleum, public utilities)	116	75,000
Distributors (e.g., wholesalers, retailers, transporters, excluding ocean shippers)	133	117,000
Labor unions	71	298,000
Professional associations	91	105,000
Sellers of services (e.g., banks, insurance companies)	172	225,000
Export associations	2	—
Total	825	1,048,000
Reporting lobbyists representing consumer interest		
In general	16	7,000
Importers	15	16,000
Ocean shippers (and organizations generally interested in more foreign trade)	19	50,000
Organizations with a genuine interest in the general welfare (in a sense which presumes some lobbying in the consumer interest)	37	147,000
Total	87	220,000
Other reporting lobbyists		
Associations of retired people (including the American Legion)	19	53,000
Other (war and peace, Indian tribes, and unclassifiable)	109	123,000
Total	128	176,000
Total reporting	1,040	1,444,000
Estimate of total nonreporting	320	443,000
Total reporting and nonreporting	1,360	1,887,000

Source: *Congressional Record*, May 24, 1972, pp. H-5021 et seq.

Classifying associations of retired people and various organizations of exmembers of this or that institution under "Other reporting lobbyists" involved some uncertainty. Retired people do have a real interest in lower prices, yet their effective lobbying is probably more in the direction of obtaining larger pensions and social security payments.

Where to put group health organizations and suchlike entities, frequently very praiseworthy, was also a problem. They are classified mainly under "Sellers of services." If that distorts the figures, it is no more anomalous than having associated third-class-mail users and the National Rifle Association in the consumer interest category. Most of the items under "Importers" are either lobbyists arguing over shares of the sugar quota or lobbyists interested in imports from Japan. Many of the lobbyists under "Ocean shippers" are probably fairly neutral between exports and imports.

In spite of all these qualifications, without applying any complicated statistical tests to the data, it seems pretty obvious that there are more lobbyists spending a great deal more money to promote producer interest in higher prices (and fewer imports) than there are lobbyists (with money) promoting consumer interest in more goods at lower prices (and more imports).

Such results follow from the type of economic organization, the institutional order, that characterizes the economy. Someone has suggested that we abolish lobbying, or that we build a high fence around Congress, or that there should be an informal understanding that members of Congress should not accept free meals or go to free barbecues or accept free vacations in Colorado. Maybe each legislative hall should have a big bulletin board on which all legislators register when they get back, saying who paid for their lunch. Uninformed as legislators may be on a certain subject, their ignorant but honest vote may be more intelligently cast, in the sense of taking better account of consumer interest, than it tends to be after they have heard an energetic statement of the case from the producer's side: they have fewer facts but clearer heads. It is a strange situation, but it is literally correct. (Or course, properly put, this should be a plea not for ignorance but for balanced knowledge.)

It is not just legislative bodies that are overwhelmed by presentations from the producer's side. Governmental regulatory agencies are likely to represent and understand producer problems better than consumer problems. Studies of the makeup of federal regulatory agencies indicate that commission members frequently come from executive positions in the companies to be regulated or go to such positions after their period of service on the commission: "More than half of the people appointed to nine Federal regulatory agencies in the last five years came from the industries they were named to regulate. . . . Of the 85 persons who left the agencies during that period, 32 have at some time during the immediately subsequent five years been employed in the regulated industry. . . . While the selection of regulators is a closed process as far as consumer groups go, . . . the White House normally cleared such appointments with the affected industry."[10]

It seems that feasible organizational arrangements in our society almost naturally result in arrangements that provide more sympathetic understanding of producer than of consumer problems. And we know why. The self-correcting value judgment process should shape up and do something about this.

NOTES

1. See Ronald H. Coase, "The Problem of Social Cost," *Journal of Law and Economics* 3 (October 1960):1–44; Richard A. Posner, *Economic Analysis of Law* (Boston: Little, Brown, 1972); Roger Leroy Miller, *Economics Today* (San Francisco: Canfield Press, 1973); Llad Phillips and Harold L. Votey, Jr., eds., *Economic Analysis of Pressing Social Problems*, 2d ed. (Chicago: Rand McNally, 1977 [1974]); Richard H. Leftwich and Ansel M. Sharp, eds., *Economics of Social Issues*, rev. ed. (Dallas: Business Publications, 1976 [1974]).

2. See H. H. Liebhafsky, *American Government and Business* (New York: Wiley, 1971), pp. 427 et seq. Instead of calling this section of his book "Public Utility Regulation," Liebhafsky calls it "Working Rules Which Replace or Modify the Operation of Market Forces." And the first chapter in the section is "Administrative Regulation," not "Public Utility Regulation."

3. See Emmette S. Redford, *American Government and the Economy* (New York: Macmillan, 1965), pt. 6, pp. 395 ff. being concerned with public enterprise.

4. See John Maurice Clark, *Social Control of Business*, 2d ed. (New York: McGraw-Hill, 1939 [1926]).

5. See Clair Wilcox and William G. Shepherd, *Public Policies toward Business*, 5th ed. (Homewood, Ill.: Irwin, 1975), pt. 4.

6. See B. Bruce-Briggs, "Rent Control Must Go," *New York Times Magazine*, April 18, 1976, pp. 19 ff.

7. See Redford, *American Government and the Economy*, in particular pt. 5, "The Regulatory System," pp. 547–590.

8. Incidentally, the lawyers and engineers learning a little economics would do better to read the Redford or Liebhafsky books on business-government relations and the problems of regulation in preference to the price theory which is the only economics many of them get. Unreasoned, unquestioning support of "free enterprise," unfortunately, seems an institutional behavior norm of engineers.

9. See Liebhafsky, *American Government and Business*, chap. 5. Liebhafsky gives many reasons why the data of table 12–1 understate the case.
10. *New York Times*, November 7, 1975, p. 14.

ADDITIONAL READINGS

Arnold, Thurman. *The Folklore of Capitalism*. New Haven: Yale University Press, 1937.

Bernstein, Marver. *Regulating Business by Independent Commission*. Princeton: Princeton University Press, 1955.

Blair, John M. *Economic Concentration*. New York: Harcourt Brace Jovanovich, 1972.

Bork, Robert H. *The Antitrust Paradox*. New York: Basic Books, 1978.

Galbraith, John Kenneth. *American Capitalism: The Concept of Countervailing Power*. Boston: Houghton Mifflin, 1952.

———. *New Industrial State*. Boston: Houghton Mifflin, 1967.

Glaeser, Martin. *Public Utilities in American Capitalism*. New York: Macmillan, 1957.

Green, Mark, ed. *The Monopoly Makers*. New York: Grossman, 1973.

Hamilton, Walton H. *The Politics of Industry*. New York: Knopf, 1955.

———. *Price and Price Policies*. New York: McGraw-Hill, 1938.

Hexner, Ervin. *The International Steel Cartel*. Chapel Hill: University of North Carolina Press, 1943.

Institute for Contemporary Studies. *Regulating Business*. Ed. Donald P. Jacobs. San Francisco, 1977.

Martin, David Dale. *Mergers and the Clayton Act*. Berkeley and Los Angeles: University of California Press, 1957.

Means, Gardiner C. *Industrial Prices and Their Relative Inflexibility*. U.S., Senate, doc. 13, 74th Cong., 1st sess. Washington, D.C.: Government Printing Office, 1935.

Myers, Gustavus. *History of the Great American Fortunes*. New York: Modern Library, 1907.

Owne, Bruce M., and Ronald Braeutigam. *The Regulation Game*. Cambridge, Mass.: Lippincott, Ballinger, 1978.

Redford, Emmette S. *The Regulatory Process: With Illustrations from Commercial Aviation*. Austin: University of Texas Press, 1969.

Sharfman, Isaiah Leo. *The Interstate Commerce Commission*. 4 vols. New York: Commonwealth Fund, 1931–1937.

Stocking, George W., and Myron Watkins. *Cartels in Action*. New York: Twentieth Century Fund, 1946.

Veblen, Thorstein. *Absentee Ownership*. New York: B. W. Huebsch, 1923.

Weidenbaum, Murray L. *Business, Government, and the Public*. Englewood Cliffs, N.J.: Prentice-Hall, 1977.

13.
The Multinationals

"Multinationals" is the latter-day term for direct investments. The activities of enterprises domiciled in one country with operations in other countries have long been a matter of concern, especially to the governments and people of the debtor or host or under-developed country but also to the governments and at least some of the citizenry of the creditor or investing country, the home country of the multinational enterprise involved.

There are many famous direct-investment case histories from the Berlin-to-Baghdad railway of pre–World War I days, through the Mexican expropriation of foreign oil companies in 1938, down to (but no doubt not ending with) the escapades of International Telephone and Telegraph in Chile in the early 1970s.[1]

Importance

To determine how seriously to take multinational enterprises and their activities, one tries to find a suitable quantitative measure. This is difficult, but a few numbers may help give a little feel for the situation.

The Industrial Union Department, AFL-CIO, reports that "in 1970, the total foreign-source income (profits) of American corporations was $17.5 billion. Of this, the U.S. Treasury collected only $900 million in taxes—an effective tax rate of 5.1 per cent."[2] This $17.5 billion was a respectable percentage of the United States corporate, before-tax profits of $71.5 billion in 1970 (on which $34.5 billion of taxes were paid). These figures may not be precise, but they are interesting.

The multinationals account for a good deal of United States exports. Raymond Vernon quotes a Department of Commerce study which "indicates that the 264 U.S. parents and their subsidiaries were responsible, whether as buyers or as sellers [in 1965], for about half of all U.S. exports of manufactures."[3]

Companies operating internationally possess large reserves of readily usable foreign exchange. The possible implications of the volatility of these funds are considerable, for good or ill, for stability or instability in the international monetary system. For example, the United States Tariff Commission has the opinion:

> As a group, private institutions on the international financial scene controlled some $268 billion in short-term liquid assets at the end of 1971—and the lion's share of these assets was under the control of multinational firms and banks headquartered in the United States. This $268 billion, all managed by private persons and traded in private markets virtually uncontrolled by official institutions anywhere, was more than twice the total of all international reserves held by all central banks and international monetary institutions in the world at the same date. . . . Because $268 billion is such an immense number, it is clear that only a small fraction of the assets which it measures needs to move in order for a genuine crisis to develop.[4]

W. I. Spencer, then president of First National City Corporation, estimated that in 1971, or thereabouts, multinational corporations produced $450 billion in goods and services, which he also estimated to be 15 percent of the gross world product.[5] United States multinationals apparently accounted for about $200 billion of the $450 billion. The numbers grow: in 1976, sales by majority-owned foreign affiliates of United States companies were reported to be $515 billion by the Department of Commerce.[6] Two things seem pretty clear. The numbers are large. But the multinationals have not taken over the world, at least not yet.

The Problem

In General

A major international problem involves the manner in which corporations can produce goods in one country and make their profits show up in, say, the Bahamas while they are United States (or Delaware) legal personalities. The possibilities created by these conditions (possibilities for irresponsible production and pricing practices and evasion of taxes) are a lively challenge to any capable business executive who is also just a bit of a shyster. However, the underdeveloped-country device for dealing with this problem—expropriation and nationalization in a setting involving generally jingoistic nationalism—is likely to be a self-defeating procedure.

For better or worse, technology decrees that the giant corporation with international ramifications is an effective device for dealing with a situation where raw materials are found in one country, labor skills or cheap labor in another, and markets in a third. This is one of the most important technology-institutions relations with which the world community has to deal. A little country may think it can deal with refractory multinationals by expropriating them and working through national or government corporations whose oyster is primarily national resources and markets but any country which tries this is simply going to lose out in terms of development, production expansion, and productivity. Retiring into a nationalistic shell based on splinters off multinationals is no way for a small country to deal with this problem: it only penalizes its own development.

Allan Gruchy has summarized Veblen's views on this matter: "In Veblen's analysis of the industrial system there was no permanent place for the nation state. Industrialism had no respect for national boundaries. The large industrial corporation drew its raw materials from many international sources, and sold its output in the markets of many countries. In this situation the national state was an anachronism."[7]

A fuller example of a particular multinational arrangement has been cited by Lester Brown:

> By far the most ambitious complementation effort conceived to date is the Ford Motor Company's project to build a new vehicle designed for the poor countries. In many ways an Asian version of the Model T, the car will be small and rugged in design, cheap to operate, and a combination car-pickup for transporting passengers and freight. Components will be produced in individual countries and then transported from country to country by what amounts to a conveyor belt of ships, with every Asian country, except Singapore, involved in assembling the vehicles for local sale. Ford expects to establish an electric and plastic parts factory in Singapore, engine foundries in Thailand and Taiwan, axle and transmission factories in Indonesia, and a diesel engine plant in South Korea. A plant is also envisaged for Malaysia, another possibly for India, and one would even be available for mainland China—if it should open up to foreign investment. By 1980, Ford plans to invest $1 billion to this regional production program.[8]

In the Host Country

From the viewpoint of the underdeveloped debtor country, the domestic role of the foreign multinational is a sensitive matter. Investment may be desired in order to increase the capital stock in order to increase production in order to improve the standard of living. But, then, a price is paid in terms of assorted psychological humiliations, real or imagined, and dependency on outside control.

The foreign investors are generally visualized as draining the debtor countries of something worthwhile, but what: profits, money, resources? These are not the same thing. The investors also appear to be serving the nationalistic and foreign policy goals of their home country. Also, they are likely, when in difficulty, to call on their home governments for protection, and the use of military force or economic pressure and debtor-country resentment may result. Examples range from sending the marines to Haiti, the Dominican Republic, and Nicaragua between 1912 and 1934 to more recent economic sanctions, such as those called for by the Hickenlooper Amendment. The phraseology of this provision has varied considerably since the Foreign Assistance Act of 1961. But, roughly, the idea has been that United States assistance should be suspended to countries that have expropriated the property of United States citizens without making provision for adequate compensation.[9]

In the Home Country

The attitude in the creditor country toward the direct foreign investments and other activities of the multinationals has had several aspects. Foreign investment and working abroad, as high adventure, also offer intriguing possibilities for making money. Providing capital funds can be a real assistance to the economic development of underdeveloped countries, and that is a praiseworthy gesture. These are two very different types of appeals.

Investors may, on the other hand, be soured on foreign investment as a result of defaults, confiscations, expropriations, and verbal insults. Or the home-country labor unions may envisage increased foreign production by national enterprises as damaging to local production and likely to result in less employment in the home country. This latter consideration has been a major concern with United States labor unions, which can inject considerable bitterness into their denunciations of "runaway plants" that "cost Americans jobs," whether they really do or not.[10]

An argument can also be made that a good deal of U.S. exports goes to the foreign branches of U.S. firms and that our domestic employment by the multinationals is rising at a more rapid rate than is our total domestic employment.[11] There are two sides, or more than two, to this issue. There are a lot of ways people can imagine they may be damaged by the activities of multinationals. Considerable human ingenuity and indignation go into denouncing them. Who bought and paid for whom? It is simply not possible to compute a definitive estimate of net gains and losses affecting all the parties that think they have an interest in this issue.

National Loyalty

One of the concerns in the debtor countries transcends the matter of money and regards the multinationals as powerful alien influences serving the interests of their home countries in a patriotic way. At the same time, at the economic level, the multinationals are visualized as siphoning profits back to the creditor country, in the selfish interest of the developed country.

That the multinationals, in fact, serve home-country national interests in this way to a significant degree is by no means established. Underdeveloped countries might be a little less frustrated in their dealings with the multinationals if they conceived a somewhat different perspective of what the multinationals are up to.

What is the actual attitude of management in a multinational corporation relative to the national interests of the nation in which it is chartered? There seems some reason to believe that the executives of multinationals are not highly mesmerized patriots:

> This is the vision held by Carl A. Gerstacker, chairman of Dow, who last week described his idea of an "anational" corporation at the White House Conference on the Industrial World Ahead. . . .
>
> "We appear to be moving strongly in the direction of what will not be really multinational or international companies as we know them today," he asserted, "but what we might call 'anational' companies—companies without any nationality, belonging to all nationalities. . . .
>
> "We will see more foreign companies with large American holdings and vice versa. They will tend for many reasons, political and economic, to become nationless companies."[12]

The Industrial Union Department of the AFL-CIO has unearthed this statement by Robert Stevenson, then head of Ford Motor Company's international division: "We at Ford Company look at the world map without any boundaries. We don't consider ourselves basically an American company. We are a multinational company. And when we approach a company that doesn't like the U.S., we always say, 'who do you like, Britain, Germany?' We carry a lot of flags. We export from every country."[13]

In January 1974 (during the original energy crisis), it became known that United States oil companies in the Middle East, under pressure from Arab governments, in particular Saudi Arabia, had been, at least since October 1973, refusing to supply oil to United States military forces around the world. "Defense Secretary James R. Schlesinger has confirmed that United States military forces had some difficulty obtaining oil as a result of the embargo."[14] In fact, it seems, the United States had to supply the Sixth Fleet in the Mediterranean during those rather crucial times by a massive air and sea lift.

C. S. Burchill has evaluated this situation:

> The nerve-center of such a corporation, the decision-making managerial team, owes its primary loyalty to the enterprise, not to any particular set of politicians nor to the governments that the politicians dominate. . . . Neither does the managerial elite feel any particular loyalty to the shareholders, regardless of their nationality. Management's function is to keep the enterprise safe, healthy and—above all—growing. . . .
>
> Similarly, it will lobby against restriction or interference by any government, and when it must accept political interference imposed by law it will submit to necessity in as comfortable a fashion as it can arrange.
>
> To classify corporations as foreign or domestic is a dangerously misleading practice. It implies that such corporations will be inspired by the same patriotic loyalties that inspire individuals. Managers, in their private capacities, are just as patriotic as any other class of men; but managers are also . . . bound by a loyalty to the corporation that they serve. The dual allegiance can lead to a conflict of loyalties. . . . The judgement of history will as often approve the trustee's loyalty as the patriot's. . . .
>
> The first step in dealing with this problem is to recognize the reality that exists—the condition of anarchy, in which each multinational corporation is very largely a law unto itself.

The third element in this reality is the fictitious nature of the "nationality" attached to the multinational corporations—the practice of designating them as American or Canadian; British or German or Japanese; is entirely misleading. In most respects, they have no nationality, are not responsible to any national government, and cannot be controlled by its laws or regulations.[15]

Pope Paul VI seems to see somewhat the same picture: "Under the influence of new systems of production, national frontiers are crumbling and new economic powers are appearing, the multinational enterprises, which as a result of their centralization and flexibility can effect independent strategies, in large measure independent of national political power and, in consequence, not effectively controlled in the public interest. As they expand their activities, these private organisms can create a new abusive form of economic domination in the social, cultural, and even political sectors. This is the excessive concentration of means and powers denounced by Pius XI on the 40th anniversary of *Rerum novarum*, which now acquires a new concrete aspect."[16]

There thus seems some basis for saying that there is a tendency among the executives of the multinational corporations to feel a prime loyalty to the corporation rather than to the nation of its origin. And, when the goals of the corporation run counter to the foreign policy objectives of the corporation's home government, it is likely to be the interests of the home government which are disregarded. Contrary to commonly held opinion in debtor countries, there is no nice identity of interests between multinational corporations and the nations in which they are based.[17] However, corporations have frequently proven very adept at suckering their home-government foreign offices into putting the national prestige on the line in supporting their frequently dubious claims against foreign governments.

A second look at some of these implications is called for. Lack of patriotism on the part of the executives of multinationals is not necessarily bad. It may be just as well for executives not to feel that they are under an obligation to serve the political interests of nation-states. Their role in the host countries would be less tainted if that were clearly understood to be the case and if the multinationals would also understand the implications of that position. In particular they should understand that, when they get into trouble, it is not appropriate for them to appeal to their home-country governments to bail them out.

Draining Profits

With regard to the alleged tendency of the multinationals to drain profits from the host country back to the home country, this much will be said here. The feverish efforts of a country, such as the United States, to have an export trade balance indicates that that country is not, in fact, carefully cultivating an import trade balance. And it has to be striving for an import trade balance for the charges of resource and profits drainage to stand up.

Pretty clearly, it is not a prime interest of the multinationals to drain profits back to Delaware. In the immediate run, they have an interest in making the profits show up in jurisdictions with low tax rates. In the long run, their interest is likely to be in transferring the profits, as new capital investment, to whatever country they view as being most propitious for their next round of expansion.

Intracorporate (Interaffiliate or Transfer) Pricing and Tax Havens

It also seems pretty clear that the multinationals are greatly interested in paying fewer taxes. Thus, it is probably a concern with them, in any given year, to arrange things so that profits appear in a political jurisdiction (not especially in the home country) with low corporate income tax rates.[18]

The so-called tax havens are a by-product of these relations. The multinationals are likely to charter one or more of their subsidiaries in such places. Transfer pricing will then be used to make a goodly amount of the profits show up there. The Bahamas, Panama, Liechtenstein, Bermuda, Luxembourg, Monaco, and the Cayman Islands are such places. It has been said that there are more corporations than cows in Liechtenstein—but you would never know it by looking around.

Transfer pricing of sales and purchases among the multinationals' subsidiaries domiciled in different countries helps accomplish this result as follows. Goods produced by one subsidiary in a country with high tax rates can be sold at lower than market prices to another subsidiary in a low-tax-rate country. Capital goods being imported into a high-tax-rate country by one subsidiary from another can be imputed to be quite high-priced.

There is every reason to believe that a good deal of such intracorporate-interaffiliate price manipulation is going on, but is it enough to make the matter a really major issue? Data for Colombia obtained by Constantine Vaitsos have been the chief evidence cited in recent years on the intracorporate pricing phenomenon.[19] Thus, a pretty small sample of data serves as the basis for major generalizations about the amount of interaffiliate price distortion going on.

However, I will vouch for the fact that the multinationals are not free with information about their pricing practices. And, until the corporations are willing to cooperate with those trying to study their practices, their bland denials of this sort of thing are not entitled to much credibility.

Previous Policies

Of Debtor Countries (Especially Expropriation and Nationalization)

Underdeveloped countries have attempted to counter the to them undesirable features of the behavior of multinationals by various means. The Drago Doctrine, fostered about 1900, tried to establish as a principle of international law (and the Calvo Clause represented insertion of a provision to this effect in contracts with foreign investors) the concept that foreign investors could not or should not appeal to their home-country foreign offices for protection if they ran into trouble in the debtor country. The United States has generally maintained that such provisions do not cancel an obligation to provide some minimum standard of justice to foreigners and to pay reasonable compensation promptly in the event of expropriation.[20] But these issues have not been resolved in a way that permits us to say confidently what the international law on the subject really is.

Other debtor-country policies have included restriction on or regulation of new foreign investments, restriction on or regulation of the transfer of earnings and the repatriation of investments. On the other hand, underdeveloped countries may encourage investments by tariff protection of new plants, by tariff reductions applicable to equipment imports, and by assorted favorable tax measures. Foreign investors may be wined and dined, or they may be targets of vituperation and rock throwing.

Recent proposals to facilitate the repatriation of foreign investments under reasonably harmonious circumstances have been made by Paul Rosenstein-Rodan and by Albert Hirschman. An expression for this sort of thing is "fade-out joint venture."[21] Under such arrangements, it would be agreed between the foreign investor and the debtor government, before the original investment is ever made, that the foreign investor will sell out much or all of the interest in some time period, such as seven to twenty years.

Fade-out joint ventures would be a fine way to deal with the economics and politics of foreign investment if the appropriate long-run situation allowed, in the words of Candide, us to tend our own garden. But the forces of nationalism, on the other hand, and irresponsible foreign investment, on the other, that have produced the proposal for fade-out joint ventures should not be allowed to lead toward autarchy-type solutions. This approach is conducive to situations where one national government and its licensed corporations square off against another national government and its corporations. This is not a pretty picture of the future, and it does not take into account the almost inevitable future of the multinational corporation, which, for all of the questions associated with its behavior, is probably going to play a major role for quite a while. It is appropriate (inevitable, natural, desirable?) that individual corporations be able to operate in many countries without being hamstrung in their activities and, certainly, without having to accomplish the impossible feat of being majority-owned by the nationals of each of the countries in which they operate.

Better let corporations be multinational and better weaken (rather than strengthen) their relations with national governments. But, then, the multinational corporation must be subjected to meaningful, international control.

The chief, and most controversial, defensive measure of the underdeveloped countries has been expropriation with compensation (or, alternatively, nationalization or confiscation). As the end result of this process, the enterprise is subsequently owned by and run by either the government or local private industrial magnates, who end up with a pretty good thing for next to nothing.

Host countries have been tempted to react to the excesses (or the imagined excesses) of foreign firms—such as meddling in local politics or domineering the local economy—with confiscation or at least with antiforeign denunciations. Such tactics gain the government favor with almost everyone—the local labor unions, the students, the army, the poor, the rich—especially those of the latter group who may end up owning or controlling the properties in question and exploiting their fellow citizens as briskly as the foreigners ever did. The other classes, meanwhile, enjoy the excitement of the antiforeign crusade, but they probably get little else for their trouble in the end. True, some of the more flamboyant popular leaders may gain power and political position.

Expropriation has not been much of a cure-all; it has not been much of a cure-anything. In fact, some of the public-utility expropriations in Latin America in recent years apparently have permitted some of the foreign companies, such as I.T.&T., to divest themselves of money-losing, undesirable properties, for example, in Brazil.

After the expropriation or confiscation, the government (or local private industrialists) may have a production facility which they may be able to use effectively in producing for the local market. It is also not unlikely that the enterprise, lacking the worldwide connections of the multinational corporation, will have trouble obtaining the necessary raw materials or intermediate goods. The personnel may have difficulty with some of the more technical aspects of the plant operation. Also, if the enterprise, in order to operate on a reasonably efficient scale, must export a substantial amount of its product, there may be additional trouble overcoming the tariff barriers of other underdeveloped (and developed) countries.

Such difficulties are especially likely to arise in connection with large, complex production facilities originally involving integrating operations in many countries. On the other hand, by expropriation, underdeveloped countries may acquire some fairly small-scale operations that can be managed successfully, for example, in industries such as textiles. They may acquire some raw-material-producing properties involving oil or various metallic minerals that will prove profitable, perhaps after some marketing problems have been worked out with certain other multinational companies that are not above capitalizing on their fellow multinational's troubles. However, small underdeveloped countries are not going to make much progress in sharing in the development of the major pathbreaking manufacturing industries of the world by such procedures.

If the underdeveloped country's primary concern is to take major steps forward in increasing productivity and improving the standard of living, generalized expropriation emerges as a "cut off your nose to spite your face" solution.

Of Creditor Countries (Especially "Send the Marines" and Guarantees)

Aggrieved investors may appeal to their home governments to send the marines to collect the customs and use the proceeds to pay the investors off. They may abstain from further investment in the offending country. They may solicit their congress to restrict further lending or other assistance to the offending country.

The home-country government, on the other hand, may establish some kind of insurance guarantee system to pay off investors who have their properties expropriated or confiscated. Such insurance arrangements may or may not involve some sort of formal agreement on behavior and/or joint participation between the two governments as a prerequisite to the making of the original, insured investment. If the potential host government does not agree to certain behavior norms or, perhaps, to some arrangement for compensation, the home government may discourage the original investment.[22]

Such measures are at best palliatives, however. They do not represent reasonable solutions to real problems under the rule of law.

Tax and Tariff Policy

The taxation policy that has been applied to multinationals and foreign investments is a whole world of additional complexity in relation to the general run of tax problems. For example, there have been the provisions in the U.S. tariff law relative to raw materials and semiprocessed goods exported from the United States, involved in some processing abroad, and then imported back into the United States. In such cases, the import tariff rate is applied only to the value added to the product in the foreign processing, not to the total value of the imported goods.[23] Especially involved are the textile, motor, and electronics industries—and don't forget baseballs.

United States labor unions complain of these provisions, alleging that they result in lost employment in the States relative to northern Mexico, East Asia, and other areas where such foreign processing is going on. The unions also object to various features of the general United States corporate income tax setup for encouraging foreign investment.

The general effect of this tax treatment is that the United States-owned subsidiaries pay no domestic corporate income tax on foreign-made profits until such profits are actually transferred to the United States—which frequently never occurs. Also, it is a general rule that, on profits actually transferred to the United States, the tax owed is tentatively computed under more or less standard procedures. Then taxes already paid to foreign governments are deducted from the domestic tax liability. This frequently virtually wipes out the tax payment obligation to the

United States. There are additional procedures for reducing tax liability to the United States under the Western Hemisphere Trade Corporation provisions: under this arrangement, a corporation chartered in the United States whose major business is outside the States but inside the Western Hemisphere is entitled to reduce its profits (for purposes of computing the United States corporate income tax) by 14/48 before the computation of the tax.

The net effect of this combination of possibilities seems to be that, on their foreign operations, U.S. corporations are likely to pay corporate income taxes at rates in the 5 to 15 percent range, while domestic firms are paying at rates approaching 48 percent. However, of course, this is not net gain to the foreign investor, who is meanwhile paying considerable tax to the foreign government.

Such favoritism to foreign investors might be (and has been) looked upon as economic assistance to underdeveloped countries. But if, in the longer run, it is desirable to eliminate as much discrimination as possible, the domestic unions may have a genuine complaint on this ground. As the Williams Commission recommended in 1971: "We believe that tax systems should not be designed to provide either an incentive or a deterrent to foreign over domestic investment, whether inward or outward."[24]

The OECD Code of 1976

In 1976, due to a general feeling that society should decree some behavior norms for the multinationals, the Organization for Economic Cooperation and Development drafted a voluntary conduct code. The code says that the multinationals should disclose more information on their activities, they should be competitive rather than collusive, they should "take into consideration the established objectives of the countries in which they operate," they should be forthcoming with the information necessary for correct determination of their taxes, they should refrain from using transfer pricing when it does not conform to "an arm's length standard," they should respect "the right of their employees to be represented by labor unions."[25] And there are some admonitions about not practicing bribery.

Probably some such rather innocuous action is necessary as a first step in getting hold of the multinationals in the social interest. But such a voluntary code can scarcely accomplish very much, even if it is observed, and, even if observed, it would actually generate only a fraction of the information needed. For example, in the area of information disclosure, Sweden pressed for disclosure of such things as profits, wages, sales, and transfer prices on a country-by-country basis. But "other countries led by the United States argued that companies would be forced to give away too much competitive information if they broke down their data in this manner."[26] The resulting compromise pretty well assures that really meaningful information will not be revealed in significant quantities.

The world community does not yet have the multinationals under control. Discussion of further possible measures should be a major concern—even if they seem a bit beyond the realm of likelihood in the atmosphere of 1980.

International Incorporation

The behemoths should not be allowed to operate without social control. The United Nations must develop machinery for such control, probably involving international agency incorporation of multinational corporations.

There is probably no satisfactory way to deal with the problem of the power of the multinational corporation (and with its facility for avoiding national laws) short of international incorporation of multinational firms and taxation by the United Nations of corporations which operate internationally. There might then be some sort of grant-in-aid arrangement for transferring much of the tax receipts down to individual nations (especially underdeveloped nations). This procedure would deal with two serious problems— controlling multinational corporations and structuring foreign aid—[27] and might facilitate underdeveloped-country acceptance of such an arrangement.

The organizations operate internationally. It is therefore desirable that their legal personality be essentially international. This means that they should be incorporated by an international agency rather than by a national government, or the state of New Jersey, or the duchy of Luxembourg. An agency of the United Nations should be empowered to charter business enterprises, much as is now done by individual nations or states within nations.

An International Corporate Income Tax and Grants-in-Aid
One feature of these arrangements should be an international corporate income tax, with tax payments being made directly by the

corporation to the international agency, without benefit of intermediation by any national government, developed or underdeveloped. Also, the United Nations police should be free to enforce the tax collection, if necessary, wherever the corporation may be approachable (and that is surely somewhere).

An independent source of revenue of this sort could be the making of the United Nations, just as the power to collect the customs directly was the making of the U.S. federal government after 1789. Even with quite moderate rates, the international corporate income tax should raise more than enough to finance the United Nations into a viable organization and to yield a substantial surplus which might well be used as grants-in-aid to underdeveloped countries to take the place of most (or perhaps all) bilateral international aid. Eliminating this bilateral foreign aid, with its unhealthy power-politics ramifications, is long overdue. Also, the possible grants-in-aid might well make underdeveloped-country governments more sympathetic to international incorporation and its implications.

If there is to be halfway equitable taxation of the giant multinationals, the geographical taxing unit has to be the world as a whole. As things have been, no taxing jurisdiction, not even the United States, is big enough to make an effective check on the books of many of these corporations. Certainly the typical small, underdeveloped country has neither the information nor the jurisdiction nor the administration to implement the imposition of fair taxes.

There should be an international treaty provision by which individual countries agree not to allow the company in question to manufacture or mine (or whatever) within their boundaries, if the company is also operating in some other country, unless it is internationally incorporated. (Perhaps purely trading companies would be exempted, at least initially, from these procedures.)

Legal Appeal
There should also be provision that corporations (and individuals) in a wide variety of circumstances should have the right to appeal the decisions of the supreme courts of the host countries to some international tribunal (but *not* to the foreign offices of the home countries of the creditors).

The possibility of receiving substantial funds in the form of grants-in-aid from the international corporate income tax (and without political strings attached) might make the underdeveloped countries both willing to cooperate in such a program and willing to allow possibly aggrieved multinationals to appeal court cases from national to international courts. Corporations occasionally do have very legitimate complaints against the treatment they get from local (even supreme) courts, local mobs, and local charismatic rulers. National governments in small countries have frequently been irresponsible, if not vicious, in their attacks on foreign enterprises. What better way for local politicians (a general who has just seized power by coup or a politician who wants to stay in power) to solidify their position than by attacking foreign investors?

The quid pro quo, for international endorsement of the principle of nonintervention (by strong countries in the domestic affairs of the weak) and for the grant-in-aid by-product of the international corporate income tax, should be an international court to which the multinational corporation can appeal in the event of possible injustice in the national judiciary of the debtor country or in the event of confiscation by the government of the debtor country.[28]

The right of appeal from local courts to international courts should help make the multinationals willing to go along with international incorporation. And the prospect of grants-in-aid should help induce the underdeveloped countries to realize that this is a better procedure than a policy of nationalization, such as is so frequently self-defeating.

Representation on Boards
In the proposal for international incorporation, there should probably also be a provision for a process that would allow more underdeveloped countries to be involved in multinational corporation management. Perhaps some sort of formula could be developed that would require representation on the board of directors by at least one national of every country in which a corporation does 10 percent of its business or 10 percent of its production. One might think it would be good judgment for multinationals to give such representation without being required to do so.

Perhaps, also, there might be a provision that one-third or one-fourth of all board members be public officials, at least if the firm is larger than a certain size. But one should not expect too much from "representation on the board" measures. Someone will need to bird-dog the bird-dogs.

Summary

The international incorporation of business firms operating across national boundaries should have several advantages. It should help make it clear that it is inappropriate for developed-country governments to try to protect such firms when they get into trouble abroad (International Petroleum in Peru or what-have-you). It should not matter what the nationality of the majority stockholder interest may be. It should be understood as a principle of international law that it is inappropriate for one sovereign state to put pressure on another in support of private corporations which are based in the pressuring country. If these principles were accepted worldwide, one of the sorest areas in international relations might play less of a role in stirring up friction between countries.

Countries (or their governments) both large and small object to giving an international organization the power to direct the behavior of a sovereign nation. Just what claim to omniscience sovereign nations possess that has entitled them to be free of external control has never been quite clear. Even stranger, in connection with the prevalent acceptance of the validity of the concept of the sovereign nation, is the insistence on the part of small, weak, underdeveloped countries on the sacredness of this concept. These are the very countries that have a stake in the rule of international law. But international law will never have the stature which will permit it to protect the small, the weak, and the underdeveloped until all countries (including especially the small) accept the duties that go with the rights in such a system. This means that they must also understand that they themselves are subject to the rule of law. The sovereign state as an entity above the law is a concept with which the earth should dispense, the sooner the better.

The incorporation of multinationals with an international agency is desirable. Multinationals should pay an international corporate income tax on the totality of their operations. Grants-in-aid back to individual governments from the receipts from the corporate income tax should, in general, take the place of "foreign aid." And corporations, and other possibly aggrieved parties, should have a right of appeal from national supreme courts to an international court, at least in a substantial range of situations.

NOTES

1. See Herbert Feis, *Europe, the World's Banker, 1870–1914* (New Haven: Yale University Press, 1931); Wendell Gordon, *The Expropriation of Foreign-Owned Property in Mexico* (Washington, D.C.: American Council on Public Affairs, 1941); Anthony Sampson, *The Sovereign State of ITT* (New York: Stein & Day, 1973); Mira Wilkins, *The Emergence of Multinational Enterprise* (Cambridge, Mass.: Harvard University Press, 1970).
2. *Viewpoint, an IUD Quarterly* 5 (Fourth quarter 1975): 3.
3. Raymond Vernon, *Sovereignty at Bay: The Multinational Spread of U.S. Enterprises* (New York: Basic Books, 1971), p. 16.
4. United States, Senate, Committee on Finance (83: 1), *Implications of Multinational Firms for World Trade and Investment and for U.S. Trade and Labor* (Washington, D.C.: Government Printing Office, 1973), pp. 8–9.
5. *New York Times*, October 25, 1972, pp. 63, 75.
6. *Statistical Abstract of the U.S.*, 1978, p. 575.
7. Allan G. Gruchy, *Contemporary Economic Thought* (Clifton, N.J.: Kelley, 1972), p. 28.
8. Lester R. Brown, *The Interdependence of Nations* (New York: Foreign Policy Association, 1972), pp. 16–17.
9. See Arthur W. Rovine, *Digest of United States Practice in International Law, 1973*, Department of State Publication 8,756 (Washington, D.C.: Government Printing Office, 1974), p. 379.
10. *Viewpoint, an IUD Quarterly* 5 (Fourth quarter 1975). This issue of the publication of the Industrial Union Department was devoted virtually in its entirety to the multinationals.
11. See Roberto Marchesini, "Impact of Multinational Corporations on Domestic Employment" (Ph.D. dissertation, University of Texas at Austin, 1974).
12. "Worldwide Companies Outgrow Nations," *New York Times*, February 13, 1972, sec. 3, p. 1.
13. *Viewpoint, an IUD Quarterly* 5 (Fourth quarter 1975): 37.
14. *New York Times*, January 26, 1974, p. 14.
15. C. S. Burchill, "The Multinational Corporation," *World Federalist* (January 1971): 7, 9, 10.
16. The apostolic letter to Cardinal Roy, "Octogesima adveniens," is quoted in Salvador María Lozada, *Empresas multinacionales* (Buenos Aires: El Colegio, 1973), p. 92.

17. See George W. Stocking and Myron Watkins, *Cartels in Action* (New York: Twentieth Century Fund, 1946).
18. See Roger Beardwood, "Sophistication Comes to the Tax Havens," *Fortune* 79 (February 1969): 95 ff.
19. Constantine V. Vaitsos, *Intercountry Income Distribution and Transnational Enterprise* (London: Oxford University Press, 1974).
20. See Gordon, *Expropriation of Foreign-Owned Property*.
21. Paul N. Rosenstein-Rodan, "Multinational Investment in the Economic Development and Integration of Latin America," in Inter-American Development Bank, *Multinational Investment in the Economic Development and Integration of Latin America* (Washington, D.C., 1968), pp. 21–31; Guy B. Meeker, "Fade-Out Joint Venture: Can It Work for Latin America?" *Inter-American Economic Affairs* 24 (Spring 1971): 25–42; Albert O. Hirschman, *How to Divest in Latin America, and Why* (Princeton: International Finance Section, Princeton University, 1969).
22. See Rovine, *Digest of United States Practice in International Law*, pp. 379–386.
23. United States, Tariff Commission, *Economic Factors Affecting the Use of Items 807.00 and 806.30 of the Tariff Schedules of the United States* (Washington, D.C., 1970).
24. United States, Commission on International Trade and Investment Policy (Williams Commission), *United States International Economic Policy in an Interdependent World* (Washington, D.C.: Government Printing Office, 1971), p. 179.
25. *New York Times*, May 27, 1976, p. 6.
26. Ibid., p. 7.
27. See George W. Ball, "Cosmocorp: The Importance of Being Stateless," *Columbia Journal of World Business* 11 (November 1967): 25–30; Edith T. Penrose, *The Large International Firm in Developing Countries: The International Petroleum Industry* (Cambridge: MIT Press, 1968), p. 273; Paul Streeten, *The Frontiers of Development Studies* (London: Macmillan, 1972), p. 231.
28. Raymond Vernon seems to take a position not greatly dissimilar from this. See United States, Congress, Joint Economic Committee, Subcommittee on Foreign Economic Policy (Hearings, 91: 1), *A Foreign Economic Policy for the 1970's, pt. 1: Survey of the Issues* (Washington, D.C.: Government Printing Office, 1970), p. 143.

ADDITIONAL READINGS

Ball, George W., ed. *Global Companies*. Englewood Cliffs, N.J.: Prentice-Hall (for the American Assembly), 1975.

Barnet, Richard J., and Ronald E. Müller. *Global Reach: The Power of the Multinational Corporation*. New York: Simon & Schuster, 1974.

Hymer, Stephen H. *The International Operations of National Firms*. Cambridge, Mass.: MIT Press, 1976.

Servan-Schreiber, J. J. *The American Challenge*. New York: Atheneum, 1968.

Tugendhat, Christopher. *The Multinationals*. London: Eyre & Spottiswoode, 1971.

United Nations. *Report of the Group of Eminent Persons to Study the Impact of Multinational Corporations*. . . . New York, 1974.

14.
The Energy-Ecology "Crisis" of the 1970s

THE POLLUTION PROBLEM has had many facets. What can be done about garbage? A good deal of it is floating down the rivers. Automobiles generate exhaust fumes and smog, with the help of trucks. Oil slicks are good for suppressing mosquitoes, but swimmers do not like them, nor do beaches, nor seabirds. Then there is cigarette smoke, and aerosol fallout, and atomic fallout. Picnickers have been known to litter, and so have a lot of people in town and along the highway. The country can almost be papered with old beer cans and bottles. And a lot of the surface of the country has gone the way of coal strip mining. The energy problem has one facet: we want more.

These are cases of undesirable results, in large measure byproducts of modern technology—examples of institutionalized practices brought into being by technology as epitomized by the internal-combustion motor. One can allege this on the basis of a value judgment connection with which there would seem to be pretty general consensus.

The Problem

There is reason for treating the ecology and the energy difficulties together. The curtailment in energy use (or the shift to other energy sources) which may be called for by petroleum, natural gas, and waterpower "shortages" could represent a significant aspect of the solution of the pollution problem. Also, industry representatives have used the ecologists as whipping boys for the energy shortage. The two problems are related.

The Reserves

In what sense is there, or may there be, an energy shortage?[1] In 1973, when the energy crisis surfaced, proven reserves in the Middle East still seemed astronomical in size. One relevant statistic concerns the number of years that presently known proven oil reserves in the ground will last at the prevailing rate of production. About 1932, United States currently known reserves would have provided for the then prevailing United States production for about sixteen years. In 1971, the figure was down to eleven years. Since the average figure for all the years since 1918 is probably something like twelve years, this is hardly a figure to become especially concerned about, hardly a figure that would explain a crisis in 1973. Nevertheless, it probably did hint at trouble in the years ahead, especially since the figure would be more like eight years if Alaskan oil were excluded.

After the development of Middle Eastern production, the equivalent figure for the world was at a peak about 1957, when the then prevailing rate of world production could be supported by the then known reserves for about thirty-five years. In 1971, the figure was down to thirty-two years. As is the case with the United States figures, this is hardly a development that could explain a crisis in 1973.

With regard to natural gas, the situation is similarly equivocal. But, also, natural gas bears a rather peculiar relation to crude oil. To an important degree, natural gas production has been a byproduct of petroleum production. Natural gas in considerable measure has been produced not because it was wanted but because gas pressure facilitated petroleum production. Over the years in the United States, unbelievable amounts of natural gas have been produced and flared—one should have seen the East Texas Oil Field at night in the 1930s to believe it. There is less waste now in the United States than there used to be, but perhaps this circumstance has more ominous rather than less ominous implications for the speedy exhaustion of natural gas in this country. It is not flared so much because it is relatively more valuable and scarce. Apparently, however, there is still major wastage in foreign fields, especially in the Middle East. And the likelihood of working out arrangements for using that gas to ease the immediate shortage in the United States seems remote indeed.

In the United States in 1949, the natural gas reserves were adequate to meet the then rate of production for 33 years. In 1971, the figure was down to 12.4 years. Meanwhile, the consumption of natural gas in the United States has been rising at a rate substantially faster than the consumption of petroleum products in general. This relationship suggests far more genuine serious trouble immediately and in the years just ahead for natural gas than need have been the situation with gasoline and other petroleum products.

However, on the world scene, between 1964 and 1971 the number of years that world natural gas reserves would supply world production was rising from thirty to forty-two years. One should probably not draw particularly encouraging implications from this relation, however. The international trade in natural gas is relatively small and may remain so, and much of the Middle Eastern gas is not marketable production. It is wasted, and it is likely to continue to be wasted. Or is it? Also, the United States plays a much larger relative role in the world natural gas picture than in the world petroleum picture. In 1972, U.S. natural gas production, of the so-called marketable or marketed type, was still over half of the world total. So, to some degree, the United States is probably going to stew in its own juice in the natural gas matter.

Estimated oil reserves in the oil shale deposits of the Green River Formation in Colorado, Utah, and Wyoming are four times the presently estimated petroleum reserves of the world. At present consumption rates in the United States, the recoverable coal reserves are estimated to last some 2,600 years. Such figures are being reestimated down, but they are still large. In the background are atomic power (fusion and fission), solar energy, geothermal energy, the energy of the wind, and whatnot. Why should the United States have succeeded in conjuring up a fuel shortage in 1973?

Conditions (Largely Involving Institutionalized Behavior) Which Have Created the Difficulties

Relative Cheapness in the United States

Petroleum, natural gas, and waterpower (and, consequently, electricity) have been relatively cheap, especially in the United States and especially since Dad Joiner discovered oil in the East Texas Oil Field in the early 1930s. Cheapness, convenience, and cleanliness have given them an advantage over coal—resulting in such mistakes as the dieselization of the railroads, which cost the United

States coal industry a fourth or more of its market. Even as late as the 1970s, the price of gasoline was substantially lower in the United States than in almost all other countries, except for a very few like Venezuela. Chiefly it has been high foreign excise tax rates that have accounted for the great differences, not high foreign production costs or high foreign demand.

At all events, in general and chiefly in the United States, petroleum and natural gas have been convenient, clean (relatively clean), and cheap. The American consumer and the American industrialist and the American laborer have exploited this godsend in profligate fashion, at prices so low that the development of alternative energy sources was inhibited until it was "too late."

After World War II, industry in the United States, especially on the Gulf coast of Texas, waxed fat, and it now seems fat on the basis of deceptively cheap petroleum and natural gas. In the United States in general, automobiles proliferated and urban mass transit almost disappeared. Freeways came to dominate city planning and city skylines—at least when one could see the skylines through the smog. Natural gas became a prime fuel for developing electric power. Coal fell into disuse, at least relatively speaking, and waterpower has never played more than a marginal role. And the promoters of natural gas succeeded in selling Texas gas in New England and the Pacific Northwest: quite a feat.

Regulation, Proration, and Allowables
The petroleum industry has "conspired" with the United States Bureau of Mines, the Railroad Commission of Texas, the Interstate Oil Compact Commission, and the labor unions to keep down the amount of imported oil and to use up United States reserves instead of foreign reserves. Of course, this conspiracy was not overt: industry leaders, and Bureau of Mines officials, and railroad commissioners did not explicitly agree among themselves to do this. In fact, some industry leaders learned long ago that discretion is the better part of valor in such matters. They probably scarcely formulated certain thoughts about the implications of what they were doing, even to themselves.

But they knew.

In a fashion, they knew. The industry developed a certain institutionalized conception of proper behavior that became a powerful influence. Some strange interplay also had a role in these developments. For example, the major oil companies, in fact, never had a real interest in keeping foreign oil out. After all, they produced, or used to produce, the foreign oil. They did have an interest in higher (but not too high) prices and profits, and they did have an interest in favorable legislation in the United States, an interest that could be furthered by the cooperation and support of the domestic independents.

So, rigging a United States price which was high by comparison with the cost of producing Middle East crude but low enough to inhibit the development of shale oil, coal, atomic power, and solar energy fitted their attitudes. This pricing policy was heartily endorsed by the independents in the United States (although they always would have liked a price higher than whatever the price happened to be). But the domestic independents got the point.

The procedure for administering the system was proration. Each month the Bureau of Mines provided the state regulatory agencies, such as the Railroad Commission of Texas, with estimates of the demand for petroleum. These estimates had to involve assumptions as to the prices at which these quantities would be demanded, but these price assumptions were not made explicit. In fact, it was customary to deny that price considerations were involved. (That this was governmental price control in the petroleum industry was vigorously denied. Nevertheless, the government was certainly influencing prices in a manner that generally won the approval of the industry.)

Each month, for example, in Texas, the Railroad Commission would hold hearings to consider the implications of the report it had received from the Bureau of Mines. Industry leaders would testify. And the commission would then issue a proration order indicating how much crude oil could be produced in Texas during the subsequent month.

The control has been precise. Production from each well in the state was specified. This was accomplished by a procedure that in fact made the essence of the monthly order fairly simple. In the interest of "conservation" and of getting, in the long run, the maximum possible production from each well, a figure for the maximum efficient rate of production from each well had been determined. So, it was known how much would be produced if all the wells were operating at their maximum efficient rates. The desirable monthly allowable could then be established as a percentage of that rate. Formerly, this figure was arrived at by specifying, in the monthly order, how many days a month a well could produce at its maximum efficient rate. Recently the procedure has been changed, and the Railroad Commission actually sets the allowable as a percentage of the maximum efficient rate. Since 1973, that figure has pretty generally been 100 percent. An era has ended.

Despite this covert oil industry endorsement of regulation, the overt theme of the industry has always been espousal of the free market system and laissez faire. The industry does want to be as free as it may judiciously be to price-gouge the public.

If the truth be told, however, there is no way that a free market can satisfactorily regulate the production and price of an exhaustible resource. Too frequently, a free market generates too rapid production, the flaring of natural gas, the waste of other by-products, and ultimate shortages. Nevertheless, regulation provides no magic solution. The problem involves the regulation of the regulators by an alert public.

The Nature of Property Rights/the Rule of Capture
The nature of property rights in United States common law explains why surface owners have had title to the oil produced from under their land. And, typically, they have received a one-eighth royalty. This is not the situation in most civil-law countries, where the oil companies obtain their right to produce in the form of concessions from the government. And the equivalent of the one-eighth royalty is paid to the government.

In the United States, in the early years of the oil industry, the provision that the surface owners also owned the oil under their land was supplemented by the Rule of Capture. By analogy with hunting wild animals, it was ruled that they got the oil who brought it to the surface, regardless of the possibility that some of the oil might have come from under a neighbor's land. More than any other thing, this version of the Rule of Capture is probably to blame for the excessive drilling of wells and for the too rapid and wasteful production of petroleum and, even more so, for the too rapid production and flaring of natural gas. Since the 1930s, proration and legal requirements regulating the spacing of wells have somewhat modified these practices. But the desirable unitization of the fields has still not become standard practice, despite the fact that ultimate recovery would undoubtedly substantially increase if each field was administered as a unit.

The Depletion Allowance
The depletion allowance has also played a role as a behavior pattern in the industry. This highly institutionalized characteristic of the petroleum industry (and of mineral production generally) had been designed to give the companies and the royalty owners a break in computing their federal income taxes. For many years, 27.5 percent of the gross oil produced was deducted before the total amount of production was taken into account for purposes of computing the tax liability of the producers and royalty owners. Industry representatives have, over the years, vigorously argued that this tax favoritism is necessary to encourage risk taking in the search for oil, the riskiness of which activity being continually pointed out. In the United States, such allowances involving a variety of rates have characterized production of most depletable natural resources: sand and gravel (5 percent), sulfur (22 percent), limestone (14 percent), bauxite (14 percent), oil shale (15 percent), iron ore (15 percent), and copper (15 percent).[2] Also, over the years, the United States permitted the application of the depletion allowance to foreign production by U.S. companies.

In recent years, the depletion allowance for oil has almost been eliminated. Thus, the issue is largely historical. The depletion allowance should never have been established, except, perhaps, on a temporary basis. Oil production has been sufficiently profitable to cover any reasonable interpretation of the risk influence.

In the 1970s, modifying the depletion allowance provisions is a little like locking the barn door after the animal has been stolen. Nothing can now undo the seventy-five years of vicious lobbying by the landowner/oil millionaires who have profited from the depletion allowance. Removing the depletion allowance now will never recapture for society the bonanzas of Spindletop and East Texas, Ranger and Scurry County, and the King Ranch, of Hunt and Getty, Rockefeller and Glenn McCarthy, or undo the damage done by the flaring of gas in the oil fields of the Southwest during the 1930s.

The depletion allowance on foreign oil was also an important issue. And the stakes were huge. The United States oil producers argued that in fact the Arab, Persian, Venezuelan, and Libyan governments ended up taking most of it away from them. Even to the extent that this was true and the depletion allowance became a form of foreign aid, it was foreign aid to the wrong underdeveloped countries. The Lord must really have been in a sadistic frame of mind the day he put the oil bonanzas in the least populated of the underdeveloped countries.

The Profitability of the Industry
It should be noted that the oil industry is more profitable, in terms of the take of its participants, than the ordinary corporate profit statements reveal. For example, in 1972 oil industry profit rates (after taxes) were about 10.8 percent. Profit rates for all manufacturing were 12.1 percent and, for all industry, 10.5 percent. These figures would seem to put the oil industry fairly close to the average for the economy or even slightly below the average. However, comparisons of this sort do not take into account the fact that a value equal to one-eighth, more or less, of the gross of all the oil produced is siphoned off as pure gravy to the royalty owners before these profit rates are computed. And one-eighth of the gross, as unearned increment to surface owners, has not been chicken feed.

Crosscurrents in 1973
What caused the blow to fall in 1973 was probably a more or less accidental juxtaposition of events which, given the institutional structure and operating norms of the oil industry, created a serious problem. It is worth looking at some of these conditions to see how they acted and interacted.

In the United States, limiting petroleum imports by an import quota system has been popular. The idea seems to have been: let us use up the domestic oil reserves rather than the Arabian reserves. "Buy the product of your friendly local merchant." The majors were willing to orient their marketing of Middle Eastern oil to Europe and to cooperate with the domestic independents in keeping oil in moderately short supply in the United States, so that the U.S. price structure could be higher than would probably have been the case in the 1950s and 1960s if Arab oil had been permitted to force down the price.

Meanwhile, with the expanded consumption in the United States in the 1960s, a shortage of domestic refining capacity developed at the same time that the environmentalists were beginning to object to the role of petroleum refineries in polluting the environment. Antipollution standards, which the companies did not want to meet, were set by law. And the companies delayed the construction of new refineries. Thus, the shortage of 1973 was in some degree caused by a shortage of refining capacity (and inadequate arrangements for importing). Then the Yom Kippur war of 1973 and the Arab oil embargo triggered a crisis.

Also, perhaps, there was another element in the picture. Subconsciously, the industry leaders probably relished the idea of a shortage and a crisis. It would give them an opportunity to put the ecologists in their place, perhaps an opportunity to force the relaxation of the antipollution standards, an opportunity to force the building of the Alaskan pipeline, and an opportunity to obtain government support in their battle with the Arab sheiks for title to the Middle Eastern properties.

The importance of the desire of the industry leaders to put down the environmentalists should not be underestimated. Many seem to have become almost psychopathic on the subject of the Sierra Club and the Wilderness Society. They had been pretty thoroughly defeated in the Battle of the Santa Barbara Channel, and they did not take their defeat with good grace. On the matter of pervasive oil slicks, they have been truculently defensive and have made no good-faith efforts to deal reasonably with the problems. It was hardly enough that the water coming out of the King Ranch refinery was pure enough for the Santa Gertrudis to drink: the water coming out of the Perth Amboy refineries needed to be reasonably clean also.

Finally, the oil companies managed to obtain a substantial spurt in profits as a result of the 1973 crisis—and also as a by-product of the 1979 crisis. The temptation apparently was strong, on the part of the companies, to net what they could from these situations. But one may be excused for wondering whether it was very good judgment on their part, in view of the public reaction.

Problems since 1973

The Arab oil embargo of 1973, the accompanying escalation by three or four times over (from three plus dollars a barrel to eleven dollars) in the price of oil, and the subsequent high cost of imports created a major balance of payments problem for the developed countries of western Europe and a significant problem for the United States. However, the willingness of the Arabs to hold their balances in the United States and western Europe as well as their interest in buying increased supplies of arms and industrial equipment from the West meant that, by 1975, the balance of payments problem resulting from the oil crisis seemed to have temporarily disappeared. (Large agricultural exports from the United States also helped in this process.) In fact, one might have surmised, from the renewed wave of purchasing large automobiles in the United States by 1976, that the problem was gone.

For the underdeveloped, non-oil-producing countries the problem has remained serious in the sense that their industrialization programs have been significantly impeded by the lack of fuel. Also, many of these countries can ill afford the more expensive oil. But the burden has been uneven: countries producing other raw materials that have also risen in price have suffered less than countries with little means to compensate. But, then, the poor have a remarkable ability to tighten their belts and survive.

And maybe they and everybody else need some such ability. There was a short-lived second-round oil crisis in the early summer of 1979, which involved another round of rising prices, shortages, and bonanza oil company profits. The groundwork for the crisis was provided by an upheaval in Iran. But some other event would no doubt have created a second-round crisis at about that time if Iran had not.

We have successfully avoided any jolt and even avoided any significant structural corrective since 1973—a rather remarkable feat under the circumstances. Between 1967 and 1978, the price of gasoline did not rise relative to consumer prices in general:[3]

	Consumer Price Index	*Price of Gasoline Index*
1967	100.0	100.00
1972	121.3	118.1
May 1978	193.2	192.3

Given the threatened exhaustion of reserves and the insecurity of sources of supply and the appropriateness of a substantial rise in gasoline prices relative to other prices, this performance has to be viewed as remarkable. Something was due to fall on us by the spring of 1979, with or without the help of the Iranians and OPEC.

And the most fabulous standard of living of any large country in the history of the world has not suffered perceptibly either:

	Consumer Price Index	Per Capita Consumption Expenditures Index
1967	100.0	100.0
1972	121.3	140.5
May 1978	193.2	249.7

And per capita gasoline consumption has risen:

	Per Capita Domestic Gasoline Product Demand Index
1967	100.0
1972	121.4
May 1978	134.2

Given the increase in miles per gallon that cars have been getting on the average, this implies an amazing increase in the mileage being driven by the average individual. We bought a few of the small cars and then figured that that proof of concern licensed us to drive more, to move out further and further into suburbia, and to junket more generously on the weekends. Little wonder that urban mass transit has not revived.

People in general do not observe the 55 miles an hour speed limit. Why should they, as they see the trucks flying by at 70 or 75 miles an hour? The truckers certainly have problems, but so also do a lot of other people not in a position to flaunt their power in ways available to the truckers since they asserted themselves in 1973.

Meanwhile the price of gasoline in western Europe is two and a half times the price in the United States, and the average European does not even own a car, and neither does the average Russian, Latin American, African, or Asian.

Offshore drilling has not produced major discoveries. The nuclear program is, to put it mildly, in trouble. The oil shale program has not evolved. The oil companies have bought a lot of coal mines, an activity which has probably not contributed much to increasing the supply of coal.

In spite of our "if we disregard it maybe it will go away" attitude, there is a problem. We are running out of oil. And we are not likely to be saved by major new domestic discoveries. It does not matter how much we subsidize the oil companies, how freely we let their prices float, how much we let the profit motive operate, or how much we denounce the oil companies.

Possible Future Energy Sources

Alternative energy sources include oil shale, tar sands, coal, nuclear fission, nuclear fusion, the sun, the winds, the tides, thermal energy from underground hot water, waterpower from dams and waterfalls, and no doubt, the list should be extended. The sun (thermal energy) is probably the most promising source for the long run. But it is not going to substitute for gasoline powering automobiles in the medium run. And various of the other possible sources will play roles of varying importance depending on how the energy technology evolves. The planet is not going to exhaust its energy sources, but it may pass through some traumatic periods accommodating needs to the nature of the types of energy becoming increasingly available.

Whichever sources of energy gain in relative importance in comparison with petroleum and natural gas (and several will), we can be sure that the resultant institutional changes which will be called forth will be major. Some suburbanites may even have to move back to town, and the layout of cities may be changed drastically. But one cannot state with assurance what form these institutional changes will take. Technological determinism permitting such precise forecasting is not possible. But that makes the whole process more interesting.

Policies

Rationing and geographical allocations and continued artificially low prices are not going to solve the problems, however much wishful thinking there may be in the Northeast on this score. I allege here, rather dogmatically, that long-run rationing on a comprehensive scale cannot be made fair and workable. A substantial increase in the prices of gasoline and natural gas relative to other prices is long overdue. That is what it will take to stimulate the development of alternative sources of energy, and to reduce consumption (or slow the rate of increase in consumption), and to hold back expansion in the use of energy long enough to get the pollution situation under control. In no event is a major increase in petroleum production in the United States likely to be the White Knight to the rescue, unless we are unbelievably lucky. A price increase will not draw out increased production in the patterns alleged by the proponents of higher prices, higher profits, higher production scenario. That argument is a ploy by the oil industry to justify higher prices and profits.

The policy measure which is immediately called for is a new federal excise tax of at least a dollar a gallon. Life will be simplified if, at the same time, the price controls on gasoline are lifted and the allocation system is abolished. No doubt the price will go up somewhat more than exactly the amount of the dollar a gallon tax. But, at least, there will not be the major bonanza to the oil industry people which would be involved if they got it all. Also, the excise will insure that the government gets the money more quickly and simply than will be the case if prime reliance is placed on an excess profits tax. (However, an excess profits tax, as a backstop, may well be desirable.)

There will be some repercussions. The price increases, insofar as they apply to business, industry, and trucking, will appropriately be passed along, with some further inflationary effects. But, fortunately, for the most part the private motorists will not be able to pass the increases along and will be induced (the hard way) to drive at least somewhat less. And a few prices might even come down, for example, the price of real estate in suburbia.

We must understand that it is appropriate that the price of gasoline rise substantially *relative* to other prices—and quickly. During recent years, we have been remarkably adept at compensating and increasing other prices and our incomes more rapidly than the gasoline price. And personal consumption expenditures have risen even faster. A favorable long-run effect of the substantial relative increase in gasoline prices should be to halt or at least to slow down the migration to the suburbs and to encourage the building of high-rise apartments (backed by extensive green areas) along arterial streets. This development is necessary as a preliminary to the revival of urban mass transit.

Fortunately for the real-estate industry, it has a good thing going and coming—promoting suburbia the past few years and building high-rise apartments for the next few.

As early as 1973, concern for the poor was cited as a reason for avoiding at all costs an increase in the price of gasoline. Seldom have the poor been so inadequately served by the concern of the affluent. Politicians interested in doing something for the poor could try to enact job guarantee legislation—and even effect the long-overdue reform of the federal income tax.

Incidentally, a dollar a gallon excise on gasoline would raise over $100 billion a year. That sum could more than subsidize a job guarantee program, or a health program, or a lot of exemptions at low levels in the income tax. It could even create the possibility of eliminating virtually all of the country's sales taxes, which come to a figure less than $100 billion. If concern for the poor was, at least for some, the real grounds for opposing a major increase in the price of gasoline, the repeal of the sales taxes (which are especially burdensome on the poor) should mollify those few who have been genuinely concerned for the poor.

In any event, there is an obvious, simple cure for the immediate gasoline crunch, a cure that will have quite a few constructive, worthwhile long-run effects. But it is a cure that no politician in Washington will endorse because they have all brainwashed each other to the effect that the voters will not hold still for an increase in the tax on gasoline. And it is true that almost any individual will be glad to wax indignant on the subject.

But the voters are going to get an increase in the price of gasoline. The only real question is whether the increase is carried out in a better or worse way—with or without rationing, with or without wholesale industry profiteering, with or without major difficulty for suburbia as suburbia tries to get to work.

The high excise tax would seem to be the urgent, high-priority, desirable policy measure which will cut back consumption at least somewhat and which should have several desirable by-product effects. But there are many other potentially useful policies. One would involve returning the railroads to the use of coal or fuels other than those derived from petroleum. Also, the railroads should be expanding their passenger service in a major way on runs of one hundred to seven hundred miles between large cities. And positive measures (probably in the form of taxes) should be taken to reduce long-distance hauling by trucks and the return of much of that business to the railroads.

The necessary structural changes can be made fairly painlessly if we will set about the task with some sense of urgency and some thoughtfulness.

NOTES

1. Sources of the statistical data used in this section include *World Oil*, particularly the February 15 and August 15 issues of any year; United States Bureau of Mines, *Minerals Yearbook*; United Nations, *Statistical Yearbook*; *Monthly Bulletin of Statistics*; *Commodity Yearbook*; First National City Bank *Monthly Letter*.
2. *Prentice-Hall Federal Tax Handbook, 1975* (Englewood Cliffs, N.J.: Prentice-Hall, 1975), p. 299.
3. Information in this and the following tables has been culled from *Statistical Abstract of the United States, 1978* (Washington, D.C.: Government Printing Office, 1978).

ADDITIONAL READINGS

Adelman, Morris A. *World Petroleum Market*. Baltimore: Johns Hopkins University Press (for Resources for the Future), 1972.

Bohi, Douglas R., and Milton Russell. *U.S. Energy Policy*. Baltimore: Johns Hopkins University Press (for Resources for the Future), 1975.

Carson, Rachel. *Silent Spring*. Boston: Houghton Mifflin, 1962.

Herfindahl, Orris C., and Allen V. Kneese. *Economic Theory of Natural Resources*. Columbus, Ohio: Charles E. Merrill Publishing Co. (for Resources for the Future), 1974.

Kasper, Raphael G., ed. *Technology Assessment: Understanding the Social Consequences of Technological Applications*. New York: Praeger, 1972.

McDonald, Stephen L. *Petroleum Conservation in the United States: An Economic Analysis*. Baltimore: Johns Hopkins University Press (for Resources for the Future), 1971.

Redford, Emmette S. *American Government and the Economy*. New York: Macmillan, 1965. Chapter 21 is an excellent statement on oil and gas.

Reich, Charles A. *The Greening of America*. New York: Random House, 1970.

Zimmermann, Erich W. *Conservation in the Production of Petroleum: A Study in Industrial Control*. New Haven: Yale University Press, 1957.

15.
The Monetary System

The Nature of Money

Money is something, but it is an understatement to say that it is difficult to say what. People like to have some, the more the better, even when its value is falling—maybe especially when its value is falling. Money is a medium of exchange, it is a measure of value (a unit of account), it is a store of value, it is a standard of deferred payment. So!

Money has intrinsic value. No, it does not. A bit of money is basically an acknowledgment of debt, an IOU. Who said so? Money is a creation of the state and has value because the government has power. What is the leverage that assures acceptance of the money after the general who issues the fiat money disappears down the road with his dusty cavalry? Money has value because it has general acceptability (I will accept it, even anxiously, because I know that you have the same attitude). But how did we both get that way? Money is legal tender. The law says that creditors must accept it in payment of debt or go without repayment. That circumstance may line the creditors up, but what about the rest of us?

Perhaps some sense may be made of these questions by viewing money alternatively as a debt instrument, something with intrinsic value, or fiat money.

Money as Debt

I may buy a lawn mower from a dealer for a hundred dollars. I may pay him, or try to pay him, with a slip of paper on which I have written "IOU $100" and signed my name. If I have a signature as well known as that of John Hancock and a reputation for wealth like Jakob Fugger, the dolt may accept the IOU as payment, at least for the present. He may succeed in his turn in buying something from a third party and using my IOU as payment. The third party may play the same trick on a fourth party, and so on far into the night. There is no absolute necessity that the original debtor ever pay off the IOU. But the piece of paper has been functioning as money.

Much the same process, done with more mirrors, is the basic way in which money now comes into existence in most countries. If one may be permitted the luxury of leaving out a few of the mirrors, the essence of the process is as follows. A government prints some bonds with an ostensible face value of $1 million. Printing the bonds is no trick. It just take a printing press. The government then sells the bonds to the central bank, which pays for them with $1 million worth of newly printed ten-dollar bills. The printing of the bills also required a printing press. The government can then use the $1 million worth of "money" to pay its bureaucrats or its suppliers of pencils and paper. And there is the money in circulation. The central bank is glad to cooperate. It has two angles or maybe more. For one, the law probably says that the bonds may serve as the legal reserve behind the money which the central bank issues. That is, the law did not permit the central bank to print the money and directly use it to buy its own pencils and paper and pay its own help. Sound banking practice requires that the central bank have reserves: somebody else's bonds. Another happy feature of this arrangement from the viewpoint of the central bank is that the government is probably paying 5 percent or so interest on the bonds as long as they are outstanding. And the central bank is the recipient of this interest, a well-earned reward for the trouble to which it has been put in printing the money.

So, the debt instrument and the money are not exactly the same pieces of paper. But the money is there as a by-product of the fact that the government has issued the bond, the debt instrument.

In many countries (and frequently), the process of creating money takes virtually this form. More commonly, however, in the "financially more developed" countries, the process is somewhat more circuitous. There are more mirrors. The reserve requirements are more complicated. And the government bonds are probably sold initially to the general public rather than to the central bank. The central bank may then buy them from the public (in the United States, this is called an open-market operation). The citizen who sold the bonds to the Federal Reserve is likely to be paid with a check which becomes the basis for a deposit, the reserve behind which, one or two degrees removed, is the bonds bought by the central bank with the check.

A somewhat different example of the relation between debt and money occurs in connection with the activation of Federal Reserve notes. As the *United States Code* cites: "Any Federal Reserve bank may make application to the local Federal Reserve agent for such amount of the Federal Reserve notes hereinbefore provided for as it may require. Such application shall be accompanied with a tender to the local Federal Reserve agent of collateral in amount equal to the sum of Federal Reserve notes thus applied for and issued pursuant to such application. The collateral security thus offered shall be notes, drafts, bills of exchange, or acceptances acquired under the provisions of sections . . . , or bills of exchange endorsed by a member bank . . . , or bankers' acceptances . . . , or gold certificates, or Special Drawing Right certificates, or direct obligations of the United States."[1] Another party, the Federal Reserve agent, has been injected into the process and, literally, is the one who receives the debt instrument and issues the money.

So, one way to look at money is as a reflection of debt. This is surely a meaningful way to look at the nature of money. Yet this explanation leaves some questions. For example, why does a dollar have more or less the purchasing power that it has? A first approximation of an answer may be that it has more or less the purchasing power that it had yesterday, with purchasing power varying with the passage of time in response to such influences as variation in the total quantity of money in circulation and other changing conditions. And everyone is caught up in a situation where, if everyone is using money as though it had such and such a purchasing power (general acceptability), it will continue to have more or less that purchasing power and no individual will be contemptuous of it. Such a state of affairs is capable of continuing as long as the monetary authorities are reasonably responsible and discreet in issuing money. Don't overdo a good thing, fellows. There still remains the question, How did things get this way? It is one thing to say that a behavior norm in being will continue to be observed. It is another matter to explain how it got that way. The present purchasing power of a unit of money got to be that way as a result of a historical process. And that historical process probably, although not necessarily, did start with a situation where the circulating money had intrinsic value and where it was, in a manner of speaking, a technological imperative to have a medium of exchange.

The Intrinsic Value of Money

Money may have intrinsic value in two directions: because of the things that can be bought with it or because it has commercial value of its own or is redeemable in something that does. It is this latter value that is at stake at the moment and that is the start of this stylized history.

The story begins, let us allege, in the early Middle Ages or earlier with gold coins, which have intrinsic commercial value, circulating as money at a value more or less corresponding to that commercial value. But gold may be readily stolen from a pocket or from underneath a mattress. Also, coins may be undesirably heavy. So, in exchange for a paper receipt, the possessor of gold coins might find it judicious to deposit those coins with a goldsmith to be held in the goldsmith's strongbox. If suitable discretion is exercised and the goldsmith's signature is sufficiently legible and well and honorably known, the receipt may even circulate as money.

Also, at a slightly later stage in the process, the goldsmith may observe that he has quite a collection of gold coins, all mixed up. He is obligated to honor a receipt when depositors request the return of their gold. Probably any gold coins will do, however—they do not have to be the specific coins that were originally deposited. Also, the goldsmith observes that all the depositors do not request their coins at the same time, and he consistently has an amount of gold on deposit that seems never to fall below a certain level. The goldsmith may also have a little of his own gold in the pile and enjoy something of a feeling of legitimate ownership.

It may be noted at this stage in the story that the purchasing power of one unit (a claim on one ounce of gold) of the paper receipts circulating as money has a direct relation to the commercial value of the gold itself. But, as the story unfolds, the relation between the number of units specified on the pieces of paper and the one-to-one correspondence with the quantities of gold at the goldsmith's gets more nebulous.

For a few days, the goldsmith may lend some of the gold continually in his custody to someone willing to pay interest. Or the goldsmith may merely lend a receipt for the gold which he actually still keeps in his possession. In either event, a given bit of the gold is now doing double duty, and we have passed into the realm of a paper money supply based on *fractional* reserves that, withal, have some intrinsic value but not enough to meet all the outstanding claims at once. And some of the paper money came into being as an aspect of the debt-creating process, with the gold really only playing a catalytic role in the background.

A bit later in the story, after a few disasters with irresponsible goldsmiths, the government may decree that the privilege of playing this particularly fruitful game should be a monopoly of governmentally chartered banks or of the central bank and that they must keep gold reserves in some fixed percentage, say 40 percent, of the ostensible amount of gold warehouse receipts (money) outstanding. (This occurred quite generally in the nineteenth century.) After a little more time, the requirement of gold reserves in some legally stated percentage of the money in circulation may be lifted. (This happened quite generally in the 1930s and in the United States in the 1960s.) Thus we have, as ongoing process, a monetary system in which new money comes into being as an aspect of debt creation in more or less the manner described in the preceding section, and the intermediation of the substance such as gold, with its intrinsic value, is lost. The paper money retains general acceptability and purchasing power, if it is not overissued.

Fiat Money
Another possibility is that a government or an army commander may print some paper money, assign to a unit of it a value equivalent to the value of some money that has already been circulating, pay the troops or the bureaucrats with it, and use police power to assure that sellers will accept it. The soldiers will shoot up the bar if the tavernkeeper refuses to accept the paper. Such money may maintain respectable value if the general who issues it wins the revolution and if it is issued in modest amounts. If he loses or if too much money is issued, it may quickly become worthless. In other cases, such fiat money has been phased out as "ordinary" money came back into use and the fiat notes were redeemed. This is what happened, for example, with Civil War greenbacks and with the occupation currency issued by the United States Army in Italy during World War II.

At all events a pure fiat money, independent of the debt instrument counterpart aspect, is conceivable, but it has not been a common form of money in "normal" times. It is a little too crude. The present situation, however, seems to justify the generalization that the tie between the paper money and something of intrinsic value has virtually been severed. In general, circulating money is either on its face a debt instrument or a promise to pay in something else.

It has as a counterpart, or as backing, a debt instrument, or an IOU, or a bit of commercial paper.

Our Domestic Monetary System

Gold Reserves and Federal Reserve Notes

The United States went off the gold standard in 1933/34. Private citizens could not thereafter exchange paper money for gold. But nominally and legally gold was priced at $35 an ounce (it was $20.67 an ounce before 1933/34). This gold value was operational in the dealings of United States monetary authorities with foreign money authorities.

In addition, following 1933/34, the United States law provided that there should be gold (or gold certificate) reserves of at least 25 percent behind Federal Reserve notes and behind deposits with Federal Reserve Banks. (The existence of such percentage reserve requirements had also been a common characteristic of the gold standards of earlier years, although the percentage had been 40 percent.) Observance of the 25 percent reserve requirement would have forced United States monetary authorities to play by the rules (contract the supply of Federal Reserve notes) if and when the gold reserves fell toward the 25 percent figure. But there was no corresponding pressure to make them expand the money supply more or less in proportion as reserves rose. And, if excess reserves existed, a government could even expand the money supply in the face of falling reserves.

In fact, as the United States gold reserves fell from $22 billion (at $35 an ounce) in 1958 to $11 billion in 1968, currency held by the public actually increased from $28 billion to $42 billion and deposits with the Federal Reserve rose from $19 billion to $23 billion. The money supply (currency plus demand deposits) rose from $128 billion to $138 billion.

Under the pressure of loss of reserves and playing by the rules of the game and observing the 25 percent reserves, the United States should have been engaged in major contraction of the money supply. The problem was dealt with differently, however. In 1965 the requirement of a 25 percent gold reserve behind deposits with the Federal Reserve was removed from the law, and in 1968 the requirement of a 25 percent gold reserve behind Federal Reserve notes was also removed.

So, during the period from 1946, when the International Monetary Fund began to function, to 1971, when the IMF system was forced into major changes by President Nixon, the United States insisted on divorcing its domestic monetary policy from the international behavior norms which were appropriate to the IMF system.

The Domestic Role of the Federal Reserve System

Meanwhile, what was the domestic policy of the United States monetary authorities—the secretary of the treasury and the board of governors of the Federal Reserve System? Since the policies of the two were not always in agreement, it is not entirely correct to speak of a coherent domestic monetary policy. Nevertheless, we will paint with a wide brush.

The Federal Reserve Banks (twelve in all), working more or less under the control of the board of governors in Washington, D.C., function more or less as a United States central bank, the system having been created by the Federal Reserve Act of 1913, during the administration of Woodrow Wilson. The system guides, controls, and regulates (or tries to) the money and credit supply of the United States, taking into account some sort of conception of the national interest (perhaps Marriner Eccles' or Arthur Burns' or Paul Volcker's).

The system has reserves. It has the quantity of gold and foreign exchange reserves which might be (but have not been) used as a guideline for regulating the supply of domestic money and credit and which are no longer required to be part of the reserves behind the money supply.

There are various channels through which the Federal Reserve may influence the supply of money and credit (demand deposits and, perhaps also, time deposits) in the country. It is directly responsible for the existence of most of the currency, particularly the Federal Reserve notes. One restraint on the quantity of these notes in the hands of the public is that somebody (with a deposit) must come up to a teller's window in a commercial bank and want to swap some of the deposit for them, or there must be some other feasible channel of issuance. Also, the reserve requirements specified in the law must be observed. But the 25 percent gold reserve requirement, as mentioned above, has been lifted. What remains? For one thing, the Federal Reserve notes in circulation must be backed 100 percent by Federal Reserve holdings of United States government bonds and/or commercial bank deposits with the Federal Reserve. The latter deposits may come into being as a result of commercial bank discounting of its "commercial paper" with the Federal Reserve. The commercial paper is Jane Doe's IOU in which she has promised to pay the commercial bank back the sum she has borrowed after, say, ninety days. The commercial bank may turn such commercial paper over to the Federal Reserve in exchange for either Federal Reserve notes or a credit account deposit on the books of the Federal Reserve.

The notes (currency) received in this way by a commercial bank are the currency it slips to depositors interested in withdrawing money. Or the deposit of the commercial bank with the Federal Reserve, created by borrowing at the Federal Reserve against the security of a customer's promissory note, may be the legal basis for its making commercial loans. That is, the existence of its deposit with the Federal Reserve permits, or justifies, the existence of deposits or loans in amounts limited by the percentage reserve requirements.

Legal reserve requirements: The law requires that commercial banks must have certain amounts of legal reserves (generally held in the form of deposits with the Federal Reserve) behind their loans and deposits. This percentage reserve figure is one of the principal money and credit control powers of the Federal Reserve. which can vary this percentage reserve requirement in a fairly wide range, the range for demand deposits being between 7 percent, the low for "other banks," and 22 percent, the high for reserve city banks. So, depending on what percentage reserve requirement is applied and to whom, the permissible money and credit supply in existence may be varied between about 14 times and 4.5 times the commercial bank's reserves (deposits) with the Federal Reserve. That is, this is the range within which the Federal Reserve can influence the commercial banking system's ability to create money and credit using the percentage reserve requirement tool and assuming a given amount of reserves.

Paul Samuelson deemphasizes the basis for original primary deposits (high-powered reserves): "Where they came from is not important. It could have come from someone's having deposited the proceeds received from his selling a government bond to the regional Federal Reserve Bank (which may have paid for it by printing off 20 fifty-dollar bills)."[2] After this brief treatment of the basic problem, Samuelson spends several pages explaining how, in the setting of a 20 percent reserve requirement, the banking system can compound such an increase in reserves into five times that much money.

Considering the overshadowing importance of the leverage and flexibility the Federal Reserve has in creating the original reserves (Federal Reserve notes or whatever) used to buy the bonds from the public in the first place, one may be tempted to question the sloughing over of that aspect and the comparative emphasis placed on determining just how much a precise amount of such a volatile item can increase the money supply. Perhaps reticence on this score is to be explained by the understandable desire of central bankers to deemphasize the tremendous power they possess to influence the amount of the original primary reserves.

Rediscounting: Commercial bank reserves (as indicated above) may be increased by commercial bank borrowing from the Federal Reserve (perhaps using its borrowers' IOUs as security) to increase its reserve account deposits at the Federal Reserve. These reserve account deposits, basically, guide how much a bank can lend at a given time. How anxious the commercial bank may be to use this facility for expanding its reserves will depend on assorted influences, which include the interest rate (or the so-called discount or rediscount rate) which the Federal Reserve charges. The commercial bank will want to charge its borrowers enough to more than cover the interest which it in turn has to pay the Federal Reserve. (But, remember, the commercial banks as a system can lend some multiple between 4.5 and 14 times what they borrow from the Federal Reserve.) At all events, another credit control power of the Federal Reserve is its ability to vary its rediscount rate. After World War II, variation was pretty much in the range between 2 and 9.5 percent until October 1979, when the rate began to skyrocket.

In the early years of the system, it was thought that the rediscounting procedure would automatically increase the money supply when business needed money and contract the money supply when business demand was less. This conception has not been so generally accepted in recent years. The latter-day opinion seems to be that too much sensitivity on the part of the money supply to the whims of business breeds instability. A concept more in vogue is Milton Friedman's, to the effect that the money supply be increased by a constant percentage each year. In any event, rediscounting is of modest importance as a credit control tool by comparison with open-market operations.

Open-market operations: Another credit control power, the one generally considered most important, is open-market operations by the Federal Reserve. These operations involve buying or selling government bonds by the Federal Reserve, and they play a role in underwriting the creation of money—viewed as a debt instrument.

Actually, there are two levels where there is an important possible connection between the public debt (U.S. government bonds) and the money supply. Since U.S. government bonds, as well as short-term commercial paper, can serve as reserves behind money, there is an immediate possible connection. Although things are not generally done this directly, the implication is that the government can print up bonds and sell them to the Federal Reserve for freshly printed legal-tender Federal Reserve notes, the bonds being the reserve that the Federal Reserve is required to have behind the notes. Debt and money supply have both increased. Everything is legal, the books balance, and the required reserves are in place. Not only that but, if the additional Federal Reserve notes are deposited in commercial banks by the individuals that the government has paid off with them, there is the basis for a further multiple expansion of the money supply by the commercial banking system as it takes advantage of the fractional reserve requirements under which it operates.

The foregoing is a not unfair statement of the underlying bonds/money supply relation. But things are generally not done quite so forthrightly. The government makes a great show of selling its bond issues initially to the general public for whatever money the general public already has in hand. And that step, prima facie, leaves the money supply unchanged. The money is just in different hands.

Open-market operations, properly speaking, then involve the purchase by the Federal Reserve, using Federal Reserve notes or maybe really just by creating new bank deposits, of old issues of government bonds. Such an operation may increase the money supply and the ability of the commercial banking system to compound the money supply against the backing of these newly created reserves. Meanwhile, the Federal Reserve carefully stores the slightly worn bonds in its vaults or, perhaps, in the vaults of the Federal Reserve agent (who may give the Federal Reserve Bank Federal Reserve notes in exchange for them).

The other half of the open-market operation involves the possible sale of its worn government bonds by the Federal Reserve for money in the possession of the public. Such action reduces the money supply and may (given the workings of the percentage reserve requirements in effect) force a reduction in the money supply in an amount much larger than was directly involved in the bond sale operation. All this is pretty much what was said earlier in the discussion of the general nature of money.

Implications for the Money Supply
The monetary authorities have other credit control powers. Perhaps these three examples will suffice to indicate the major possibilities and the nature of the process.

One of the major precepts in evaluating the implications of these possibilities is that the monetary authorities and the government must be reasonably discreet in using their power to expand the money supply (and to profit themselves from such expansion) if the public is to retain confidence in the currency. It is this confidence which gives paper money that all-important characteristic: general acceptability, in a setting of price stability.

Money supply is usually defined as currency in circulation plus demand deposits. (A loan actually typically takes the immediate form of a book entry saying that the borrower now has a demand deposit with the bank. And, of course, how much monetary creation the banking system can effect this way is influenced both by the reserve requirements and by the desire of people to borrow.) Money supply defined this way is currently called M-one (M_1). If time deposits or savings deposits are also included in the concept, it is called M-two (M_2). Which is the better concept is a matter of some debate.

Model building in monetary theory is likely to start with an assumption that the money supply is determined by the monetary authorities—that is, its supply is given. But the demand of the general public for the given money supply is thought of as being a result of several influences, such as the size of the national income and the liquidity preference of people (the desire of people to hold money). Much econometric-statistical work has gone into estimating the demand for money. If the demand equation can be so estimated, and if the supply is given—and somebody, for sure, is holding all the money—and if demand must equal supply at the prevailing price (price in this case being the interest rate), one has a model of demand and supply and price in the money market. And one can combine the money market with the other markets in the economy (the securities market and the commodity market) and construct a model of the whole economy. A fantastic amount of such model building has been going on.[3]

Surely, however, it is not true that the real money supply (the nominal quantity of money corrected to allow for inflation) is effectively set by the monetary authorities and that the other elements in the picture (interest rates, price levels, and so on) adjust to conform to that given quantity. The real money supply in fact is itself one more *variable* in this hodgepodge.

There is another side to the story. It is not only that people must be willing to hold the money that government creates for the government to be able to create money. People can quite meaningfully create money by being willing to buy and sell on the basis of credit instruments which they may create without the necessity, at all, for government participation in the process. The mere use of a credit card issued by a private commercial bank or by American Express is enough to indicate the importance of this possibility. And the possibilities for private proliferation of purchasing power are enhanced by NOW (negotiable order of withdrawal) accounts, ATS (automatic transfer service) accounts, overdrafts (on the part of at least the favored few and allowed or even encouraged by banks), bank providing of credit facilities (and automatic borrowing facilities) at all hours of the day or night, easy transfer of funds from savings to checking accounts and back, and so on. The facilities are there and the public has been using them to mushroom its effective buying power (and the rate of inflation). Things have changed considerably since the good old days when banks closed at 2:00 P.M. on Friday and did not reopen until 10:00 A.M. on Monday and one might have to wait a considerable period of time before one would be permitted to take money from a savings account.

Between 1967 and 1979, the basic money supply (currency plus demand deposits) increased by only 2.1 times, while outstanding consumer installment credit increased by 3.8 times, and the bank debits to demand deposits increased by 8.1 times. The private sector (the public with the help of the commercial banks) has been ingeniously figuring out ways to get "more bang for a buck" and to escalate inflation.

Conclusion

Money matters. Money is not neutral. There is such a thing as a free lunch, at least for some people. And there are plenty of scroungers out on the town. The trouble is that the free lunch is not available to everybody. Concerned citizens would do better to look around and see how the system really works, instead of just assuming the truth of the mystique that "the market works." It works all right. And really works over some of the actors. This is not necessarily the best of all possible worlds, but it is a quite interesting place, although you may occasionally want to hold your nose.

The creation of money by an interchange of government bonds for money between the government and the monetary authorities may be inflationary (or may not, depending), represents a source of government revenue, occasions income redistribution, and may be used to effect productive resource reallocation. All these are important effects, with both monetary and real implications.

NOTES

1. *United States Code: 1970 Edition* (Washington, D.C.: Government Printing Office, 1971), title 12, sec. 412, pp. 2363–2364.
2. Paul A. Samuelson, *Economics*, 10th ed. (New York: McGraw-Hill, 1976 [1948]), p. 302.
3. See, for example, Robert L. Crouch, *Macroeconomics* (New York: Harcourt Brace Jovanovich, 1972).

ADDITIONAL READINGS

Cassel, Gustav. *Money and Foreign Exchange after 1914*. London: Constable, 1922.
Friedman, Milton. *Money and Economic Development*. New York: Praeger, 1973.
————. *A Theoretical Framework for Monetary Analysis*. New York: Columbia University Press (for the National Bureau of Economic Research), 1971.
————, and Anna Jacobson Schwartz. *A Monetary History of the United States, 1867–1960*. Princeton: Princeton University Press (for the National Bureau of Economic Research), 1963.
Neale, Walter C. *Monies in Societies*. San Francisco: Chandler & Sharp, 1976.

Niehans, Jürg. *The Theory of Money*. Baltimore: Johns Hopkins, 1978.

O'Bannon, Helen B., David E. Bond, and Ronald S. Shearer. *Money and Banking*. New York: Harper & Row, 1975.

Prather, Charles L. *Money and Banking*. 9th ed. Homewood, Ill.: Irwin, 1969 [1937].

16.
Inflation

INFLATION, which had not been a real problem in the United States for many years, became one in the late 1960s and early 1970s.

Concerns

People are likely to be concerned about inflation for various reasons. First, it is natural to be indignant because the price of some item is discovered to be higher than it was the day before.

Second, price-level changes redistribute income and wealth. Debtors, who find that the money they need to pay off debts is easier to come by, are benefited. Creditors are likely to be injured, being on the other side of the same process. People on fixed incomes and pensions, including especially the elderly and the handicapped, are likely to be hurt because their fixed incomes will buy less and less. Typical business owners, to the extent that they are debtors, are likely to gain from inflation. People on wages and salaries, especially if they are nonunion, are likely to lose because wages and salaries usually adjust with a lag relative to prices.

Finally, the country whose prices are rising relative to prices in the rest of the world (at given foreign exchange rates) is likely to experience balance of payments troubles because its citizenry will be interested in importing relatively more and more and the rest of the world will be desirous of buying relatively less and less of its exports. It will consequently exhaust its foreign exchange reserves and will no longer be able to defend the given foreign exchange rate. The loss of ability to defend a foreign exchange rate may, however, be no great loss—as losses go.

Explanations

The Quantity Theory of Money

The idea that there is some sort of relation between the quantity of money and inflation has been around for a long time.[1] But discussion and disagreement as to the cause and effect nature of the process and as to the closeness of the relation remain very much in vogue.

Milton Friedman says: "On the average, a change in the rate of monetary growth produces a change in the rate of growth of nominal income about six to nine months later. . . . The changed rate of growth of nominal income typically shows up first in output and hardly at all in prices. . . . The effect on prices comes some nine to fifteen months after the effect on income and output. . . . In the short run, which may be as much as five or ten years, monetary changes affect primarily output. Over decades, on the other hand, the rate of monetary growth affects primary prices. . . . *Inflation is always and everywhere a monetary phenomenon* in the sense that it is and can be produced only by a more rapid increase in the quantity of money than in output." But Friedman is opposed to using monetary policy in the business-cycle run to influence income and employment: "Monetary policy is a poor instrument for this purpose, thanks to the length and variability of the lag in the effect of monetary policy, and the limitations of our knowledge about the factors responsible for such lags. . . . The wisest policy . . . would be to shape monetary policy to meet longer run objectives; to aim, in the short-run, at steady monetary growth."[2]

More simply put, the Chicago people seem to claim that, in the long run, there is a precise correspondence between the rate of change in the money supply and in the price level. In this process the money supply change comes first, is the first act in the drama, and is causal as to the price-level changes. Regarding these allegations, one can probably say they are "not so" in this rigid form. A relation, no doubt, exists, but it is far from precise. And it is by no means certain which way the causation runs or whether the story should start with a change in the money supply rather than with a labor contract or a stock bonus to executives.

International Interrelations

The prevailing situation is not one where a combination of set foreign exchange rates and a smoothly working adjustment mechanism in fact works to assure equal rates of inflation everywhere. In the real world, different countries have been increasing their money supplies at different rates, the citizenries have been reacting in different ways to these increases, and there have been varying rates of inflation in different countries and varying patterns of change in the foreign exchange rates between different pairs of countries.

Domestically, the relation between the will to increase the money supply, the actual increase in the nominal or real money supply, and the rate of inflation is a highly institutionalized phenomenon which works differently in each country. One of the most obvious patterns is the basic case of a country in which the populace becomes aware that substantial expansion in the money supply and inflation are going on and will probably continue to go on. The people may do two things: (1) they may try harder to increase their own income to offset or exceed the inflation rate, and (2) they will probably spend their money more and more rapidly in anticipation of further inflation which will, they become acutely aware, decrease the real value of the money they retain. These two influences may reinforce each other with the result that, once inflation has started, it may compound at a rate faster than the immediately preceding rate of increase in the money supply. Once this sort of process gets going, it is extremely difficult to stop. Meanwhile, the money supply may well be expanding at an increasing rate, despite high interest rates (and government efforts to curtail inflation), because people believe that the money necessary in the future to pay off the borrowing which is increasing the money supply will be easy to come by.

Among United States economists (relatively unfamiliar with the actual workings of inflation until recently), the business cycle used to be described as characterized by rising and high prices during recovery and prosperity phases and by falling and low prices during collapse and depression. Certainly this is a possible pattern. But it is not a necessary pattern, as indicated by the many countries characterized by more or less chronic inflation through prosperity and depression, war and peace, famine and relative abundance, dictatorship and democracy.

Nor, it seems, is it a necessary feature of the United States scene, despite the (probably useful in its setting) Keynesian assumption that, during a period of depression characterized by unemployed resources, the effect of additional investment on income and employment can be appraised meaningfully using the Keynesian multiplier in an analytical model that assumes the absence of monetary inflation.

A point not too well appreciated is that the investment talked about in the Keynesian model should be real and effective new investment which genuinely expands production and/or gets money into the hands of people who need it to buy goods. An increase in the money supply scattered to the four winds (or to the bankrupt railroads under the aegis of the Reconstruction Finance Corporation in the early 1930s) does not necessarily have any useful effect on production (in manufacturing) or consumption (of agricultural surpluses).

It does make a difference who gets the additional money and how it is used. This fact of life may be illustrated by some rather likely trains of events in underdeveloped countries. A case history that has been repeated over and over runs somewhat as follows. The central bank increases the supply of money and credit. It may rationalize this action on the grounds that additional money is desirable to finance economic development. Also the increase in the money supply, it is thought, will operate somewhat like autonomous investment in the Keynesian national income theory model. The marginal propensity to consume will determine the size of the multiplier. And national income will be increased by a corresponding multiple three or four times the original increase in the money supply. Other factors influencing the central bank to increase the money supply may be that important friends of the government want to borrow money, speculators need funds to finance inventory hoarding to permit them to make a killing by cornering the market in some necessity, and so on. The interaction of the various elements in this motivation process may result in some increase in goods production, and such increase, if it occurs, will be a factor inhibiting inflation. However, much of the monetary expansion will be purely inflationary in its effect. As mentioned above, prices then rise in the country in question relative to the rest of the world. This makes the underdeveloped country a relatively unattractive place in which to buy. Consequently, imports rise relative to exports, and the foreign exchange reserves are decreased. After this process has gone sufficiently far, the central bank will no longer have foreign exchange reserves adequate to defend the foreign exchange rate which, by agreement with the International Monetary Fund, it used to be obligated to defend. Devaluation is the standard patent medicine for dealing with such a problem. And one devaluation may well lead to another as the fact of the devaluation itself gestates lack of confidence in the currency.

A matter that is likely to be left out of account in discussing the effect of a currency devaluation is its role in influencing income distribution. The result of devaluation is likely to be a shift in income to the merchants in the export sector and, if they pass a little of the increase along to their workers, a shift of income to people in the export sector in general. Money income is shifted to the export sector and, since real income in the country may well be decreased by the worsening terms of trade that are a rather likely counterpart of the devaluation, the shift in real income to those in the export sector is likely to be even more marked than the monetary shift. This is an especially serious result of devaluation because of the fact that the export sector is likely to be a relatively high-income sector anyway. A likely effect of devaluation is: "To those who have shall be given."

Pretty clearly, the interrelation between the rules of the international monetary system (in its various manifestations) and the behavior of the various national monetary systems is not of a nature to assure that inflation will occur at the same rate in all countries. There may be implications of inflation in some countries that cause inflation in others. The 1973 increase in petroleum prices by the oil-producing countries almost certainly contributed to inflation in the consuming countries. Also, however, factors connected with inflation in one country may lead to deflation in another (gold flows among countries playing by the rules of the game, for example). Thus, inflation has international implications, but it is probably not usefully analyzed as though it tended to be a common phenomenon going on at more or less the same rate in all countries.

Various Nonmonetary Influences, Including Cost Push
Some years ago, among economists concerned with Latin American economic problems, a major topic of discussion was the so-called monetarist-structuralist debate. The monetarists held to a rather pure quantity theory of money, while the structuralists argued that the chief influence occasioning inflation was the working out of structural relations and difficulties among various economic institutions.

Gardiner Means has been especially interested in the institutionalized rigidity of the administered prices of the great oligopolies in comparison with the much freer price fluctuation in connection with agricultural products and the products of more competitive industries. He says that the administered-price thesis "was first developed in 1934–35 to apply to the cyclical behavior of industrial prices. It specifically held that in business recessions administered prices showed a tendency not to fall as much as market prices while the prevailing decrease in demand worked itself out primarily through a fall in sales, production, and employment. Similarly, since administered prices tended not to fall as much in a recession, they tended not to rise as much in recovery while rising demand worked itself out primarily in a rising volume of sales, production, and employment."[3]

There is an additional facet to the Means thesis: "The new price data give a new dimension to the administered-price thesis by disclosing a substantial number of prices which tend to rise with cyclical recessions and a substantial number which tend to fall with cyclical recovery."

Means speaks of the explanation for this phenomenon: "Non-classical inflation also rises from the exercise of 'market power,' but can occur whether employment is full or less than full and can occur in a period of recession, in a period of stagnation, or in one of recovery. . . . This type of inflation may be initiated by management in an effort to widen profit margins, and could then be properly called 'profit push' inflation. It could also be initiated by labor in an effort to obtain unwarranted wage increases which would, in turn, be called 'cost push' inflation. To avoid any implication of its specific source, it will be called here 'administrative' inflation. . . !"[4]

At any rate, in the underworld of economics there have been explanations of the influences on the purchasing power of money which have assigned a role to factors other than the quantity of money. These explanations might include conditions that would cause change in the quantity of money as part of the process. But they would not begin the story with the increase in the quantity of money playing the role of original sin.

In particular, administrative or administered inflation, or let us call it cost push inflation, would seem to be a phenomenon to be reckoned with. In fact, this phenomenon may well be of new, basic, and increasing importance. More and more economic common-interest groups are recognizing communities of interest; they are organizing and pressing for measures favorable to the interest of their group. Employers and particular industries were already pretty well organized and had an understanding of the nature of various common interests, especially in higher prices and profits, by the nineteenth century. Labor unions had sufficiently organized and consolidated their position by the 1930s, at least in the United States and western Europe, to be able to press effectively for higher wages. Doctors and lawyers have pretty well been able to administer their own fees all along.[5] A major development of the post–World War II period has been the organization of teachers and other white-collar workers in a manner that permits them also to press effectively for higher salaries. And very little has happened to undermine the ability of corporation officers to pad expense accounts, allot themselves stock options, and so on.

In the postwar period the track record of the steel industry for raising steel prices when the demand for steel falls is reasonably well known. The *New York Times* has cited a similar procedure on the part of newsprint producers,[6] and the examples could be multiplied almost to the point of justifying the claim that they represent the rule rather than the exception. Even social security benefits are escalated generously, without much double checking, as part of a similar process.

Also, increasingly in the underdeveloped countries, the various economic groups are more and more effectively organized for pressing their interest in higher incomes. And, as countries, the oil-producing bloc in the early 1970s discovered that it had the leverage to press effectively for higher earnings for their countries as a group. Meanwhile, consumer interest groups have not found the leverage necessary for creating effective organization for holding down or reducing prices.

What happens when virtually all groups in society acquire the leverage necessary for obtaining higher income? All groups are pressing, all are increasingly ingenious about finding reasons why their incomes should be increased—and increased relative to other groups. The path of least resistance, for whoever is under pressure to permit the increase, is to grant it—if the costs can be passed along as higher prices or higher taxes. And they generally can be.

There has been a tendency in some circles to call this phenomenon wage push inflation rather than cost push inflation and to blame the labor unions. But the workers have scarcely been the chief beneficiaries of cost push. Between 1970 and 1979 per capita disposable real income in the United States rose by 24 percent. Average real gross weekly earnings in total private nonagricultural employment fell by slightly over 4 percent. Some people, no doubt, are thriving under inflation. But the run-of-the-mill worker is not. There is major income redistribution going on to the benefit of . . . whom?

The nominal increases can always be granted (at least by the system, if not always by particular members of the system). The employers grant increases to their workers and to themselves and raise prices and borrow from banks to cover themselves. The banks are happy to lend, or they generally are. Meanwhile, the government is responding to similar pressures by increasing taxes and borrowing and yielding to wage and price increases exceeding government "guidelines." And the borrowing not only covers the additional outlays the government is committing itself to make, it also provides the base for an expansion of the money supply by the banking system. So, more funds can be made available, at interest, to employers who need more money to meet the administered increase in costs.

The relation of this increased swirl in the monetary area to increased production of goods is problematical rather than neutral. This is especially true since the increases in nominal income, to a considerable degree, have been related to the ability of various groups to apply pressure, rather than being related entirely to productivity or equity in income distribution considerations.

It may be noted that this sort of story also results in a high correlation between expansion in the money supply and inflation. However, it involves a bit more effort to search out explanations as to why the money supply increases in the first place. This story does not start, and the story of inflation should not start, with an assumption of an initial, unexplained increase in the money supply.

This is not to say that an alternative, simple, complete explanation of the cause of an increase in the money supply can be found. But all this does seem to mean that attention to institutionalized pressures that cause an increase in the money supply should be a prime concern. Such influences have always been of overriding importance, back to the days when generals printed fiat money to pay their soldiers and kings debased the coinage to profit themselves.

The most devout monetarist should understand that even a monetary standard where gold coins were the only circulating money was not immune from coin clipping, debasing the coinage, or putting a lot of gold coins in a bag and shaking the bag.

Worldwide inflation, if such is going on (albeit at different rates in different countries), is probably a response to effective institutionalized pressuring for far greater increases in income by groups which are more and more effectively organized for making such pressures meaningful, at least in nominal terms. The monetary system is also increasingly adjusted to supply the corresponding amounts of money. (The assumption commonly used these days, in monetary theory, of a governmentally set money supply simply does not wash.) But the productive system does not necessarily respond in kind. And neither the world nor its individual nations are equipped to cope reasonably with the income distribution problem that is a by-product of all this.

If demand falls, prices may well fall. The possibility also exists that, faced with falling demand, producers may say to themselves that they need to charge higher prices to compensate for lost revenues. The institutionalized organization of the industry may be such that they can do exactly that. Imagine the United States steel companies in 1958, and on quite a few other occasions also, raising prices in the face of falling demand. Imagine the Mexican hotel industry and other tourist-associated industries in 1976 raising prices generally to compensate for the loss in revenue caused by the falling tourist trade connected with the Jewish boycott, the Jewish boycott being a result of Mexico's voting in the United Nations to identify Zionism with racism.

Sometimes, when confronted with such arguments, the neoclassical price theorists will respond that certainly such "irrational" pricing may occur in the short run but that very soon the underlying forces will assert themselves and prices will adjust properly. Maybe so. But such an allegation is more an article of faith than a relation that can be proven to exist. It is also quite possible that behavior reinforcement phenomena may propel inflation along after its gets started. And the tendency to equilibrium simply may not work effectively as a brake on a succession of mutually reinforcing inflationary tendencies.

Policy

Freely Fluctuating Exchange Rates

So, inflation is with us. It will go on at a more rapid rate in countries less able to control the institutionalized pressures and leverages for higher income and more money and less effective in expanding production. It will go on at a less rapid rate (and perhaps even decline from time to time) in countries less intimidated by such institutionalized pressures and more effective in expanding production. Real standards of living will be basically controlled by real production, not by the monetary value of production. Nevertheless, this confusion in the monetary area will no doubt influence real production—favorably and unfavorably.

Also, because inflation goes on at different rates in different countries, it is appropriate for foreign exchange rates to vary. (Subjecting the world to a system of set pars and a set of behavior norms calculated to make price levels correspond to those pars is an open invitation to traumatic experiences with international monetary crises.)

Let us allow the foreign exchange rates to fluctuate more or less freely until such a time as the world is willing to work with a genuinely international legal-tender currency acceptable everywhere.

Constant Percentage Increase in the Money Supply

For Milton Friedman, inflation is a great evil, and its avoidance should be the major policy concern. He does not trust public officials and central bankers to deal competently with the problem with discretionary tools. Friedman believes that slow expansion of the money supply is appropriate to maintain a stable price level as the economy grows. To do this he advocates a rule of thumb: "My own prescription is still that the monetary authority go all the way in avoiding such swings by adopting publicly the policy of achieving a steady rate of growth in a specified monetary total. . . . I myself have argued for a rate that would on the average achieve rough stability in the level of prices of final products, which I have estimated would call for something like a 3 to 5 percent per year rate of growth in currency plus all commercial bank deposits or a slightly lower rate of growth in currency plus demand deposits only."[7]

One may sympathize with the desirability of an automatic, slow rate of growth in the money supply yet not particularly trust the discretion of the monetary authorities. Even with good intentions, the monetary authorities cannot increase the money supply (either nominal or real) by such and such a precise percentage by fiat. It is difficult to understand how Friedman visualizes that this automatic accretion in the money supply by preplanned amounts will occur (you can lead a horse to water but you can't make it drink). Things monetary authorities can do include setting the rediscount rate, and the reserve requirements, and engaging in open-market operations. Such measures influence the amount of change in the money (and credit) supply, but they do not fine tune the amount of that change. There is no way, ex ante, that the planners can know that they will get that mandated 4 percent increase (or whatever they decide the percentage shall actually be) in the money supply by raising the discount rate by 1.25 percent, by changing the reserve requirements by two percentage points, by buying $1 billion worth of government bonds from the public, or even by asking the Federal Reserve agent for a given amount of Federal Reserve notes in exchange for a given amount of government bonds as collateral.

For better or worse, Friedman's policy measure is not operational, quite apart from the fact that he does not really know what rate of expansion in the money supply would actually result in a zero rate of inflation. But his cause is worth something—his cause presumably being to eliminate (or at least ameliorate) inflation and to do it with nondiscretionary or automatic policy tools. He is surely correct that there is a meaningful relation between the change in the size of the money supply and inflation—but it may well be a changeable relation. The monetarists surely have better things to do with their time than trying to prove that there is an equiproportionate, constant, automatic relation between percentage increase in the money supply and percentage rise in prices in the long run. Yet this activity has been taking up a good deal of their time.[8]

In this imperfect and unpredictable world, perhaps an operational, automatic (more or less nondiscretionary) policy which would be feasible and which would work in the right direction without promising the impossible would be somewhat as follows. The monetary authorities, perhaps once every six months, should review the statistics on money and prices. If prices in the preceding six months have risen by more than, say, 1.5 percent, the monetary authorities will be required to make a modest increase in the rediscount rate, to make another modest increase in the basic reserve requirement figure, and to sell a modest amount of government bonds to the public. The direction of change in the policy measure and the fact that the authorities have to take steps are prescribed. They are admonished to be moderate (to underreact rather than overreact), but the actual amount of the reaction remains discretionary.

At least such a policy is worth trying. The veil of secrecy over the whys and wherefores of monetary policy should be removed. The direction that the policy measures have to take should be automatic. However, it should also be clearly understood that it is not the ordinary job of the planners to turn trends around, only to slow them down—while letting nonplanned influences take the blame for turning points.

Indexation (Monetary Correction)

Another Friedman proposal is indexation. At least, his suggestion of this procedure in 1973 or 1974 gave the idea wide appeal. Whether Friedman himself was in favor of the idea either then or now is not entirely clear to me.

It is tempting to believe that the problem of inflation can be dealt with by increasing the value of all assets and the return to all income recipients in proportion to the rate of inflation.[9] To accomplish this, the government would compute the appropriate index numbers to describe the rate of inflation and take the appropriate administrative measures to assure that the value of assets and incomes rose in proportion.

Particular groups, some labor unions for example, have succeeded in setting up such arrangements applicable to their group. Escalator clauses in labor contracts may provide for wages rising in step with inflation. Some (but not many) bond issues, especially in underdeveloped countries, have provided for increasing the principal value of the bond in proportion to the change in some more or less appropriate price-level index.

About 1973 or 1974, Milton Friedman seems to have gotten the impression that Brazil was employing such a procedure successfully on an across-the-board basis to the whole economy. And suddenly the idea of general indexing acquired a vogue. However, there are several reasons why this procedure does not and probably cannot work in practice in a reasonably satisfactory way.

It is probably both appropriate and desirable that the prices of different commodities rise and fall at different rates. Yet here is a system geared to forcing them all to vary at the same rate. There cannot help but be serious problems of leads and lags in computing the index numbers and taking the administrative measures necessary to see to it that each citizen is appropriately compensated. In fact, even if the problems of computing the appropriate index numbers and timing the payments currently could be dealt with, there would be major sectors of the economy where it would simply be impossible to compute with even rough equity how much compensation was appropriate and how it could be paid. Perhaps the indexing of weekly wages is feasible, but how about the indexing of the profits of small shopkeepers or the income of farmers whose crops come in only once a year? The face value of bonds might be indexed, but how about the value of stock?

At best, very different methods of compensation would have to be used in the various sectors. In all reason, the effectiveness with which the different sectors actually received compensation corresponding to the inflation rate would vary greatly. And one might well question whether the most effective bureaucracy in the world could administer such a scheme. The administrative complications pass belief. That such a libertarian as Milton Friedman could even temporarily have considered such an arrangement to be desirable or possible is hard to understand.

It would seem pretty likely that if such a scheme were ostensibly in effect but sloppily administered, as would almost certainly be the case, it would in and of itself feed the fires of inflation as all the involved groups worked to make sure that they were not the group slightly undercompensated. As a result, most groups would manage to get somewhat overcompensated, and inflation would proceed apace.

One may be sure that general indexing is not a solution to the inflation problem. The argument that inflation exists, that we have to live with it, and that this is a possible way to get along simply will not wash. The general problem cannot be dealt with satisfactorily this way. However, during periods of continuing inflation, it may be possible to identify particular sectors that are especially hurt and assist them with some indexing. This has been done and may be done in the future on varying scales. It is up to the citizenry in the process of making its self-correcting value judgments to decide what it wants to do along this line. Some indexing, using publicly agreed-on criteria, applicable to only some sections of the economy, may be judged to be better than nothing when the setting is one of major continuing inflation.

May we be preserved, however, from a comprehensive effort to implement across-the-board indexation.

Other Possible Policies
Where does all this leave us? It is hard to believe that inflation is a situation about which nothing can be done. It is too patently an

artificial phenomenon for that. It is also too easy to say that responsible limiting of the money supply plus putting the lid on groups that overreach themselves in their pressuring to impose higher prices and to realize higher incomes can solve the problem. Yet these are relevant policy areas.

In addition, taxes should not be decreased, and certainly they should not be decreased by arbitrary across-the-board amounts. Tax decreases give people more money to spend and thus stimulate inflation. In general, taxes should be maintained at present levels or increased. The Republicans are correct for once about balancing the budget. This is the time (1980) to balance the budget or operate at a surplus—but at a maintained level of government employment. With unemployment at high levels, this is no time for government to fire people or to reduce welfare expenditures. Capital expenditures by the private sector and by all levels of government should, on the other hand, generally be financed out of current revenue rather than by borrowing. Concern about productivity and efficiency calls for approaching those problems directly, fairly, and courageously—not with an ax.

Meantime, consumer credit should be drastically controlled. This means curtailing the use or availability of credit cards, NOW accounts, ATS accounts, overdrafts, easy transfer of funds from savings to checking accounts, and the availability of banking and credit facilities at all hours. Expense-account living should be gotten hold of by allowing only transportation and lodging (not food and drink) coverage. After all, we have to eat three meals a day whether we are on company business or not.

And maybe it will help if we all understand what is going on (what we are doing to ourselves) instead of blaming the government, and business, and OPEC. Maybe it will help. Maybe. Maybe not.

NOTES

1. See Marjorie Grice-Hutchinson, *The School of Salamanca, Readings in Spanish Monetary Theory, 1544–1605* (Oxford: Clarendon Press, 1952); Earl J. Hamilton, *American Treasure and the Price Revolution in Spain, 1501–1650* (Cambridge, Mass.: Harvard University Press, 1934); Joseph A. Schumpeter, *History of Economic Analysis* (London: George Allen & Unwin, 1954), p. 311.

2. Milton Friedman, *Money and Economic Development* (New York: Praeger, 1973), pp. 27–28, 39.
3. Gardiner C. Means, "The Administered-Price Thesis Reconfirmed," *American Economic Review* 62 (June 1972): 292–306, especially p. 292.
4. Ibid., p. 304; Gardiner C. Means, "Simultaneous Inflation and Unemployment: A Challenge to Theory and Policy," *Challenge* 18 (September 1975): 6–20, especially p. 11.
5. Louis M. Kohlmeier, "Price Fixing in the Professions," *New York Times*, April 18, 1976, p. F3.
6. *New York Times*, November 22, 1976, p. D3.
7. Milton Friedman, "The Role of Monetary Policy," *American Economic Review* 58 (March 1968): 16.
8. See Robert L. Crouch, *Macroeconomics* (New York: Harcourt Brace Jovanovich, 1972), pp. 162–186.
9. See Milton Friedman, "Monetary Correction," in American Enterprise Institute for Public Policy Research, *Essays on Inflation and Indexation* (Washington, D.C., 1974); Jack D. Guenther, "'Indexing' versus Discretionary Action—Brazil's Fight against Inflation," *Finance and Development* 12 (September 1975): 24–29.

ADDITIONAL READINGS

Cuddy, J. D. A. *International Price Indexation*. Lexington, Mass.: Heath, 1977.
Hirschman, Albert O., ed. *Latin American Issues*. New York: Twentieth Century Fund, 1961. Pp. 69–124 deal with the "monetarist-structuralist" controversy.
Kaldor, N. "Inflation and Recession in the World Economy." *Economic Journal* 86 (December 1976): 703–714.
Krause, Lawrence B., and Walter S. Salant, eds. *Worldwide Inflation*. Washington, D.C.: Brookings, 1977.
McCulloch, J. Huston. *Money and Inflation*. New York: Academic Press, 1975.
Means, Gardiner C., John Blair, et al. *The Roots of Inflation: The International Crisis*. New York: Burt Franklin, 1975.
Sherman, Howard J. *Stagflation*. New York: Harper & Row, 1976.

17.

The Job Guarantee

ABOUT 1919, John Dewey wrote:

> The first great demand of a better social order, I should say, then, is the guarantee of the right, to every individual who is capable of it, to work—not the mere legal right, but a right which is enforceable so that the individual will always have the opportunity to engage in some form of useful activity, and if the ordinary economic machinery breaks down through a crisis of some sort, then it is the duty of the state to come to the rescue and see that individuals have something to do that is worth while—not breaking stone in a stoneyard, or something else to get a soup ticket with, but some kind of productive work which a self-respecting person may engage in with interest and with more than mere pecuniary profit. Whatever may be said about the fortunes of what has technically been called socialism, it would seem to be simply the part of ordinary common sense that society should reorganize itself to make sure that individuals can make a living and be kept going, not by charity, but by having productive work to do.[1]

Years later, little has been done to implement this quite straightforward and simple concept. Instead, a fantastic and expensive bureaucratic monstrosity exists for dealing with the unemployment problem without dealing with it.

The worker has a legitimate fear of unemployment, technological and otherwise. But, since technical progress means increased welfare, it needs to be implemented. The solution has to involve making available to the worker a guarantee against technological unemployment (and against unemployment from other causes) without inhibiting productivity.

The Nature of the Job Guarantee Proposal

The problem of income adequacy needs to be divided into two parts: the problem as it applies to those ready, willing, and able to work and the problem as it applies to the handicapped. Of course, there is a gray zone between these two groups, and individuals frequently move from one group to the other. Nevertheless, there is an important basic difference in the circumstances of the two groups, and their problems should be handled in markedly different ways. This chapter concerns itself with those able to work.

It is about time for a bit of neopuritanism in economic policy formulation. At least, this is surely true as far as those ready, willing, and able to work are concerned. They should have the opportunity to work.

The important policy which offers the prospect for improving the welfare of the poor with some speed (and for making all people, especially the young, genuine participants in society) is the job guarantee for the able.[2] The United Nations Universal Declaration of Human Rights of September 24, 1948, says: "Everyone has the right to work, to free choice of employment, to just and favourable conditions of work and to protection against unemployment."[3]

Maybe, also, most people would really prefer work to charity—at least work that involves some degree of gratifying self-expression. Thorstein Veblen wrote of the instinct of workmanship: "For the present inquiry it is enough to note that in human behaviour this disposition is effective in such consistent, ubiquitous and resilient fashion that students of human culture will have to count with it as one of the integral hereditary traits of mankind."[4]

The job guarantee is the crux of the matter because of the desirability of creating a set of conditions that permits everyone who wishes to be a responsible member of society to function as such. Society, if it is able (and it *is* able), owes the individuals it has permitted to be born the opportunity to earn a reasonable living and the insitutional order needs to be restructured to permit them to do so. Individuals, on the other hand, are obliged to earn their keep if they are able.

The Government as the Employer of Last Resort

The essence of the job guarantee has to be that there is an employer of last resort—some institution that is bound to hire the able workers that no other employer is willing to hire and is bound to hire them at a wage level no lower than the basic minimum wage, whatever that may be, that a given society can afford at a given time and place. (The minimum should carry a supplement for a nonworking spouse and for each dependent.) In all reason, the employer of last resort has to be the government. The government (or governments: federal, state, and local) has to stand ready to employ anyone, any marginal person, at the minimum wage. And the government must understand that it has this continuing obligation.

The Initial Job Productivity Problem

It behooves the government to organize itself so that these employees of last resort obtain jobs involving reasonably useful labor. Of course, at the inception of the program, there could well be difficulties on this score, just as there were difficulties with the public works program in the early days of the New Deal in the 1930s. But, as the program is put on a permanent basis, it should be possible to classify jobs better and to make sure they are reasonably productive and gratifying. We are not going to get to heaven in one jump, but neither is the matter all that difficult.

The Basic Procedure

A procedure which might make the job guarantee system work could be something like the following. The job guarantee would operate primarily at the county level. A federal (or federally supervised) agency in each county would receive the request of unemployed individuals to the effect that they wished to take advantage of the job guarantee. Ongoing communication with the various governmental activities in the county would keep this county job guarantee agency informed of available jobs. The government at the county level would have a firm obligation to assure that a job would be made available to unemployed individuals at the basic minimum wage. In the actual operation of the program, the individual job might be provided by any agency of any level of government in the county. But if, at the moment, no agency would admit to having a suitable vacancy, the county job guarantee agency, using funds provided by the federal government, would hire and pay the individual and assign some basic type of work with some agency. In cases where placement was extremely difficult, it would employ the individual itself and assign tasks itself. Cleaning up a little pollution is useful work, as is mail collecting, or working in day nurseries, or garbage collecting, or picking up litter, or mowing the grass, or tending the garden. It would be helpful if various private employers in the county would also agree to participate in the ongoing aspect of the job guarantee program and accept quotas of the unemployed as might be feasible. A lot of plants could stand to have their grass cut and their buildings painted. And there are few companies that could not tend the grounds around their buildings better. The ultimate responsibility for picking up the slack, however, must rest with the government. And the government must *continually* restructure its operations to make a reservoir of assorted jobs *continually* available in each county. In the United States, the federal government would be the level of government responsible for providing a job in the more difficult cases.

Minimum Age
The minimum-age criterion for coverage under the job guarantee might well be age eighteen or graduation from high school— whichever comes first. Youths aged twelve to eighteen might, however, be eligible to work one-quarter time under the job guarantee if they so desired (or, alternatively, to work full time during the summer), although their basic pay might well be less than the ordinary legal minimum. Both husband and wife should be eligible for coverage under the job guarantee if they desired, but in such a case one spouse would not receive the salary supplement applicable in the case of the dependent spouse.

Minimum Wage
The effect of the government's functioning as the employer of last resort under the job guarantee and paying the federal minimum wage would make $2.90 an hour, the minimum in 1979, or whatever the minimum happens to be, the meaningful minimum wage for everybody—including black maids in the South, and farm laborers, and state government employees. Pressure that would bring up the wage rates of these exploited people is long overdue.

Some of the most exploited people in the United States are the female black and Mexican American heads of families working as maids or in laundries. However, the variety of their problems hardly lends itself to one simple solution.

There is the woman whose husband left home because he did not have a job and because, under the rules of the welfare system, if there were no man in the house the wife would be entitled to welfare. The job guarantee should mend some broken homes of this type.

Then there is the woman with several children, in a fatherless home, who wants to tend the home rather than work outside it.

She is certainly entitled to respectable support, but the job guarantee is not the patent medicine for that problem.

The female head of household who wants to work should come under the job guarantee and should have the opportunity to utilize free day-nursery care. (The possibility that the woman is being irresponsible as to the number of her children may raise other types of problems. But that is pretty much neither here nor there as far as the job guarantee is concerned.)

At a minimum wage of $2.90 an hour (the 1979 figure), a person working fifty-two weeks a year and forty hours a week would make $6,032 a year. The federal government's poverty index in 1977 estimated $6,191 as the poverty-line income for a nonfarm family of four.[5] The supplements for spouse and dependents should be calculated to bring the minimum wage at least above the poverty line. In 1972, in the affluent United States, there were 25 million people in families (and similar groups) with incomes below the poverty line for the size of their household.

It is more than high time to be much more concerned about the problems of the willing to work, conscientious, concerned poor—those who are ready, willing, and able to try and *are* trying. The Commission on Income Maintenance Programs said: "Very few people seem poor because they are shiftless." It also said: "We have concluded that more often than not the reason for poverty is not some personal failing, but the accident of being born to the wrong parents, or the lack of opportunity to become non-poor, or some other circumstance over which individuals have no control."

Using the job guarantee not only to guarantee a job to all those able to work but also to guarantee it at a wage which is not below the poverty line is important. One of many troubles with most recently proposed income-support programs is that they do not provide a decent income.

The Role of Private Enterprise

In the job guarantee program, the government is the employer of last resort, but this does not mean that its role in providing employment should be artificially large and growing: it need not be if private enterprise bestirs itself and provides virtually all of the employment most of the time. It is now technically feasible for the private sector to provide full employment to all workers and to do so in jobs with ever rising productivity. The difficulty in doing this is institutional.

A program for implementing the job guarantee might involve

two chief features in relation to private business. One would be the maintenance by the government of a register of the names of those who are able to work, but who are unemployed, and those who are employed by the government in its role of employer of last resort. Information about the numbers of these people, their skills, their geographical location, their willingness to move would be made available as an ongoing proposition to prospective employers.

In the second place, the economic planners would also provide the business and banking sectors with information about possible productive activities that have more profit-making potential than some activities actually being engaged in. So, the economic planners would provide information on the labor force and on the production possibilities, on a continuing basis, to the trade associations, to the private business sector, and to the banks.

The private sector should understand that, as a collective entity, private enterprise has an obligation to use this information and to give jobs to all the registered people. Perhaps private enterprise in both developed and underdeveloped countries should be more impressed than it has been with the proposition that, if it is going to minimize government regulation (or socialism), it is going to have to provide jobs for most people. Also, the private sector needs to provide more job stability and more thoughtful rewarding of diligent and conscientious workers than has frequently been the practice in the past, when the standard rule has been "Fire them" when demand slacks off or when retooling is in order. The automobile industry has been a prime sinner in this regard.

A program of government subsidies to business owners who wish to expand an operation or begin a new one should be available under carefully controlled conditions that, among other things, obligate the employer to thoughtful cooperativeness in giving jobs to the employees of last resort.

That the government will become the employer of a larger and larger percentage of the work force is a possibility in the job guarantee system, a possibility that needs to be guarded against. The chief insurance against this danger is for private interprise to hire more and more people at higher and higher salaries. If private enterprise will not or cannot, the government can and should—and that is all there ought to be to that.

The Freedom to Fire
Another difficulty is that some workers protected by the job guarantee may malinger on the job. The implications of the deadbeat

and malingerer issue should not be brushed aside lightly. Those who are conscientiously trying to work and to do a good job are entitled not to be, in effect, discriminated against in the sense that other people are getting something for nothing or next to nothing and being inconsiderate, or worse, at the same time. Diligent workers are entitled to this measure of consideration.

Many well-intentioned people advocating the income guarantee (in contrast to the job guarantee) to the contrary notwithstanding, there are deadbeat, truculent people. They represent a serious problem, which is not dealt with by pointing out that there are also a lot of nice people out of work or inadequately employed, who would make good use of an income guarantee. In fact it is crucial, for the viability of society, that the problem of the malingerer be effectively dealt with.

Strangely enough, it may be possible to combine the job guarantee with freedom to fire (for cause) in a manner that will solve the problem.

A mild verbal reprimand just does not get the message through to some people. If an employee does unsatisfactory work, the employing corporation or government agency would be entitled to discharge him or her on the spot. In fact, the psychology of such situations (and such people) indicates that this is frequently the only way to handle the problem. The bum just has to be discharged then and there for *everybody's* self-respect—including the bum's. But the employer must be prepared, ex post, to show cause.

A period of one month (the length of the time period is arbitrary) might then pass before the individual would be entitled again to take advantage of the job guarantee. (Whether it is desirable to have a system of soup kitchens, which will give the individual who is destitute a minimum diet during the month of unemployment, may be left as a pending question). At any rate, the idea is that there be a time period when a bit of discomfort may encourage the not necessarily incorrigible person to do some soul-searching. It will probably be desirable that the individual's second go-around of employment not be with the same employer—although that issue might also well be one in which circumstances alter cases. And the handling of the itinerant should probably differ from the handling of those who have a roof over their heads. The itinerant might, rather summarily, be told to go to areas of expanding employment.

It would probably be desirable to classify regions of the country in terms of areas of expanding employment and areas of static or declining employment possibilities. After two or three (or four) go-arounds in which individuals end up being fired in their home county, they might be required to migrate to one of the centers of expanding employment possibilities if they are to take advantage of further job guarantees. Individuals already in such centers can stay there. The county job guarantee agencies in the centers of expanding job opportunity could be staffed with individuals with a good deal more professional competence in social work and in handling problem cases than would be necessary in many of the counties with small population and largely rural orientation.

Given these conditions, the job guarantee program might work indefinitely. The occasional period of one month off the job might continue to apply to malingerers. But it is also possible that some individuals might be sufficiently vicious or antisocial to make it desirable to change their status to handicapped. Two or three go-arounds of the on and off routine might cause some people who had been contemptuous of their jobs and slovenly and ill-humored about their work to have second thoughts and, at least, to adjust to an attitude that involves behaving in a minimally presentable way on the job. This procedure just might have some pretty favorable effects on the on-the-job attitudes of some people.

This would be the complete story of the handling of some types of malingerer cases. A person whose problem is ineptitude (perhaps caused by low intelligence) but who is willing to try is entitled to special assistance. Also, people with psychological problems are entitled to special assistance. But people who are aggressively truculent, or mean, or completely uncooperative, or have a chip on their shoulders, or feel a need to compensate for small physical size may require handling with a firmer hand. Combining firmness with fairness in handling such people is a skill that society needs to cultivate. Also, as mentioned above, their classification might have to be shifted to that of handicapped.

The county job guarantee agencies themselves should provide a major field of job openings for professional psychologists and welfare workers. As we move into the era of the affluent society, one of our serious problems may actually turn out to be how to handle the inherently truculent or combative people to whom affluence gives greater latitude for expression of their unpleasantness. Up to now the institutionalized attitude of society toward boors has been that, until the offense gets to be pretty serious, it is not the duty of one human being to admonish or discipline another. The boor has the right of way until another comes along, and then they have a wreck.

In any event, for one individual to reprimand another is tricky business. Peer-group approval or disapproval, indirectly expressed, works better. Peer approval is a powerful sanction. In certain circumstances, the groups to which the noncooperating individuals belong may be worked on and lined up, where individuals cannot be. And group attitudes then line up individuals.

In terms of psychology, perhaps some human characteristics (truculence or aggressiveness) are biologically determined. However, the manner in which people express truculence or aggressiveness is institutionally or socially determined. They will drive with abandon if that is the thing to do. But, whether the psychological characteristic is inbred or socially cultivated, the manner in which it is expressed is very largely socially or institutionally controlled. If society wants, it can condition even the meanest of people out of the habit of expressing their meanness in certain ways. But the social and peer-group sanctions have to be there. The conditioning cannot necessarily be done by law, and it can rarely be done by preaching.

However, access to a decent standard of living takes away most of the defensible basis for massive dissatisfaction in society. Perhaps social pressures will then effectively discredit most forms of public obnoxiousness. It should be hoped that this will happen. If it does not, we will have to cross that bridge when we come to it. Meanwhile, the possibility that the job guarantee may not solve all the problems of all the people in this world is hardly a very strong argument against the program.

The Freedom to Quit
There are two sides to the getting-along business. The job guarantee would permit employees to deal effectively with offensive employers under circumstances where, up to now, the employers have pretty much had the employees at their mercy. The employees can simply quit an objectionable employer en masse with the assurance that they can find alternative employment immediately while spending more time looking for more desirable jobs.

Training and Retraining Programs
The job guarantee is the hard-core, basic tool for dealing with the employment problem, the economic development problem, and

the business-cycle problem. But this hardly means that it is the only tool. Certainly the business-cycle problem may continue to exist in a degree that will make it desirable to use fiscal and monetary policy tools in the macroeconomic area. Also, it may be desirable to deal with some aspects of the employment problem by encouraging substantial population shift from relatively depressed to expanding areas or to poles of development near depressed areas—if such can be found.

It is certainly going to be important to have readily available training facilities to permit people, with the will to do so, to improve their skills. In fact, inexpensive or free training and retraining facilities will contribute a great deal to the success of the job guarantee program.[6]

Cost

Senator John Williams, in the interest of the taxpayers of Delaware, used to be entitled to be concerned and to ask the age-old question (or he might have been if he had voted against the Antiballistic missile system): how much will it cost?

In reply, one might say that there is a sense in which the job guarantee program will not cost anything. The laborer is worthy of his hire, provided he is assigned to a reasonable job and does it. The country is getting something for its "money." In fact, it is getting something that would be permanently lost if the individual had not worked that day. Herbert Simon has claimed: "Likewise when a private business employs an unemployed person his wage is an ordinary cost; while when the government employs such a person [who would not otherwise be employed] it makes use of a resource that would otherwise not be utilised, and hence the wages of those employed do not involve any real cost from the standpoint of the community."[7]

However, there are organizational problems and an institutional adjustment problem. The involved administrators had better be engaged in a continuing program of reappraisal to make sure that the jobs they are providing are worth doing. There is worthwhile work to be done. It takes just a little arranging to get organized to do a lot of it.

There is also the more immediate direct-cost problem. How much additional federal funds would be needed the first few years? Six million unemployed (in December 1978) times $6,032 each is over $36 billion. But the lesser number of unemployed of three

years earlier would have cost only about $12 billion.[8] Someone
who recalls the sixteen million unemployed of the Great Depression may imagine a far higher price tag. But $36 billion is a good
deal less than the Department of Defense budget ($126 billion pro-
jected for 1979–80). And the total outlays for 1979–80, in the
federal budget, are projected to be $532 billion. Who can really be-
lieve that this country cannot afford $36 billion to assure decent
jobs for everyone reasonably able to work, especially when that
amount is a genuine, net addition to the gross national product?
What are our priorities in this country anyway?

Of course, the gross cost of the program would not be net cost.
As an aspect of creating the job guarantee program, certain thence-
forth unnecessary programs or parts of programs could be discontinued. The unemployment-insurance program, for one thing,
could surely be dispensed with. That involved $16.9 billion in 1977.
Then there is the food stamp program running $6 billion, and so
on. How much saving in unnecessary programs could be effected if
we had a meaningful job guarantee program? Considerable—
probably more than the cost of the job guarantee program! In fact,
a rough estimate for 1977 runs $55 billion. But the desirability of
the program is hardly contingent on determining beforehand exactly how much it will cost, a determination which cannot be
made.

It is worth remembering that, even if the economy had those
sixteen million unemployed of the Great Depression again, it
would have to do something about them—or they would do something about the Establishment. The job guarantee, in all reason,
would be a far better and cheaper way of handling them than the
standard alternatives. It would surely be better than the dole, better than unemployment insurance, better than breadlines, better
than income maintenance. It may be worth remembering that the
Great Depression reduced the United States national income by
something approaching half for several years, and a depression of
similar magnitude now would reduce it by between $500 billion
and a trillion a year. If the job guarantee can take the sting out of
depression, it is surely some of the best-spent money—ever.

In fact, there is some reason to believe that, if there were a job
guarantee program, unemployment would not be likely to reach
the abysmal levels of yesteryear. The job guarantee is preventive
medicine. It is the best of the possible built-in stabilizers. The

money expended to support the job guarantee would finance consumer goods purchases which would finance other jobs. And unemployment would be less. Additional production is also part of the process, and the national product is increased, unlike the situation with unemployment insurance and income support and the dole.

At least one transition-period problem should be recognized, however, which will initially seem worse than it will turn out to be in the long run. There may now be about ten million jobs in the United States paying salaries less than the federal minimum wage. It is a merit of the job guarantee approach, in the form recommended here, that it will tend to force even the lowest wage rates up to the minimum. However, quite conceivably, an undetermined number of jobs paying less than the minimum will be discontinued during the early years of the program. The employers will not be able or, more likely, willing to pay the higher wage. Unknown numbers of such unemployed people may be a burden on the job guarantee program in its early years. But, when the chips are down, a lot of employers who now loudly say they cannot pay more will decide that they can, just as, despite initial protestations to the contrary, they have generally found that they could pay the various levels of minimum wage which have been imposed since the middle 1930s. Forecasting how much initial cost will fall on the job guarantee program as a result of this circumstance is difficult.

It is impossible dogmatically to state the cost of the program. No useful purpose is served by conjuring up an ostensibly firm estimate that may be wide of the mark. The cost might decline to a very low figure just because of the security that the existence of the program would give. But maybe not. At any rate, $20 to $60 billion is a rough estimate of what the program would cost per year the first few years (at 1979 prices). As an offset, it would save at least $15 to $30 billion or more in other programs, such as unemployment insurance. (And the gross national product was well over $2 trillion and government expenditures well over $500 billion in 1979.)

The job guarantee program would be worthwhile if it cost several times this amount. It is surely worth the lesser amount that it will probably actually cost once it is effectively playing its built-in stabilizer role.

Alternatives

Income Maintenance

It seems common sense that the job guarantee rather than income maintenance or the negative income tax ought to be the basic approach to the problem of the able-to-work poor.

It is important that somehow the message get through to people in general and to policy makers in the United States in particular that the difference between the job guarantee approach on the one hand and the income guarantee and negative income tax approaches on the other is significant. The Speenhamland and Roman circus implications of these other approaches do matter. The choice among these alternatives is probably the most important public choice that will be made in this half century. And we are in danger of being stuck for a long time to come with whichever of these devices we opt for first. This is true because of the sheer complexity of making a change later. It is worth appreciating that there is a clear-cut, unambiguous choice, on their merits, among the options.

Some argue that everyone should be guaranteed a decent living, whether the person works or not. I am tempted to allege that, before that bridge is crossed (or not crossed), there should be agreement that everyone ready, willing, and able to work and desirous of having a job should have one. With a very much lower priority, society might later consider other alternatives for the able-bodied.

The Negative Income Tax

As for the negative income tax, this is a worse proposal than the income guarantee. It is a gimmick, a gimmick calculated to make the already too complicated personal income tax yet more complicated. It would be difficult to administer. And, like the guaranteed income proposal, it would almost certainly provide submarginal income in the common difficult situations.

Unemployment Insurance

An unemployment-insurance program is, of course, already in existence, but it does not work well or give adequate protection. It is administratively awkward, based as it is on contributions determined by wages based on prior earnings. In 1975, only about two-thirds of the unemployed were actually receiving unemployment compensation under the system. This is a complex, inflexible system involving a fantastic amount of bookkeeping. It does not get the job done, and there are no practical modifications of the program that would permit it to get the job done. The unemployment-insurance program should be scrapped. This alone would probably release over half of the funds needed to underwrite the job guarantee program, which makes a contribution to output while unemployment-insurance payments do not.

The Job Guarantee in the Underdeveloped Countries

The job guarantee should be basic policy in underdeveloped countries as well as in developed countries. But there are additional problems in the underdeveloped countries. One is not entitled so glibly to assert that a job that would justify paying a living wage can readily (or even with a little difficulty) be made available for everyone in those countries.

Certainly, the programs in such countries as India could not start off paying the real wage equivalent of anything remotely like $2.90 an hour. Also, the problems of organizing the job guarantee program will be serious in the typical underdeveloped country— shorthanded as it is in terms of competent public administrators.

But conditions are grave in the underdeveloped world. Massive unemployment and underemployment are characteristic of its cities, to which youths are migrating in droves from the countryside and finding frustration rather than jobs. Overt unemployment in Latin America probably ranges from 10 to 30 percent of the labor force; in other underdeveloped countries, it is similarly high.[9] Those are pretty high figures, especially for nondepression times, and the figures are generally thought to be rising. In 1979 the United States is, or should be, concerned about a 6 percent rate. Unemployment is serious business all over the world.

The job guarantee is a program which the underdeveloped countries can get their teeth into now. It does not require major amounts of foreign aid for implementation (although it could certainly use some public administration advisers). And it is a program that can be built on small beginnings. In the very poor countries, the transition to the job guarantee should involve providing jobs up to a close approximation of full employment before the job guarantee, as a worker right, goes into effect.

The first step, then, would be the providing by the government of an expanding number of jobs spread widely over the country; road maintenance in the countryside and street-cleaning, custodial, and day-nursery work in the cities are examples of types of work with almost unlimited ability to sop up labor. Also, there should perhaps be subsidization of private employers willing to provide more jobs (especially apprenticeship and custodial jobs) during the early phase of the program.

From the very inception of the program, major emphasis should be placed on arrangements for effective supervision. Keeping ahead of the game in this respect, as the program develops, will go a long way toward solving the public administration aspect of running the program later.

Initially, however, in spite of best efforts, the job supervision might be pretty lax and the productivity of the laborers low. Productive, useful work should still be involved, and the wage should be paid in cash, not in kind, and the law should provide that the job guarantee (as a worker right) go into effect with some speed—perhaps within five years of the enactment of the basic law. At that time, the highest-priority business the leaders will have will be the meaningful implementation of the job guarantee. They had better forget about baiting foreign investors, baiting Tío Sam, the politics of the cold war, running the Israelis into the sea, foreign adventures, soccer wars, and suchlike diversions and get down to work.

As for the cost of the implementation of the program, I will be a bit irresponsible. Since the wage will be paid in the domestic currency, there is no need for monetary foreign aid to finance the program. The local currency has never been in short supply in the underdeveloped countries. So, the possibility of creating, by hook or by crook, the necessary funds exists. At this point some economists will shudder at the inflationary implications. Certainly the program should be financed in ways that have as little inflationary impact as possible. The progressive income tax would be a basic source of funds. Also important would be qualitative credit control devices which would compel banks to be more alert to the real productivity of the projects for which they lend money. Administrators of the program should be concerned about inflation. But worry about the possibility of inflation should not be allowed to prevent the implementation of the program.

Once the job guarantee is in actual operation (with or without a little accompanying inflation), the chief ongoing task of the planner is the continual implementation of the shifting of productive resources from less to more productive activities.

Can it really be true that, within a decade or two, under-developed countries generally can provide jobs for all workers, jobs involving productivities that will permit the paying to all of wages that are not too miserably low? One answer is, if it can be done, fine; if it cannot, underdeveloped-country leaders had better try again—because this is the essential meaning of economic development in these countries.

In addition, one may be reasonably optimistic that, if planners will approach their problem in this light and get their hands dirty at the level of small projects, some real miracles can be performed. Take housing as an example (but not as a major fraction of the whole story). Inadequate housing (for example, a situation where six people live and sleep in one room) is commonplace in the underdeveloped countries. What are the possibilities for putting a goodly number of the unemployed to work on housing? Are lack of capital and the expense of purchasing raw materials an almost insuperable hurdle preventing this in the near future? Maybe not.[10] The matter can stand some double checking.

There are new procedures for making quite durable bricks out of some common clays using very simple equipment. Expansion of cement production might be given a much higher priority in many of the underdeveloped countries. Many countries have local building materials, unique to the area, which offer possibilities for imaginative use. Also, housing construction has the especial advantage of providing jobs requiring relatively little capital per worker.

Food preservation (canning and packing) is another area. The saving resulting from checking food spoilage could be tremendous. Estimates of the amount of food spoilage in underdeveloped countries run almost unbelievably high—20 to 40 percent of the production. (A lot of the spoiled food, however, is also eaten.)

Apropos of the possibility of finding reasonable work rather readily for the unemployed, Gunnar Myrdal cites examples of useful work where little capital is required:

> Such work as, for instance, building roads, bridges, irrigation canals, soil conservation terraces, warehouses for storing crops and farm supplies, draining ditches, wells, and tanks, and laboring on afforestation and pasture improvement is all highly labor intensive and requires few resources to complement labor beyond those locally available.
>
> Other uses of the villagers' spare time relate more directly to consumption: construction of school buildings, dispensaries, village priv-

ies, and gutters; clean wells for drinking water and other household uses; paving of village streets to do away with dust and mud; improving the houses; manufacturing simple furniture; killing rats; or merely washing the children, and keeping flies away from their eyes. It is generally recognized that these undertakings in the service of consumption are also highly productive. . . .

The difficulties are several. For one thing these undertakings presuppose collective action, and hence organization, as the scale of effort required mostly surpasses the immediate interests and resources of individual households. The understanding of the common advantage of such collective action and organization assumes a degree of rationality and social cohesion that is often absent in a faction-ridden village.

Such action, moreover, immediately raises questions of the distribution of benefits and costs and thus the equality issue. . . . Should the landless workers be paid, and if so how much, when the benefits mainly accrue to the landowners and others in the higher strata, who often are not willing either to work or to pay others for working?[11]

Keith Griffin also believes that there are major possibilities for low-capital-requirement productive work in agriculture: "It has been conclusively demonstrated in several countries that properly organized labour-intensive rural investments (a) are an excellent way to mobilize the bases for development, (b) are inexpensive, (c) can have a very short gestation period, and (d) provide large returns on capital expenditure. The author has personal experience in Algeria with projects of the type recommended."[12]

More and more the evidence mounts that the crux of the matter in raising standards of living is the redeployment of effort at the local level, a process that requires intelligent and thoughtful guidance, not necessarily a lot of capital or a lot of sophisticated model building. Some antisocial but institutionalized behavior patterns have to change (or be changed). Jobs need to be provided for all. And thoughtful use, by planners, of industry studies as an aid in shifting productive activity into ever more desirable lines of activity is, or ought to be, the meat and drink of the development planner.

Conclusion

Let us put our money where our mouth is on this proposition that we want to get able-bodied people off of welfare and into jobs. However, we are going to have to work out a lot of the details the hard way. That is the way of life. The Articles of Confederation did not work, but the Constitution did. The country tried again.

We are fond of talking about bold, new initiatives. Let us try one. And let the country just dig up some decent jobs for the unemployed minorities, for the teenage unemployed, for the older unemployed as well, and even for the professional people who are unemployed.

Really assure everybody of a job and an income that provides a decent living and forswear most other economic controls (especially price controls and international trade controls). The thing to do is to create better institutions and then let people alone to help themselves. At least, let the able-bodied alone—and be genuinely and pleasantly helpful to the disadvantaged.

The poor generally do prefer jobs to charity (or income maintenance). At any rate, Leonard Goodwin says they do:

> Evidence from this study unambiguously supports the following conclusion: poor people—males and females, blacks and whites, youths and adults—identify their self-esteem with work as strongly as do the nonpoor. . . .
>
> The picture that emerges is one of black welfare women who want to work but who, because of continuing failure in the work world, tend to become more accepting of welfare and less inclined to try again. . . .
>
> The plight of the poor cannot be blamed on their having deviant goals or a deviant psychology. The ways in which the poor do differ from the affluent can reasonably be attributed to their different experiences of success and failure in the world.[13]

It is about time that something was done to implement the full-employment pledge made in the Employment Act of 1946.[14]

NOTES

1. John Dewey, *Intelligence in the Modern World: John Dewey's Philosophy* (New York: Modern Library, 1939), pp. 420–421.
2. For somewhat similar views see Melville J. Ulmer, *The Welfare State: U.S.A.* (Boston: Houghton Mifflin, 1969), p. 95.
3. *Everyman's United Nations*, 8th ed. (New York: United Nations, 1968 [1948]), p. 589.
4. Thorstein Veblen, *The Instinct of Workmanship* (New York: Augustus M. Kelley, 1964 [1914]), pp. 27–28.
5. *Statistical Abstract of the United States, 1978* (Washington, D.C.: Gov-

ernment Printing Office, 1978), p. 465; also see the text of the Report of the President's Commission on Income Maintenance Programs (Ben W. Heineman, chairman), *Poverty amid Plenty* (Washington, D.C.: Government Printing Office, 1969), and *New York Times*, November 13, 1969, p. 34.

6. See Ray Marshall, *The Negro and Organized Labor* (New York: Wiley, 1965), p. 402; United States, Congress, Joint Economic Committee (92: 2), *Report . . . on the January 1972 Economic Report of the President* (Washington, D.C.: Government Printing Office, 1972), pp. 27–30.

7. Herbert A. Simon, *Administrative Behavior*, 2d ed. (New York: Macmillan, 1957 [1948]), p. 175.

8. See Garth L. Mangum, "Government as Employer of Last Resort," in Sar A. Levitan, ed., *Towards Freedom from Want* (Madison: Industrial Relations Research Association, 1968), p. 153.

9. See United States, Congress, Joint Economic Committee, Subcommittee on Foreign Economic Policy Hearings (91:2), *A Foreign Economic Policy for the 1970's*, pt. 3: *U.S. Policies toward Developing Countries* (Washington, D.C.: Government Printing Office, 1970), p. 700; *Visión*, May 22, 1971, p. 41.

10. See United States, Congress, House of Representatives, Subcommittee on Inter-American Affairs, Hearings, *New Directions for the 1970's* (Washington, D.C.: 1969), pp. 402–430.

11. Gunnar Myrdal, *The Challenge of World Poverty* (New York: Pantheon, 1970), pp. 88–89.

12. Keith Griffin, *Underdevelopment in Spanish America* (Cambridge, Mass.: MIT Press, 1969), p. 84.

13. Leonard Goodwin, *Do the Poor Want to Work?* (Washington, D.C.: Brookings, 1972), pp. 112–118.

14. Leon H. Keyserling, "For a Full Employment Act by 1976," *Challenge* 18 (July 1975): 22–25.

ADDITIONAL READINGS

Cain, Glen G., and Harold W. Watts, eds. *Income Maintenance and Labor Supply*. Chicago: Rand McNally, 1973.

Copeland, Morris A. *Toward Full Employment in Our Free Enterprise Economy*. New York: Fordham University Press, 1966.

Graham, Frank D. *The Abolition of Unemployment*. Princeton: Princeton University Press, 1932.

Haskell, Mark A. *The New Careers Concept*. New York: Praeger, 1969.

Lampman, Robert J. *Ends and Means of Reducing Income Poverty*. Chicago: Markham, 1971.

Marshall, Dorothy. *The English Poor in the Eighteenth Century*. New York: Augustus M. Kelley, 1969 [1926].

Orr, Larry L., Robinson G. Hollister, and Myron J. Lefcowitz, eds. *Income Maintenance*. Chicago: Markham, 1971.

Rose, Michael E. *The English Poor Laws, 1780–1930*. Newton Abbot, Devon: David & Charles, 1973.

Turnham, D. *The Employment Problem in Less Developed Countries: A Review of Evidence*. Paris: Organization for Economic Cooperation and Development, 1970.

Ulmer, Melville J. "How to Fight Inflation." *Atlantic* 234 (October 1974): 39–47.

18.
The Larger Picture

LET US SUPPOSE that the universe alternately expands and contracts. In one phase it contracts into a black hole which is fantastically concentrated, and this black hole has such powerful attractive force that, while it is forming, light and everything else flows in but not out. Then, at some stage in the process of concentration, the universe has had enough and explodes far and fast. The concentrated mass of the black hole expands and disintegrates in the process, eventually evolving into nebulae and stars and planets circumnavigating stars. Meanwhile everything, except possibly the center, whatever that is, is flying outward. When the universe has dispersed as far as it can or wants to, it may proceed to contract again back into the fantastically concentrated black hole. (As a by-product of this process, some minor black holes, such as seem to have been observed, may come and go along the way.)

Also, the possibility exists that occasionally (maybe thousands of times in the course of one of the cycles of expansion) some one or another of the planets circling some one or another of the stars may generate life. In some of these instances the life may evolve into something capable of thinking and acting. And that planet is then participating in a process involving the evolution of the biology of the beings, the accumulation of knowledge, the institutionalization of behavior, and the use of the available natural resources, resources which will be more or less practicable depending on the current state of technical knowledge. The look of the culture at any given time is dependent on how these influences have interacted up to that time.

Such a society evolves from simple beginnings up to some level of competence in appreciating the nature of this (sociological) process, and its members may acquire some degree of appreciation as to what is happening to them and to the universe.

The beings' appreciation of all this evolves through a process of self-correcting value judgments. And they acquire some degree of ability to influence the process itself. They may even acquire an ability to influence their own biological evolution to some degree. They may even acquire the capability for traveling some distance through space to other planets, where they may not be fried or frozen or, indeed, where they may be. They may even be able to tune in on societies much further away.

Nevertheless, they are at the mercy of the great overriding physical phenomenon that is the expansion and contraction of the universe. At some point in the process the society is wiped out. Or it might wipe itself out before its time with some injudicious use of the technical knowledge it possesses.

There is no Garden of Eden, no paradise, no utopia, however, into which the beings of this society can settle in eternal bliss. They perform upon the stage, make much or little of themselves along the way, and pass on back into the black hole from which they came. Yet along the way they exercise certain options, and they may themselves make being a more or less pleasant experience.

Or this may not be the way things are at all. Perhaps there is some supergod standing on a solid chunk of concrete somewhere, operating this expansion-contraction process like a giant yo-yo. It may or may not care particularly about the beings that, along with their societies, appear and disappear in this process. It may have one hip pocket that it calls paradise where it can put the nice people and another one called hell where it can put the others. Or it may just let the beings disintegrate into dust which later collapses into the great primal black hole, which is where the yo-yo is on the extreme of the downswing. In this case, of course, one may well ask where the supergod came from and where it is going.

In the other case, one may well ask which is the chicken and which the egg: the black hole or the limits of expansion. Reading Matthew Arnold's "Dover Beach" may or may not give one much comfort in thinking about these cosmic possibilities.

In any event, the decision still rests with any one of these groups of beings, after it sort of gets squared away with itself, as to how it wants to exploit its allotted time, cussing each other out or trying to make the operation a reasonably satisfactory experience while it lasts.

ADDITIONAL READINGS

Gingerich, Owen, ed. *Cosmology + 1: Readings from "Scientific American."* San Francisco: W. H. Freeman, 1977.
Weinberg, Steven. *The First Three Minutes*. New York: Basic Books, 1976.

Index